COMMERCIAL DISPUTE RESOLUTION

COMMERCIAL DISPUTE RESOLUTION

Kevin Browne LLB, Associate Professor and Senior Lecturer

Published by

College of Law Publishing,
Braboeuf Manor, Portsmouth Road, St Catherines, Guildford GU3 1HA

British Library Cataloguing-in-Publication Data
A catalogue record for this book is available from the British Library.

ISBN 978 1 915469 58 8

Typeset by Style Photosetting Ltd, Mayfield, East Sussex
Tables and index by Moira Greenhalgh, Arnside, Cumbria

Preface

This book is intended to build on the introduction to civil dispute resolution practice and procedure in England and Wales as detailed in the Legal Practice Guide, *Civil Litigation*. I hope that it will be of use to students studying in this area, as well as practitioners who are new to the various topics covered or who wish to update their knowledge.

After a short, practical introduction to the nature of commercial dispute resolution in **Chapter 1**, the book deals with key early considerations in **Chapter 2**. This is followed by an introduction to the three specialist courts at the heart of the Business and Property Courts, namely the Commercial Court (**Chapter 3**), the Chancery Division of the High Court (**Chapter 4**) and the Technology and Construction Court (**Chapter 5**). The next four chapters then address key aspects of injunctions, starting with the relevant law and procedures (**Chapters 6** and **7**) followed by a detailed analysis of freezing injunctions (**Chapter 8**) and Search Orders (**Chapter 9**). The practicalities of handling evidence in commercial cases are addressed in **Chapter 10**. The appeals system, settlement and alternatives to litigation, arbitration and mediation are dealt with in **Chapters 11–14**. Enforcement and insolvency are considered in **Chapter 15**. Much commercial litigation occurs cross border, and foreign elements of proceedings and enforcement are outlined in **Chapters 16** and **17**.

Although I am responsible for this edition, I remain indebted to Mike Waring and the late Graham Beecher who were responsible for earlier versions of this book. I should also like to thank Russell Binch who provided the first draft of Disclosure under CPR 1998, PD 57AD for **Chapter 10**.

Significant developments in law and procedure included in this edition are funding of commercial litigation (**Chapter 2**), the just and convenient test for an interim injunction (**Chapter 6**), contempt proceedings (**Chapter 7**), freezing injunctions (**Chapter 8**), disclosure under CPR 1998, PD 57AD (**Chapter 10**), appeals procedures (**Chapter 11**), arbitration proceedings (**Chapter 13**) and service of proceedings out of the jurisdiction (**Chapter 16**).

New cases in this edition include: *Ascension Asset Management Ltd v Sky Solicitors Ltd* [2023] and *Candey Ltd v Bosheh* [2022] (conditional fee agreements), *Candey Ltd v Tonstate Group Ltd* [2022] (damages-based agreements), *R (on the application of PACCAR Inc and others) v Competition Appeal Tribunal* [2023] (third party funding), *Seedo v El Gamal and others* [2023] (limitation), *Hayden v Associated Newspapers Ltd* [2022] (Norwich Pharmacal order), *Atos IT Services UK Ltd v Secretary of State for Business, Energy and Industrial Strategy* [2022] (consolidation), *University of Brighton v Persons Unknown Occupying Land* [2023] (quia timet injunction), *Jaldhi Mideast DMCC v Al Ghurair Resources LLC* [2023] and *Deutsche Bank AG v Sebastian Holdings Inc* [2023] (contempt), *CRO v REC* [2023] (freezing injunction), *Olympic Council of Asia v Novans Jets LLP* [2023] (search order), *Emirates NBD Bank PJSC v Hassan Saadat-Yazdi* [2023], *Republic of Mozambique v Credit Suisse International* [2022] and *Morina v Scherbakova (Re Estate of Vladimir Alekseyevich Scherbakov)* [2023] (disclosure), *Palladian Partners LP v Republic of Argentina* [2023] (Part 36), *Global Aerospares Ltd v Airest AS* [2023] (arbitration) and *Pantheon International Advisors Ltd v Co-Diagnostics Inc* [2023] (service out of the jurisdiction).

I would like to thank David Stott, Sue Hall and the team at CLP for all their hard work on this title.

I would also like to thank my wife, children, colleagues and past students for their support and inspiration.

This edition is dedicated to Alistair, Mary, Chris, Tom, Phil, Harry and Rene. All much missed.

KEVIN BROWNE
The University of Law
London

August 2023

Contents

Table of Cases

Table of Statutes

Table of Secondary Legislation and Court Guides

Table of Abbreviations

AA 1996	Arbitration Act 1996
ADR	alternative dispute resolution
AJA 1920	Administration of Justice Act 1920
ATE	after the event (insurance)
B&PCs	Business and Property Courts of England and Wales
CDR	commercial dispute resolution
CEDR	Centre for Effective Dispute Resolution
CFA	conditional fee agreement
CMC	case management conference
CMO	costs management order
CPR 1998	Civil Procedure Rules 1998
DBA	damages-based agreement
DRD	Disclosure Review Document
ENE	early neutral evaluation
EU	European Union
FJ(RE)A 1933	Foreign Judgments (Reciprocal Enforcement) Act 1933
GLO	Group Litigation Order
ICC	International Chamber of Commerce
LA 1980	Limitation Act 1980
NDR	negotiated dispute resolution
PD	Practice Direction
SRA	Solicitors Regulation Authority
TCC	Technology and Construction Court
UNCITRAL	United Nations Commission on International Trade Law
WFO	worldwide freezing order

PART I

COMMERCIAL DISPUTE
RESOLUTION

CHAPTER 1

THE NATURE OF COMMERCIAL DISPUTE RESOLUTION

LEARNING OUTCOMES

After reading this chapter you will understand:

- the approach of business clients to commercial dispute resolution
- the specialist courts available in commercial litigation
- the main alternatives to commercial litigation as methods of resolving commercial disputes
- the importance of being able to advise the client on appropriate methods of dispute resolution.

1.1 INTRODUCTION

This chapter introduces the factors which need to be taken into account in the field of commercial dispute resolution (CDR) and the different methods of dispute resolution available. Every lawyer working in this field must be aware of all the available options to resolve the client's problem. Commercial disputes come in all shapes and sizes of course, ranging from fairly straightforward debt collection cases to extremely complex international disputes involving a multitude of parties.

This book deals with the three main types of CDR:

(a) commercial litigation;

(b) arbitration (the most well-established form of alternative dispute resolution (ADR));

(c) other methods of ADR, with particular emphasis on mediation.

Whilst this book concentrates on commercial litigation, the alternatives to litigation, particularly ADR in all its manifestations, are becoming increasingly important.

It is important to realise that in considering how to resolve any dispute, a businessperson is making a commercial decision. They therefore need a solicitor who is aware of the constraints of business on the conduct of whichever method of dispute resolution is chosen. These constraints are mainly time and money. There is a limit to the amount of time that a businessperson can devote to the resolution of the dispute. There is a limit to the amount of money they can afford, or wish, to spend on legal costs. They want a satisfactory resolution of the dispute at reasonable and proportionate expense.

In view of this, the solicitor needs to keep numerous points in mind, including the following:

(a) What is the appropriate method of dispute resolution to best achieve the client's aims?

(b) Is the client's priority a quick settlement – possibly to avoid incurring legal costs 'unnecessarily'?

(c) Does the client want to preserve the business relationship with the other party?

(d) How will the dispute, and possibly the chosen method of resolution, affect relationships with other customers or suppliers? Clients will not generally want to be seen as a 'soft touch'.

(e) Will the knowledge that your client is willing to resort to litigation in order to enforce or preserve their rights deter others from attempting to infringe those rights?

(f) Is the other party involved in the dispute solvent?

(g) Does the client want the legally correct solution to the dispute, the cheapest solution, the quickest solution, or the best combination of the three?

These are matters which a dispute resolution lawyer must consider with the client at the beginning of the case. They also have to be kept under review as the case progresses. As more is known about the opponent's strengths and weaknesses, the strategy and tactics may have to be changed.

1.2 COMMERCIAL LITIGATION

The term 'commercial litigation' is a very broad term and not easy to define. This book uses it in the context of the resolution of commercial disputes by litigation or the threat of litigation. Litigation to resolve business disputes is carried out in the County Court and the King's Bench Division of the High Court throughout England and Wales, but the following courts may be said to provide specifically for the resolution of such disputes:

(a) The Commercial Court. The Commercial Court in London was established in 1895, intended as a court which would have a great familiarity with the subject matter of commercial and mercantile disputes, and to provide procedures which would enable those disputes to be determined justly, expeditiously and efficiently. The practices of the court are discussed in **Chapter 3**.

(b) The Admiralty Court. Based in London, this deals with shipping and maritime disputes.

(c) The London Circuit Commercial Court. This was established to deal effectively with commercial claims where the most convenient venue is London, but which are less complex or of smaller value than those claims dealt with in the Commercial Court.

(d) The regional equivalents of the Commercial Court are the Circuit Commercial Courts in the High Court district registries of Birmingham, Bristol, Cardiff, Leeds, Liverpool, Manchester and Newcastle.

(e) The Technology and Construction Court (TCC) (formerly known as the Official Referee's Court), as its name suggests, is the appropriate venue for construction and engineering disputes as well as those of a 'technical' nature such as computer disputes. The TCC is part of the High Court and sits in London. Outside London, TCC claims should be issued in one of the following District Registries in which a TCC judge will usually be available – Birmingham, Bristol, Cardiff, Chester, Exeter, Leeds, Liverpool, Manchester, Newcastle upon Tyne and Nottingham.

The practices of the court are discussed in **Chapter 5**.

(f) The Chancery Division. The specialist parts of the High Court referred to above are part of the King's Bench Division. Many commercial claims are, however, of a nature which makes them suitable for trial in the Chancery Division (eg claims relating to commercial property or intellectual property). The particular rules and procedures applicable to the Chancery Division are considered in **Chapter 4**.

All of these courts operate under the single umbrella of the Business and Property Courts of England and Wales (B&PCs). Those courts in London are all housed at the Rolls Building in

Fetter Lane, making it the largest specialist centre for financial, business and property litigation in the world.

There is an advisory note about issuing proceedings in the B&PCs. Although this was produced in 2017 and has not been updated, it still provides useful guidance about which particular court or list in which to issue proceedings. There are 10 of these as follows:

(1)   Admiralty Court (KBD)

(2)   Business List (Chancery Division)

(3)   Commercial Court (KBD). This includes the option to issue in the London Circuit Commercial Court or those outside London

(4)   Competition List (ChD)

(5)   Financial List (ChD/KBD)

(6)   Insolvency and Companies List (ChD)

(7)   Intellectual Property List (ChD)

(8)   Property, Trusts and Probate List (ChD)

(9)   Revenue List (ChD)

(10)   Technology and Construction Court (KBD)

The Advisory Note appears at **Appendix 19** and the Practice Direction for the B&PCs is at **Appendix 20.**

1.3   ALTERNATIVES TO LITIGATION AS A METHOD OF DISPUTE RESOLUTION

It is important to appreciate that litigation is not always the appropriate solution to a client's problems.

Many disputes are resolved without the need to commence proceedings and, where litigation is used, most proceedings are settled before trial. Alternatives to litigation, such as ADR and arbitration, are becoming increasingly popular.

1.3.1   Alternative dispute resolution

Litigation can be very expensive, very slow and it causes antagonism. Often, the business client will need to continue to deal with the person with whom they are in dispute. Such dealings are unlikely to be happy while litigation continues between the two of them.

The most common type of ADR is mediation, the principal feature of which is that it enables a neutral third party to discuss the problem and possible solutions with both parties. This may lead to a quick and painless solution. Disputes are often caused by misunderstanding rather than bad faith, and when the parties come to realise how the problem came about, they may find it easier to see the other side's point of view and to reach agreement. The different forms of ADR are considered later on in this book (see **Chapter 12**).

Courts have become increasingly supportive of using ADR as a means of resolving disputes even after litigation has commenced. Rule 1.4(2)(e) of the Civil Procedure Rules 1998 (CPR 1998) identifies one of the court's case management powers as

> encouraging the parties to use an alternative dispute resolution procedure if the court considers that appropriate and facilitating the use of such procedure ...

Examples of court orders which encourage or facilitate ADR include:

(i)   an order refusing to grant permission for proceedings to commence until the parties had engaged in a meaningful way with a professional mediator (*Hussain v Chowdhury* [2020] EWHC 790 (Ch) at [18]);

(ii)   an order for a stay of the whole or part of the proceedings for mediation or some other ADR procedure, for example the 12-month stay ordered in the *Grenfell Tower Litigation* [2022] EWHC 2006 (QB) and the 8-month stay ordered in *Hamon v University College London* [2023] EWHC 1812 (KB); and

(iii)   ordering early neutral evaluation (even if one of the parties objects: *Lomax v Lomax* [2019] EWCA Civ 1467).

A solicitor who fails to advise about the availability of ADR may be negligent. It could also amount to a breach of Principle 7 of the SRA Code of Conduct 2019 if a solicitor does not act in the best interests of their client.

1.3.2   Arbitration

Many business contracts contain an arbitration clause requiring the parties to refer their disputes to arbitration rather than litigation. Even if there is no arbitration agreement, after the dispute arises the parties will often agree to refer the matter to arbitration, in preference to litigation.

In arbitration, a dispute is decided by one or more arbitrators who are usually experts chosen from a particular field or professional body. The decision of the arbitrator(s), called the arbitration 'award', is binding on the parties and enforceable through the courts.

Arbitration has many advantages over litigation:

(a)   The parties can choose their own arbitrator (or arbitrators). This means that they can choose an expert from within their own trade or profession to resolve the dispute. The arbitrator will have personal experience of the matters in question and (unlike a judge) they will not have to be educated by the parties and their experts on the subject matter of the dispute. For example, an engineer who is a member of the Institute of Civil Engineers might be chosen as an arbitrator for a large construction dispute. As a result, there is little risk of a wrong decision on the facts and there is less need for the parties to call their own expert evidence. There is also a saving of time and a corresponding saving of cost.

(b)   The arbitration can be conducted with the convenience of the parties in mind. There are no fixed rules of procedure like CPR 1998 (although many standard form contracts incorporate arbitration rules which are quite detailed). Instead, the parties may have a preliminary meeting with the arbitrator when they will work out the timetable for the arbitration and the procedure they want to follow.

(c)   The arbitration can take place at a time and place which suits the parties rather than being fixed by the dictates of the court listing system (although other calls on the arbitrator's time may sometimes limit the parties' freedom of choice).

(d)   The dispute can be resolved in total privacy so that, for example, trade secrets can be protected.

(e)   Arbitration is binding on the parties. If the arbitrator's award is not complied with, it can be enforced through the courts.

(f)   Arbitration offers a range of procedures. The parties may opt for a formal hearing, an informal site meeting, or for the case to be resolved on documents only.

(g)   There is greater finality because there is no appeal on questions of fact.

(h)   It can be easier to enforce an arbitration award in a different jurisdiction than it is to enforce a court judgment in a different jurisdiction. This is because many countries are signatories to the New York Convention – see **13.1**.

Not all cases are suited to arbitration, however. If the dispute is about a point of law, it is best resolved in the courts. In some cases, the claimant may need remedies which only a court can give (eg assistance in the enforcement of an injunction). Section 44(2) of the Arbitration Act 1996 (AA 1996) enables the court to supplement the arbitrator's powers in such cases, but they are usually best dealt with by litigation.

Arbitration is not cheap. Lawyers are usually instructed by each party and charge as much for their services in an arbitration as they do in a court case. In litigation, the State provides the judge and the courtroom in return for ever-increasing fees. In an arbitration, the parties have to hire a room for the hearing and they have to pay the arbitrator's fee. Because the arbitrator is an experienced professional, their time will not come cheaply.

1.4 WHICH METHOD OF DISPUTE RESOLUTION?

The most appropriate method of resolution for a particular dispute will depend on all the circumstances and, ultimately, the client's wishes – assuming that there is indeed a choice. Sometimes the best option will be clear-cut – for example, if the client needs an injunction then court proceedings must be taken. If the client wants as quick a resolution as possible, then some form of ADR will clearly be the best option. An arbitration clause in the contract may mean that arbitration must be pursued. The essential attribute for the commercial dispute resolution lawyer is that they understand the scope and characteristics of the available options and can advise the client accordingly.

CHAPTER 2

EARLY CONSIDERATIONS IN COMMERCIAL LITIGATION CASES

LEARNING OUTCOMES

After reading this chapter you will understand:

- the methods of funding commercial litigation
- limitation issues which may arise in commercial litigation
- the scope of pre-action disclosure and when it may be appropriate to apply for a *Norwich Pharmacal* order
- how the rules provide for the conduct of complex actions involving more than two parties
- the difference in approaches when acting for an insurer client or a trade union
- the ways in which the court can impose sanctions for failing to comply with the Practice Direction on Pre-action Conduct
- basic jurisdiction issues
- the approach of the courts to case management.

2.1 INTRODUCTION

When the solicitor is first instructed in relation to any dispute or potential dispute, there are a number of factors which they must explore with their client at a very early stage (during or shortly after instructions are received) in order to protect their client's position.

This chapter seeks to introduce in checklist form some of the more important of those factors and act as a summary of points which the solicitor must run through or discuss with their client. It does not attempt to do more than raise points which may be applicable. Some of the topics, such as jurisdiction, are dealt with in detail in later chapters of this book; others are only mentioned here. In practice, the onus is then upon the individual solicitor to explore the issue in the required depth and to determine whether any action is in fact appropriate. (The more basic considerations which apply in relation to all litigation are examined in Chapter 2 of the Legal Practice Guide, **Civil Litigation**.)

In all cases of course the solicitor needs to identify the client's objective in the matter. In particular, does the client want the best business solution (usually yes) or the 'correct' legal outcome? The solicitor and client must then agree on a strategy to achieve that objective.

2.2 FUNDING THE ACTION

2.2.1 Conditional fee agreements

Conditional fee agreements (CFAs) have traditionally been used almost exclusively in personal injury actions. However, they are of course available for use in commercial litigation, although the potential risk and level of costs in such cases undoubtedly makes them less attractive to solicitors. It is one thing to lose a case, and therefore your costs, in a fast track personal injury case; it is rather different to face the prospect of losing your costs exceeding, say, £500,000 in a substantial commercial case. A solicitor is, however, under a duty to discuss all possible methods of funding the case with a client, and in certain situations a CFA may be the best option but invariably in commercial cases this is at a reduced hourly rate (a 'discounted CFA'). Under a discounted CFA, the solicitors are paid by the client at a reduced hourly rate whatever the outcome of the proceedings. If the client loses, nothing further is payable, but if the client wins, the full hourly charge becomes payable, usually with a success fee.

A client who settles their case through an ADR mechanism such as mediation but on the basis that each side pays its owns costs may consider no payment is due under the CFA signed with their solicitor. The answer will be in the wording of the CFA, as in *Ascension Asset Management Ltd and another v Sky Solicitors Ltd* [2023] EWHC 875 (KB).

A CFA may potentially be unenforceable on the grounds of illegality for significant breaches of the conducting solicitor's obligations in the SRA Code of Conduct (particularly to act with integrity and in the best interests of the client) in the making and performance of the CFA (*Winros Partnership v Global Energy Horizons Corporation* [2021] EWHC 3410 (Ch)).

Is a solicitor entitled to avoid the terms of their own CFA by seeking to recover costs against a former client in reliance on an implied duty of good faith, on the client's part, not to settle the claim on terms that are disadvantageous to the solicitor? No, held the Court of Appeal in *Candey Ltd v Bosheh and another* [2022] EWCA Civ 1103. A client is entitled to settle a claim on terms that are favourable to itself but disadvantageous to its solicitor.

Note that whilst it is not common, a CFA can be used to fund arbitration proceedings.

2.2.2 After the event insurance

Similarly, the possibility of obtaining after the event (ATE) insurance should also be discussed with the client. ATE insurance is most commonly used in personal injury cases but is available from various insurers for commercial litigation. The cover required, ie the amount of the indemnity for the other side's costs, may well run into hundreds of thousands of pounds in commercial litigation, which will be reflected in the size of the premium.

2.2.3 Damages-based agreements

A damages-based agreement (DBA) allows a solicitor to enter into a fee agreement with the client, where the solicitor can take an agreed percentage of the monies recovered for costs.

To be enforceable the DBA must comply with the requirements of s 58AA of the Courts and Legal Services Act 1990 and the Damages-Based Agreements Regulations 2013 (SI 2013/609), which came into force on 1 April 2013. Under reg 3 of the Regulations, the agreement (which must be in writing) must specify:

(a)   the claim or proceedings or parts of them to which the agreement relates;

(b) the circumstances in which the representative's payment, expenses and costs, or part of them, are payable; and

(c) the reason for setting the amount of the payment at the level agreed.

In non-personal injury cases the maximum percentage permitted is 50% of the sums recovered. This must include VAT and counsel's fees but does not include other disbursements.

As costs under a DBA are recoverable only from monies recovered, this means that the case has been successful, at least in part. Usually, therefore, there will also be a costs order in favour of the client. Credit must be given for costs recovered from the losing party.

> **EXAMPLE**
>
> Claimant enters into a 40% DBA with solicitor.
>
> Claimant recovers £500,000 in damages.
>
> Claimant recovers £100,000 in costs. This figure includes disbursements incurred (eg court fees and expert fees).
>
> 40% of £500,000 is £200,000.
>
> Credit is given for the £100,000 costs recovered.
>
> Solicitor is entitled to a further £100,000 out of the damages.
>
> Client receives £400,000.

Of course if the case had been lost the solicitor would receive nothing. The client would be liable to pay the defendant's costs (subject to having the benefit of any ATE insurance). The risk for the solicitor in running a commercial case on a DBA is therefore similar to running it on a CFA – perhaps even higher, because they will be paid only from monies recovered from the other party. For that reason acting on a DBA may not be very popular, except where the potential rewards justify the risk taken. Also note that a DBA can be used only when acting for a party who may recover money in the action, ie the claimant or a counterclaiming defendant (*Candey Ltd v Tonstate Group Ltd* [2022] EWCA Civ 936).

2.2.4 Third party funding

Another type of funding which may be available in commercial litigation is 'third party funding' or 'litigation funding'. This is where a third party – usually a specialist litigation funding company – agrees to finance all or part of the legal costs of the litigation. In return, it will take a fee from any money recovered in the litigation – often expressed as a percentage. This can be used in conjunction with a solicitor acting under a CFA or DBA. This type of funding is becoming increasingly common in England and Wales, and there are now a large number of such companies operating in the market. Whilst this is an expensive method of funding the claim for the commercial client, they may well be attracted to the idea of sharing the risk with the third party.

In R (*on the application of PACCAR Inc and others*) *v Competition Appeal Tribunal and others* [2023] UKSC 28, the Supreme Court had to determine if litigation funding agreements pursuant to which the funder is entitled to recover a percentage of any damages recovered constitute DBAs (see **2.2.3** above). The assumption had been that third party funding arrangements, which assign a passive role to the funders in relation to the conduct of the litigation, are not DBAs within the meaning of s 58AA, not contrary to public policy, and so are enforceable as ordinary binding contractual arrangements. But the Court held that these funding agreements are DBAs and have to meet the formal requirements to be enforceable. As a result, we may see some significant changes to third party funding in the future.

2.3 LIMITATION ISSUES

This topic is raised in the Legal Practice Guide, **Civil Litigation** as one of the considerations to be borne in mind at the first interview with the client, and the basic limitation rules are set out there. Limitation is a complex area of the law, and this section seeks only to remind the solicitor of its importance in the litigation process and to ring some warning bells. If there is a potential limitation problem, the solicitor should refer to specialist texts such as McGee (see **2.13**) so that they may be sure that all possible arguments are pursued. The principal statutory authority is the Limitation Act 1980 (LA 1980).

In the majority of cases, the limitation period commences on the date the cause of action arises. The basic rule for claims founded on contract or tort is that the claimant has six years from the date of the cause of action to commence proceedings.

In commercial litigation, issues of limitation may arise because the limitation period is about to end; because the time the cause of action arose is not clear-cut; or because some of the extensions and/or exceptions to the basic limitation rule may apply. A number of those extensions/exceptions are considered briefly below.

2.3.1 Initial considerations

Failure to issue proceedings or take other steps within the limitation period has always been a major source of negligence claims against solicitors and should therefore remain foremost in the solicitor's mind. All necessary checks must be put in place to ensure that any time limits are not missed (eg a duplicate diary system), and also that any relevant exceptions to the basic rule are claimed on behalf of the client. (Remember that limitation must be specifically claimed, whether as a defence or as an extension to the basic rule.) If there is any doubt as to whether the limitation period has expired, or if the time period left is short, a solicitor should issue proceedings to protect the client's position. The solicitor must look at the problem from all angles to establish what type of claim they are dealing with, whether more than one claim (and thus potentially more than one limitation period) is involved, and what points on limitation might be raised by the other side. Even if the most obvious claim is time-barred, an alternative claim might be available. Solicitors acting for potential defendants should pay equal attention to this consideration when first approached by their client. If limitation can be pleaded as a defence, it is a very effective tool for a defendant.

2.3.2 Exceptions

There are a number of exceptions to the basic limitation periods, notably the latent damage exception for a claim in negligence when the initial time limit can be extended under s 14A of the LA 1980 to the date three years after the claimant first had knowledge of all the facts relevant to the cause of action, with an ultimate longstop date of 15 years from the alleged breach of duty. Section 14A applies *only* to negligence claims in tort and not to claims which can only be framed in contract (see *Société Commerciale de Reassurance v Eras International (formerly Eras (UK)); The Eras Eil Actions (Note)* [1992] 2 All ER 82).

Some other points are worthy of a brief mention:

(a)   *Fraud.* Section 32 of the LA 1980 contains a similar exception to that contained in s 14A, namely that in the event of fraud, concealment or mistake, the limitation period is postponed until six years from the claimant discovering the fraud, etc.

In *Seedo v El Gamal and others* [2023] EWCA Civ 330, the Court had to answer the following question: if a defendant tells two lies to induce a claimant to enter into a contract, does a new limitation period start running on the claimant's later discovery of the second lie? The Court found that this depended on whether the second lie gave rise to a different cause of action, as limitation operates by barring different causes of action. Nugee LJ explained the answer in the following way (at [70] and [71]):

Take the case where a vendor sells a house to a purchaser. If in order to induce the sale the vendor tells the purchaser two distinct and unconnected lies, I would readily accept that they gave rise to different causes of action. Suppose for example the vendor untruthfully said that there were no ongoing disputes with the neighbours, and also that the house did not suffer from subsidence. The purchaser discovers soon after moving in that the first statement was untrue, but reaches an accommodation with his neighbour such that he does not think it worth suing the vendor for that deceit. Then some years later he discovers that the second statement was also untrue, with far more serious consequences. In my view that would be a separate complaint of a separate deceit; it would constitute a separate cause of action; and the purchaser would have 6 years from when he discovered (or could with reasonable diligence have discovered) that statement to be untrue, even if his right of action on the first deceit was statute-barred.

But it is not obvious that the same applies where the vendor tells two related lies as part of the same overall deceit. Suppose for example that the vendor tells the purchaser untruthfully that the house does not suffer from subsidence, and also that he has not made any insurance claim in respect of the house. In fact the house not only suffers from subsidence but the vendor made a claim on his policy for it. The purchaser discovers that the house does suffer from subsidence and that the vendor knew that, but fails to bring a claim within 6 years. He then happens to discover that the vendor also lied about not making an insurance claim. I would think it very surprising if that could give him another 6 years to bring what would in essence be a claim for the same deceit. In my judgment he could not do so, and that would be because the second lie did not give rise to a separate cause of action. Both lies, although different in their detail, were designed to conceal from the purchaser the same thing.

(b) *Consumer.* Claims under the Consumer Protection Act 1987 are subject to a statutory 10-year longstop date after which claims cannot be brought.

(c) *Contribution.* Where a claim for contribution is brought by way of separate proceedings (ie not by way of an additional claim under Part 20), under the Civil Liability Contribution Act 1978 the limitation period is two years from the date of judgment or, if none, from the date of any agreement to settle reached between the parties. The court has the power to apportion liability between two or more persons who are liable for the same damage (whether in tort, contract or otherwise).

(d) *Pending actions.* Lastly, s 35 of the LA 1980 and r 19.5 of CPR 1998 restrict the ability of a party to defeat the rules on limitation by adding a new claim to existing proceedings when it would be too late to start a separate action (whether a Part 20 counterclaim, new party or new cause of action etc – see further **2.7.1** and **2.7.2**).

2.3.3 Other time limits

There are other time limits of which a solicitor needs to be aware. These include those applicable under the Companies Act 2006, the Insolvency Act 1986, and the Financial Services and Markets Act 2000.

Very often, commercial contracts alter the limitation period by specifying very short periods for notifying the other party of claims. If, for example, a contract between A and B says that any party must notify the other within six months of any dispute or potential dispute, the courts are likely to enforce that contract. If A complains even a day late about an alleged breach of contract by B, they will probably find that they will have lost the right to sue B. It is vitally important for solicitors acting for a party to a potential dispute to check the contract and related documents to make sure that there are no such time limits. It is equally important to comply with those time limits, even if the limitation period under the LA 1980 has not expired. As you will see in **Chapter 13**, a similar issue arises in arbitration agreements.

2.3.4 Agreeing to extend limitation periods

In some cases, it may not be desirable to commence proceedings against another party or to join another party at the outset of the action. This may, for example, be because the claim against such parties is not strong or because, for commercial reasons, it is preferable to sue another person. The danger, however, is that due to problems of limitation, it may not be possible to take steps at a later stage to sue or to join that other party. In such circumstances, the parties will often in practice try to agree a stay of the limitation period. The agreement will stop time running as between the parties for a specific purpose, dispute or case as set out in the agreement. If either party then wishes to bring a claim (because the original defendant is held not liable or because further facts emerge changing the whole face of the litigation), they are not prevented from doing so. It is therefore essential for a solicitor to be aware of all persons against whom such a potential claim might be made. They must consider whether any other parties should be sued or joined to the main action and, if not, whether a stay should be agreed (see **2.7**).

2.3.5 Foreign element

Another area which should always be borne in mind in commercial litigation is the question of whether any foreign limitation period might apply. If so, foreign legal advice should be taken as early as possible to ensure that any claim is not time-barred as a result of a foreign time limit. Where (eg as a result of a contractual choice of law clause) the English courts apply foreign law, then under the Foreign Limitation Periods Act 1984 the limitation period will be that governed by the foreign law. The foreign limitation period will be determined by the judge as a matter of fact on hearing expert evidence on the question from the parties.

2.4 CAPACITY

A solicitor must be satisfied, before bringing any claim, that their client has legal capacity under English law to sue and, equally importantly, that the intended defendant can be sued. The same consideration will of course apply if acting for the defendant; the solicitor should immediately check that the claimant has the right to sue and that their client can be sued. The solicitor should never make any assumptions, particularly where the limitation period is about to expire or where a foreign party is involved. A foreign party may well be recognised under foreign law but not have the right to sue in England and Wales.

When acting for or against individuals, remember that special rules exist to protect children and patients, and that they must be followed strictly where such persons are sued or intend to sue. Equally, if the client or intended other party is dead, the solicitor should consider whether the claim will survive (it does not, eg, in relation to a potential defamation claim) and should also check that any necessary approvals have been correctly obtained from the representatives of the deceased.

The question of legal capacity is equally important when dealing with some other form of legal body (which will be far more common in commercial litigation). In cases involving partnerships, make sure that all the relevant partners involved at the time of the cause of action are named in the action. If a party is neither a company nor a partnership, the solicitor will need to determine whether the body constitutes an unincorporated body (eg a trade union) for the purposes of English law. If not, then it cannot sue or be sued.

Finally, the solicitor should confirm whether the approval of any third person is required before litigation can be brought either by or against the intended party. The approval of a liquidator or an administrator (or possibly the permission of the court) would normally be required, for example, for an insolvent person to commence court proceedings. Alternatively, the approval of a trustee (eg for a charity) might be required. If any approval is required, it should be obtained at the outset. Do not make any assumptions and do not wait until the limitation period has almost expired in the hope that there will be no problem.

2.5 IN-HOUSE LEGAL DEPARTMENTS

Many large commercial clients will have their own legal departments. In this situation, instructions to a firm to act for the company will usually come from its lawyer. The in-house lawyer may well deal with the initial stage of the dispute before taking the decision to instruct an outside firm.

2.6 DISCLOSURE OBLIGATIONS AND PRE-ACTION DISCLOSURE

2.6.1 Advising the client

Once a client is aware that they may become a party to proceedings in the Business and Property Courts, they are subject to certain duties including the preservation of documents pursuant to CPR 1998, PD 57AD, paras 3 and 4. In particular, the client must be advised to suspend their document deletion or destruction processes, notify relevant employees and former employees who may be in possession of disclosable documents which are not also in the client's possession and require agents or third parties who may hold documents on their behalf not to delete or destroy documents that may be relevant to an issue in the proceedings.

2.6.2 Pre-action disclosure

Rule 31.16 of the CPR 1998 gives the court the power to make an order for disclosure before commercial proceedings are issued where the respondent is likely to be a party to the subsequent proceedings (see Legal Practice Guide, *Civil Litigation* at **3.9**). However, where a party needs an order for disclosure against a respondent who is unlikely to be a party to the potential proceedings then it can make use of what is generally known as a *Norwich Pharmacal* order. The ability of the court to make such an order was established by the House of Lords in *Norwich Pharmacal v Commissioners of Customs & Excise* [1974] AC 133. In that case the applicant, Norwich Pharmacal, wanted to obtain information from Customs & Excise about the importation of a particular chemical compound (patented by Norwich Pharmacal) that had been imported into the country without a licence from Norwich Pharmacal. Norwich Pharmacal had no cause of action against Customs & Excise but sought disclosure of the names of the wrongdoers who had imported the chemic3l compound. The House of Lords held that Customs & Excise was indeed under a duty to disclose the information sought. In order to obtain a *Norwich Pharmacal* order, the party will generally have to show:

(a)   there are no other relevant CPR 1998 provisions;

(b)   the respondent is likely to have relevant documents or information;

(c)   the respondent is involved in the wrongdoing;

(d)   the respondent is not merely a witness who could be called to give evidence or produce documents;

(e)   the order is necessary in the interests of justice.

The court may also require the applicant to provide a cross-undertaking in damages.

Many applications fail to jump the hurdles in (c) and (d) above. For example, in *Hayden v Associated Newspapers Ltd* [2022] EWHC 2693 (KB) the claimant sought an order for disclosure against His Majesty's Courts and Tribunal Service (HMCTS) of documents that would identify the person who had obtained a copy of a Court order that had subsequently been posted, anonymously, on the website of KiwiFarms. The claimant's contention was that the person who obtained the order was likely to be the same person who had posted it on the website. The application was refused by Nicklin J, stating at [73]:

> [HMCTS] has not in any way participated in or facilitated the publication of the KiwiFarms Post. [Its] provision of a copy of the [Order] – in discharge of the duty under CPR 5.4C(1) – no more 'facilitated' the KiwiFarms Post than would a stationery shop selling someone a pen and paper 'facilitate' the sending of a defamatory letter.

Applications for *Norwich Pharmacal* orders should be made by issuing a claim form in accordance with CPR 1998, r 8 with the respondent as the defendant. The application must be supported by evidence which will usually be in the form of a witness statement. The applicant should give full and frank disclosure of all material facts. The application will usually be made on notice unless there is a need for secrecy or urgency. That might apply, for example, where the respondent is likely to be under a duty to inform the intended defendant (in the proposed main action) of the application. Where the application is going to be made on notice then it would be sensible for the applicant to contact the respondent asking for voluntary disclosure of the information requested to save the costs of the application to the court.

2.7 COMPLEX ACTIONS

It is commonplace for commercial litigation disputes to involve a number of different parties and/or causes of action. The Legal Practice Guide, **Civil Litigation** introduces the provisions in Part 20 of CPR 1998 which govern the circumstances in which a defendant may bring a claim against:

(a)   the claimant (a counterclaim);

(b)   another defendant (a claim for a contribution or indemnity); or

(c)   someone who is not already a party (a Part 20 'Third Party' claim).

This section considers the rules other than those in Part 20 by which the court manages disputes involving a number of parties or causes of action. As a starting point, it is worth remembering that the aim of the court is to have as few actions as possible, with as few parties as possible. This reduces duplication of work, ensuring that the dispute is resolved as quickly as possible and without incurring unnecessary costs, all of which is in accordance with the overriding objective. It also avoids the risk of inconsistent judgments on related matters. On the other hand, there is a limit to what can appropriately be dealt with in a single action. The purpose of the court rules is to enable the court to strike a sensible balance.

2.7.1 Causes of action

It is not at all unusual for a number of causes of action to be dealt with in a single action. Under r 7.3 of CPR 1998, the claimant may use a single claim form to start all claims which can be conveniently disposed of in the same proceedings. For a detailed discussion of this provision, see *Abbott v Ministry of Defence* [2023] EWHC 1475 (KB).

However, the claimant may run into difficulties if they wish to introduce a new cause of action after they have served the particulars of claim. The claimant cannot amend the particulars of claim without obtaining either the written consent of all the other parties or the permission of the court. Broadly, the court is likely to allow the amendment, provided the new cause of action can conveniently be dealt with as part of the original proceedings. Important factors are whether the amendment would necessitate an alteration in the arrangements for trial and whether it is fair for the defendant to face a new claim given the stage the proceedings have reached.

More stringent considerations apply where the claimant is seeking to introduce a cause of action after the expiry of the limitation period. The court has a discretion to allow the amendment if the new claim arises out of the same facts or substantially the same facts as an existing claim.

EXAMPLE

C sues D for breach of contract, issuing the claim form on 1 March. In December, C decides they also wish to bring a claim against D for negligence, but the limitation period for this expired in June. If C issued a separate claim form, D would have an impregnable defence. If, however, C is allowed to amend the original claim form and particulars of claim, the negligence claim will be treated as having been made on the date the original claim form was issued. The court may allow the amendment only if the negligence and contract claims arise out of the same or substantially the same facts.

2.7.2 Addition, substitution and removal of parties

Part 19 of CPR 1998 states that once a claim form has been served, the court's permission is required to remove, add or substitute a party. An application to the court may be made, either by an existing party or by a person who wishes to be added as a party.

2.7.2.1 Adding a party

The court may add a new party to the proceedings if:

(a)   it is desirable for resolving the matters in dispute; or

(b)   there is an issue involving the new party and an existing party which is connected to the matters in dispute in the existing proceedings, and it is desirable to add the new party so that the court can resolve that issue.

A party cannot be added as a claimant unless their written consent has been filed at court. The court may, however, require such a party to be joined as a defendant.

2.7.2.2 Removing a party

The court can order any person to cease to be a party to proceedings if it is not desirable that they should be one.

2.7.2.3 Substituting a party

The court may order the substitution of one party for another, provided this is desirable and the original party's interest or liability has passed to the new party.

Where the court makes an order removing, substituting or adding a party, it may also make any consequential directions that are necessary, such as the serving of relevant documents on a new party.

2.7.2.4 Limitation

Special considerations apply where a party wishes to add or substitute after the expiration of a limitation period.

The court may add or substitute a party if the relevant limitation period was current when the proceedings were started and the addition or substitution is necessary. Rule 19.5(3) provides that it is only necessary if the court is satisfied that:

(a)   the new party is to be substituted for a party who was named in the claim form in mistake for the new party; or

(b)   the claim cannot properly be carried on by or against the original party unless the new party is added or substituted as claimant or defendant; or

(c)   the original party has died or has had a bankruptcy order made against them and their interest or liability has passed to the new party.

There are further provisions relating to personal injuries claims which are not within the scope of this book.

2.7.3 Consolidation

As part of its general management powers (see further **2.12.1**), the court may direct that two or more actions shall be consolidated into a single action (r 3.1(2)(g)). The purpose of consolidation is to save costs by avoiding unnecessary duplication of work during the interim stages and by holding a single trial. Alternatively, the court may leave the actions as separate proceedings but order that they are tried together (r 3.1(2)(h)).

In both cases, the court can make the order on its own initiative or on the application of a party. The claims must be pending in the same court, but where they have been started in different courts, they can be transferred so that the order can be made.

When considering whether to consolidate proceedings, the court will consider a number of factors: first, the extent of the overlap of the facts and issues; second, the extent to which consolidation might avoid the risk of inconsistent findings; third, the cost and delays involved in a multiplicity of proceedings, of pleadings, of pre-trial steps taken by the parties and of interim applications that might be avoided if consolidation were ordered; fourth, the stage in the proceedings in which consolidation is sought, it being more likely that consolidation will avoid cost and delay if it is sought earlier rather than later; fifth, the extent to which the advantages of consolidation might be achieved by other means, including but not limited to an order under CPR 1998, r 3.1(2)(h) for the claims to be tried on the same occasion; and, sixth, whether the claimants in the consolidated claim can be jointly represented by the same legal representatives: see generally *Atos IT Services UK Ltd v Secretary of State for Business, Energy and Industrial Strategy* [2022] EWHC 787 (TCC) at [15] to [16].

2.7.4 Multi-party actions

This is intended only as a brief introduction to this topic. The solicitor handling a case should consider at the outset of a dispute whether a multi-party approach is appropriate. If so, specialist advice, or at least further research into CPR 1998 will be required.

Part 19 identifies two categories of proceedings that can be described as multi-party:

(a)   proceedings taken or defended by representative parties; and

(b)   group litigation.

2.7.4.1 Representative parties (r 19.8)

Where more than one person has the same interest in a claim, one of them may, with the permission of the court, pursue or defend the claim as representative for the others. In *Lloyd v Google LLC* [2021] UKSC 50, Lord Leggatt, giving the judgment of the Court, stated at [71] and [75]:

> The phrase 'the same interest', as it is used in the representative rule, needs to be interpreted purposively in light of the overriding objective of the civil procedure rules and the rationale for the representative procedure. The premise for a representative action is that claims are capable of being brought by (or against) a number of people which raise a common issue (or issues): hence the potential and motivation for a judgment which binds them all. The purpose of requiring the representative to have 'the same interest' in the claim as the persons represented is to ensure that the representative can be relied on to conduct the litigation in a way which will effectively promote and protect the interests of all the members of the represented class.

> Where the same interest requirement is satisfied, the court has a discretion whether to allow a claim to proceed as a representative action. As with any power given to it by the Civil Procedure Rules, the court must in exercising its discretion seek to give effect to the overriding objective of dealing with cases justly and at proportionate cost: see CPR rule 1.2(a). Many of the considerations specifically included in that objective (see CPR rule 1.1(2)) - such as ensuring that the parties are on an equal footing, saving expense, dealing with the case in ways which are proportionate to the amount of money involved, ensuring that the case is dealt with expeditiously and fairly, and allotting to it an appropriate share of the court's resources while taking into account the need to allot resources to other cases - are likely to militate in favour of allowing a claim, where practicable, to be continued as a representative action rather than leaving members of the class to pursue claims individually.

Unless the court directs otherwise, any judgment or order that is made against the representative party is binding on all the persons represented in the claim. However, the judgment or order may be enforced by or against anyone other than the representative only with the permission of the court.

2.7.4.2 Group litigation (r 19.21–r 19.26)

Where there are a number of claims that give rise to common or related issues of fact or law, the court may make a Group Litigation Order (GLO). Such orders are intended for large-scale litigation involving multiple parties. Their purpose is to ensure that all the claims which fall within the scope of the group litigation are properly coordinated. For example, a GLO might be suitable where a large number of individuals and/or businesses have been damaged by an environmental disaster caused by a particular company, or, alternatively, where a pharmaceutical company faces hundreds of claims as the result of the alleged ill-effects of one of their drugs. In both instances, it is advantageous to both the claimants and the defendant(s) to ensure that the mass of claims is effectively managed and that work is not duplicated.

Where a GLO is made, a register is established of all the claims that form part of it and a direction may be made as to how the GLO should be publicised. The court will set a date by which those wishing to take part in the group litigation should register. Anyone wishing to register after the cut-off date will be permitted to do so only with the permission of the court.

All the claims within the GLO will be allocated to the multi-track. They are managed by a single court, which has the power to make directions to ensure that the litigation is handled effectively. To assist in this, a managing judge is appointed with overall responsibility for the claim. A single solicitor may be appointed as the 'lead' solicitor. Practice Direction (PD) 19B of CPR 1998 recommends that their role and their relationship with the solicitors representing the other group litigants should be carefully defined in writing.

In order to reduce duplication, the court may order group particulars of claim to be prepared. The allegations common to all the claimants are set out in the main body of the document, with the facts relating to individual claimants being contained in a schedule. Another way the court can reduce costs is by ordering one or more claims to proceed as test cases.

A judgment or an order that is made in relation to any claim in the register will be binding on all the parties to all the claims which are on the register at the time it is made. It is for the court to direct whether and how the order or judgment should affect claims that join the register after it was made. A party who is affected by an order or judgment may apply for an order that they should not be bound by it.

2.8 DERIVATIVE CLAIMS (CPR 1998, r 19.14)

This is the name for a claim made by one or more members of a company, other incorporated body or trade union for a remedy to which the company, body or union claims to be entitled. The company, body or union for whose benefit the remedy is sought must be a defendant to the claim.

For example, if the minority shareholders in a company want to sue the directors for breach of the duties that they owe to the company, the minority shareholders would issue a derivative claim against the directors. The company would also be named as a defendant.

After the claim has been issued, the claimant is obliged to apply to the court for permission to continue the proceedings.

2.9 ACTING FOR INSURERS OR TRADE UNIONS

Throughout the course of any proceedings, whether they take place in court or elsewhere, a solicitor acting for insurers or trade unions (on behalf of their insured and members respectively) will have a number of additional factors to bear in mind. Similarly, there are different considerations if acting against such bodies.

The essential thing to remember is that insurers and trade unions have interests other than those of the actual party itself and are keen to keep costs to a minimum. They are in business and have relatively large sums of money at their disposal with which to fight a case if necessary. They will not hesitate to use those advantages in order to force favourable settlements and they will negotiate hard. Solicitors need to be alert to those interests whichever side they are acting for.

Most insurance policies contain a 'control of defence' clause. This means in simple terms that the insurer is entitled to bring or defend an action in the name of the insured. (The action must still be brought by or against the insured by name and not against the insurer but the insurer is usually entitled to enforce this result under the insurance contract, ie make the insured lend their name to the action.)

Solicitors need to be alive to the possibility of a conflict of interest between the client (insurer) and the insured. The solicitor owes many of the same duties to the insured but their primary responsibility is to the insurer. If there is likely to be a conflict of interests, it may well be that the solicitor cannot represent the insured, and they must bear this consideration in mind throughout the life of the litigation. Depending on the circumstances, it may also be the case that it is inappropriate for them to continue acting for *either* party, ie for either the insurer or the insured.

2.10 PRE-ACTION CONDUCT

The general principles governing pre-action conduct are set out in Practice Direction – Pre-action conduct and protocols, which applies where there is no specific pre-action protocol.

The objectives are set out in para 3:

3.   Before commencing proceedings, the court will expect the parties to have exchanged sufficient information to—

(a)   understand each other's position;

(b)   make decisions about how to proceed;

(c)   try to settle the issues without proceedings;

(d)   consider a form of Alternative Dispute Resolution (ADR) to assist with settlement;

(e)   support the efficient management of those proceedings; and

(f)   reduce the costs of resolving the dispute.

Proportionality is dealt with in paras 4 and 5:

4.   A pre-action protocol or this Practice Direction must not be used by a party as a tactical device to secure an unfair advantage over another party. Only reasonable and proportionate steps should be taken by the parties to identify, narrow and resolve the legal, factual or expert issues.

5.   The costs incurred in complying with a pre-action protocol or this Practice Direction should be proportionate (CPR 44.3(5)). Where parties incur disproportionate costs in complying with any pre-action protocol or this Practice Direction, those costs will not be recoverable as part of the costs of the proceedings.

Settlement and ADR are dealt with in paras 8–11:

8.   Litigation should be a last resort. As part of a relevant pre-action protocol or this Practice Direction, the parties should consider whether negotiation or some other form of ADR might enable them to settle their dispute without commencing proceedings.

9.   Parties should continue to consider the possibility of reaching a settlement at all times, including after proceedings have been started. Part 36 offers may be made before proceedings are issued.

10.   Parties may negotiate to settle a dispute or may use a form of ADR including—

(a)   mediation, a third party facilitating a resolution;

(b)   arbitration, a third party deciding the dispute;

(c)   early neutral evaluation, a third party giving an informed opinion on the dispute; and

(d)   Ombudsmen schemes.

(Information on mediation and other forms of ADR is available in the Jackson ADR Handbook (available from Oxford University Press) or at—

•   https://www.gov.uk/guidance/a-guide-to-civil-mediation

11.   If proceedings are issued, the parties may be required by the court to provide evidence that ADR has been considered. A party's silence in response to an invitation to participate or a refusal to

participate in ADR might be considered unreasonable by the court and could lead to the court ordering that party to pay additional court costs.

The approach of the courts towards compliance is dealt with in paras 13–16.

13.   If a dispute proceeds to litigation, the court will expect the parties to have complied with a relevant pre-action protocol or this Practice Direction. The court will take into account non-compliance when giving directions for the management of proceedings (see CPR 3.1(4) to (6)) and when making orders for costs (see CPR 44.3(5)(a)). The court will consider whether all parties have complied in substance with the terms of the relevant pre-action protocol or this Practice Direction and is not likely to be concerned with minor or technical infringements, especially when the matter is urgent (for example an application for an injunction).

14.   The court may decide that there has been a failure of compliance when a party has—

(a)   not provided sufficient information to enable the objectives in paragraph 3 to be met;

(b)   not acted within a time limit set out in a relevant protocol, or within a reasonable period; or

(c)   unreasonably refused to use a form of ADR, or failed to respond at all to an invitation to do so.

15.   Where there has been non-compliance with a pre-action protocol or this Practice Direction, the court may order that

(a)   the parties are relieved of the obligation to comply or further comply with the pre-action protocol or this Practice Direction;

(b)   the proceedings are stayed while particular steps are taken to comply with the pre-action protocol or this Practice Direction;

(c)   sanctions are to be applied.

16.   The court will consider the effect of any non-compliance when deciding whether to impose any sanctions which may include—

(a)   an order that the party at fault pays the costs of the proceedings, or part of the costs of the other party or parties;

(b)   an order that the party at fault pay those costs on an indemnity basis;

(c)   if the party at fault is a claimant who has been awarded a sum of money, an order depriving that party of interest on that sum for a specified period, and/or awarding interest at a lower rate than would otherwise have been awarded;

(d)   if the party at fault is a defendant, and the claimant has been awarded a sum of money, an order awarding interest on that sum for a specified period at a higher rate, (not exceeding 10% above base rate), than the rate which would otherwise have been awarded.

An example of the imposition of sanctions came in *Digicel v Cable and Wireless* [2010] EWHC 888 (Ch) (see **10.5.1**) where the court ordered the unsuccessful claimant to pay the defendant's costs on the indemnity rather than standard basis. One of the reasons for the court's decision was the failure by the claimant to comply with the Practice Direction, in particular by failing to send a letter of claim before issuing proceedings.

It is important to note, however, that the Practice Direction accepts that in certain situations the general principles cannot or should not apply. An example of this is freezing injunctions (see **Chapter 8**), where telling the other party in advance of your intentions would defeat the whole purpose of the application.

Similarly, if the limitation period is about to expire, proceedings must be issued without delay. In that situation, following the issue of proceedings, the parties should seek to agree to apply to the court for an order staying the proceedings whilst the parties take steps to comply.

What if proceedings are issued in breach of a contractual dispute resolution clause? The court is likely to stay the proceedings. For example, in *Ohpen Operations UK Ltd v Invesco Fund Managers Ltd* [2019] BLR 576 (TCC), O'Farrell J stayed proceedings which were commenced in breach of a contractual mediation scheme. She observed at [58]:

There is a clear and strong policy in favour of enforcing alternative dispute resolution provisions and in encouraging parties to attempt to resolve disputes prior to litigation. Where a contract contains valid machinery for resolving potential disputes between the parties, it will usually be necessary for the parties to follow that machinery, and the court will not permit an action to be brought in breach of such agreement.

2.11   JURISDICTION

One of the most important tactical considerations to bear in mind at the outset of any dispute is the choice of forum of any proceedings (whether they are to take place in court or elsewhere).

In commercial litigation, there is very often some foreign element involved and thus, since the forum can be very important to the client and to the outcome of the action, it is essential, at the outset, to take all necessary steps to try to ensure that the chosen forum is the best for the client. Such steps may involve issuing proceedings before another party takes the initiative to sue elsewhere, or indeed making a challenge to jurisdiction, where appropriate. Considerations of cost and practicality will of course have to be borne in mind and discussed with the client. It may be necessary to obtain foreign legal advice. (This topic is dealt with in more detail in **Chapters 16** and **17**.)

Sometimes it may be possible to bring a claim in the United States of America. Claimants are often attracted to this jurisdiction as a result of the high levels of damages in certain cases which have attracted media coverage.

2.12   CASE MANAGEMENT

Closer control of cases through the exercise of the court's management powers is a very important feature of CPR 1998.

In today's climate of commercially aware clients and in an increasingly competitive marketplace, solicitors need to be prepared to 'manage' the litigation for the client as if it were any other business project. The more the solicitor can plan up front, the better prepared the solicitor and their client will be for all eventualities. This means that the solicitor will need to spend an additional amount of time at the outset planning the expected life of the litigation, discovering exactly what the client wishes to do and anticipating the likely moves by the other side, rather than simply waiting to react later. Steps can then be taken to avoid or frustrate likely action by the other side, for example to issue proceedings first in a location convenient for the client.

Costs are always an overriding concern of the client (and rightly so, given the average price of commercial litigation today). It is essential to determine what price the client is prepared to pay in respect of the claim or dispute. Obtaining justice or proving a principle may seem less important to the client as the costs of litigation spiral. The client is running a business and the litigation is merely one element of it. The solicitor must be prepared to discuss this 'costs/ benefit analysis' with the client on a regular basis. A realistic costs estimate may result in the client deciding not to proceed with the claim, but that client is far more likely to return in the future than a dissatisfied client who has been faced with a series of 'unpleasant surprises' by way of costs.

Under para 8.7 of the SRA Code of Conduct, clients must receive the best possible information, both at the time of engagement and when appropriate as their matter progresses, about the likely overall cost of their matter. To what extent is a solicitor bound by any estimate of the likely overall costs? In *Mastercigars v Withers LLP* [2007] EWHC 2733 (Ch) the defendant solicitors had given their client an estimate of just over £206,000 to take the case through to trial. This was not updated. The final costs were in the region of £1 million. The court held that although the estimate was an important factor to take into account on the assessment of costs as between solicitor and client, it did not bind the solicitor absolutely.

However, in *Reynolds v Stone Rowe Brewer* [2008] EWHC 497 the court came to a rather different conclusion, holding that the solicitor was bound by the original estimate even though he had updated it from time to time. The basis for this was that the client had relied upon the original estimate in deciding how to approach the litigation.

The general provisions about costs management and costs budgets are set out in the Legal Practice Guide *Civil Litigation* at **9.7**. As stated there, the budget must be in the form of Precedent H, which is annexed to PD 3D of CPR 1998. It must be filed with the court and served on the other side either with their directions questionnaire if the value of the claim is less than £50,000, or at least 21 days before the first case management conference (CMC). Failure to do so will result in a very severe sanction – CPR 1998, r 3.14 states that unless the court orders otherwise, any party which fails to file a budget despite being required to do so will be treated as having filed a budget comprising only the applicable court fees (as to relief from the sanction see **2.12.1**).

Following the filing of the budgets, the parties must file an agreed budget discussion report (usually in the form of Precedent R) no later than seven days before the CMC. In most cases the court will then make a costs management order (CMO) pursuant to CPR 1998, r 3.15. This will record the extent to which the budgets are agreed between the parties, and, in respect of budgets which are not agreed, record the court's approval after making appropriate revisions. If a CMO is made, the court will thereafter control the parties' budgets in respect of recoverable costs.

Cost-capping orders, now dealt with in CPR 1998, rr 3.19–3.21, are likely to be fairly rare now.

2.12.1 Case management under CPR 1998

Part 26 of CPR 1998 deals with the first aspect of case management. This is the allocation of a case to the appropriate track, which is dealt with in the Legal Practice Guide, *Civil Litigation*.

Once a case has been allocated to the correct track, Part 3 of CPR 1998 sets out the court's case management powers. The general powers of the court are set out in r 3.1(2) which provides that the court may:

(a) extend or shorten the time for compliance with any rule, practice direction or court order (even if an application for extension is made after the time for compliance has expired);

(b) adjourn or bring forward a hearing;

(c) require a party or a party's legal representative to attend the court;

(d) hold a hearing and receive evidence by telephone or by using any other method of direct oral communication;

(e) direct that part of any proceedings (such as a counterclaim) be dealt with as separate proceedings;

(f) stay the whole or part of any proceedings either generally or until a specified date or event;

(g) consolidate proceedings;

(h) try two or more claims on the same occasion;

(i) direct a separate trial of any issue;

(j) decide the order in which issues are to be tried;

(k) exclude an issue from consideration;

(l) dismiss or give judgment on a claim after a decision on a preliminary issue;

(ll) order any party to file and exchange a costs budget;

(m) take any other step or make any other order for the purpose of managing the case and furthering the overriding objective, including hearing an Early Neutral Evaluation with the aim of helping the parties settle the case.

Rule 3.1(3) states that, when the court makes any order, it may specify the consequences of non-compliance. Under r 3.8, any sanction for failing to comply with any rule, practice direction or court order takes effect automatically unless the party in default applies for and obtains relief from that sanction. Where the court has set a deadline for complying with an order, it is possible for the parties to agree to extend such a deadline for up to a maximum of 28 days, provided always that any such extension does not put at risk any hearing date – r 3.8(4).

Rule 3.9 requires all applications for relief to be supported by evidence, which will usually be witness statements from the parties and their lawyers. See further the Legal Practice Guide, **Civil Litigation** at **9.4**.

2.13 SUMMARY

When the solicitor first receives instructions from their client in relation to a commercial dispute, there are a number of preliminary considerations, which it is essential for them to run through, before they can think about issuing proceedings. In general, any time (within reason) which the solicitor spends planning the litigation is time well spent and should help achieve the client's aims, reduce the chance of unwelcome surprises and result in a satisfied client.

In most cases a costs budget must be prepared, and the solicitor should ensure that during the conduct of litigation all rules and orders are complied with.

To conclude, the solicitor needs to be prepared to discuss the realistic level of costs and to show a plan for the litigation in order to prepare their client. The client's objectives need to be aired in full at the outset and a strategy agreed. This plan and the level of costs must be kept under constant review throughout the life of the litigation.

CHAPTER 3

THE COMMERCIAL COURT

LEARNING OUTCOMES

After reading this chapter you will understand:

- the nature of the Commercial Court
- the importance of the Commercial Court Guide
- case management in the Commercial Court
- the disclosure process in the Commercial Court
- interim applications in the Commercial Court
- trial in the Commercial Court
- the role of the Circuit Commercial Courts.

3.1 INTRODUCTION

As stated at **1.2**, much commercial litigation is conducted in the Commercial Court. This chapter explains the role of the Commercial Court and its special practices and procedures.

3.1.1 The Commercial Court

The Commercial Court is part of the Admiralty and Commercial Court Registry which is itself part of the King's Bench Division of the High Court. The Commercial Court was established in 1895 to provide a court which was familiar with commercial disputes and which would have procedures to enable such disputes to be resolved quickly and efficiently. It was restructured in its present form in 1970. Since October 2017, it has been a key part of the Business and Property Courts of England and Wales.

The Commercial Court provides a specialised service for businesspersons. The judges of the Commercial Court are specifically assigned to that court. They practised in the Commercial Court before they became judges and are experts in the types of cases dealt with by the Commercial Court. Although the court can be, and is, used for relatively straightforward matters, it also attracts cases which are highly complex and involve vast sums of money. Much of the court's specialised practice arises from the need to prevent these 'heavy' cases from becoming 'bogged down' by the weight of the evidence. Slow progress to a lengthy trial is discouraged.

3.1.2 The Commercial Court Guide

Part 58 of CPR 1998 and the accompanying Practice Direction deal specifically with the Commercial Court. These set out the basic differences of procedure in the Commercial Court as compared with the 'general' courts. By r 58.3:

> These Rules [ie CPR 1998 as a whole] and their practice directions apply to claims in the commercial list unless this Part or a practice direction provides otherwise.

However, that does not reflect the whole picture because practitioners in the Commercial Court must also be fully acquainted with, and follow, the provisions of the Commercial Court Guide (or, to give it its full title, The Commercial Court Guide (incorporating The Admiralty Court Guide) (the Guide)).

The Guide is prepared by the Commercial Court Committee ('the Committee'). The Committee is made up of judges and representatives of practitioners and users of the court. It receives and discusses suggestions for improving Commercial Court practice and makes recommendations to the judges, who approve the final version of the Guide.

The Guide can be found online at the Courts and Tribunals Judiciary website.

This chapter will concentrate on those aspects of practice in the Commercial Court which depart from the norm under the CPR 1998.

3.1.3 The practice of the court

Proceedings in the Commercial Court follow the same order of events as other court actions. All the usual interim steps (eg security for costs, interim payments, etc) can be taken in the Commercial Court in the same way as in any other case. This chapter simply highlights the extent to which proceedings in the Commercial Court differ from other civil proceedings.

The court's practice places great emphasis on cooperation between the parties' lawyers (many of whom are specialists in commercial litigation). They are expected to show a sense of realism in their handling of the case. This applies to dealings (including correspondence) between the parties' legal representatives, as well as to their dealings with the court. For example, the court encourages them to give advance disclosure of information and to provide written summaries which can be read by the judge before the hearing of an application or during the course of a trial in order to save time.

3.2 COMMENCEMENT

A case should be commenced in the Commercial Court only if it fulfils the characteristics of a 'commercial claim'. Rule 58.1(2) states that a 'commercial claim' means any claim arising out of the transaction of trade and commerce, and includes any claim relating to:

(a)   a business document or contract;

(b)   the export or import of goods;

(c)   the carriage of goods by land, sea, air or pipeline;

(d)   the exploitation of oil and gas reserves or other natural resources;

(e)   insurance and re-insurance;

(f)   banking and financial services;

(g)   the operation of markets and exchanges;

(h)   the purchase and sale of commodities;

(i)   the construction of ships;

(j)   business agency; and

(k)   arbitration.

Apart from arbitration claims, proceedings in the Commercial Court are commenced by practice form N1(CC) for Part 7 claims and practice form N208(CC) for Part 8 claims. The claim form should be marked in the top right-hand corner: In the High Court of Justice, Business and Property Courts of England and Wales, King's Bench Division, Commercial Court.

3.3   TRANSFER

Cases which have not been commenced in the Commercial Court may be transferred there, if appropriate. Alternatively, an action started in the Commercial Court may be transferred to another court if it is found to be an unsuitable case for the Commercial Court. Rule 30.5(3) states that an application for the transfer of proceedings to or from a specialist list must be made to a judge dealing with claims in that list, but, in addition, r 58.4(2) provides that a Commercial Court judge may order a claim to be transferred to any other specialist list.

3.3.1   Transfer into the Commercial Court

A case can be transferred to the Commercial Court by an application to a judge of that court. The judge considers whether the case is a suitable matter for the Commercial Court. The judge has a virtually unfettered discretion. At the same time, if appropriate, the judge can also give case management directions.

3.3.2   Transfer out of the Commercial Court

If the claimant commences proceedings in the Commercial Court when it is inappropriate to do so, the action can be removed from the court by the judge on their own initiative or on the application of another party. Such an application should be made promptly and normally not later than the first case management conference.

Although there is no rigid financial limit, a claim for less than £200,000 is likely to be transferred out of the Commercial Court unless it involves a point of special commercial interest.

Cases transferred out of the Commercial Court are likely to be transferred to the London Circuit Commercial Court or, if a venue outside London is more appropriate, to one of the other Circuit Commercial Courts (see **Chapter 1**). Guidance on practical steps for transferring cases to the Circuit Commercial Courts is set out in Appendix 19 to the Guide.

3.4   STATEMENTS OF CASE

Guidance as to drafting statements of case in the Commercial Court is set out in Section C of the Guide. Generally speaking, these guidelines do not depart significantly from Part 16 of CPR 1998 and the accompanying Practice Direction. In particular, it should be noted that para C1.1(e) of the Guide stresses that 'evidence should not be included' in statements of case in the Commercial Court.

3.4.1   Content

Paragraph C1.2(a) of the Guide states that statements of case should be limited to 25 pages in length. The court will only exceptionally give permission for a longer statement of case to be served where a party shows good reason for doing so. In that situation, the court may require that a summary of the statement of case is also served.

3.4.2   Service

By para 9 of PD 58, unless the court orders otherwise, the Commercial Court will not serve documents or orders and service must be effected by the parties.

The normal rules for service of the particulars of claim under r 7.4 (particulars of claim to be served with the claim form or within 14 days of service of the claim form and no later than the latest time for serving the claim form) do not apply in the Commercial Court. Although a claimant can do so if they wish, there is no obligation to serve the particulars of claim as provided by r 7.4. Instead, by rr 58.5 and 58.6, the defendant is obliged to file an acknowledgement of service in *every* case, within 14 days of service of the *claim form*, rather than within 14 days of service of the particulars of claim. Failure to do so entitles the claimant to enter a default judgment. For this reason, details of any claim for interest must be set out in the claim form.

If an acknowledgement of service is filed indicating an intention to defend, the claimant must then serve the particulars of claim within 28 days of the filing of the acknowledgement (r 58.5(1)(c)).

By para C2.1 of the Guide, the parties may agree extensions of the period for serving the particulars of claim. Any such agreement and brief reasons must be evidenced in writing and notified to the court. The court may make an order overriding any agreement by the parties varying a time limit.

3.4.3 The defence

Where the defendant has filed an acknowledgement of service indicating an intention to defend, the time limit for serving and filing the defence is 28 days after service of the particulars of claim. By para C3.2 of the Guide, that period can be extended, by agreement between the parties, by up to 28 days. Again, any such agreement and brief reasons must be evidenced in writing and notified to the court. An application to the court is required for any further extension, although if the parties are in agreement a consent order should be lodged.

3.4.4 The reply

Under CPR 1998, r 58.10, the time for filing and serving a reply is 21 days after service of the defence. If a longer period is necessary, the claimant should make a written application to the court for an extension of time because an extension will almost inevitably result in the postponement of the case management conference (see **3.5.5**). The details of the procedure can be found in para F.4 of the Guide.

3.4.5 Amendments

All amendments to a statement of case in the Commercial Court must be verified by a statement of truth.

Instead of colour-coded amendments, the amendments can be made by footnotes or marginal notes. In such cases the statement of case should retain the original text. Paragraph C5.1(d) of the Guide does, however, recommend that, if the amendments are extensive, the document should be retyped and accompanied by a copy showing where and when the amendments were made.

3.5 CASE MANAGEMENT

3.5.1 Allocation

By r 58.13, all proceedings in the Commercial Court are treated as being allocated to the multi-track. Part 26 does not apply and so the parties do not file directions questionnaires.

3.5.2 The approach of the court

Paragraph 10 of PD 58 and Section D of the Guide deal with case management, and CPR 1998, Part 29 is almost entirely excluded.

Paragraph D.2 of the Guide identifies 13 key features of case management in the Commercial Court:

    (a)   statements of case will be exchanged within fixed or monitored time periods;

(b)   a case memorandum, a List of Common Ground and Issues and a case management bundle will be produced at an early point in the case. The parties will be expected to agree the case memorandum and the List of Common Ground and Issues;

(c)   the case memorandum, List of Common Ground and Issues and case management bundle will be amended and updated or revised on a running basis throughout the life of the case and will be used by the Court at every stage of the case. In particular the List of Common Ground and Issues will be used as a tool to define what factual and expert evidence is necessary and the scope of disclosure;

(d)   the Court itself will approve the List of Common Ground and Issues and may require the further assistance of the parties and their legal representatives in order to do so;

(e)   a mandatory Case Management Conference will be held shortly after statements of case have been served, if not before (and preceded by the parties filing case management information sheets identifying their views on the requirements of the case);

(f)   at the Case Management Conference the Court will (as necessary) discuss the issues in the case and the requirements of the case with the advocates retained in the case. In a case where expert evidence is proposed the Court will consider whether to grant permission for that evidence and how that evidence should be controlled. The court will set a pre-trial timetable and give any other directions as may be appropriate, including as to the use of information technology;

(g)   at the first Case Management Conference, the Court will review and approve, amend or reject as may be appropriate the parties' proposals for disclosure;

(h)   before the progress monitoring date the parties will report to the Court, using a progress monitoring information sheet, the extent of their compliance with the pre-trial timetable;

(i)   on or shortly after the progress monitoring date a Judge may (without a hearing) consider progress and give such further directions as she or he thinks appropriate;

(j)   if at the progress monitoring date all parties have indicated that they will be ready for trial, all parties will complete a pre-trial checklist;

(k)   in appropriate cases the Case Management Conference will be restored and/or there will be a pre-trial review;

(l)   the parties will be required to prepare a trial timetable for consideration by the Court;

(m)   throughout the case there must be regular reviews of the estimated length (including reading time) of trial.

If a party needs to apply for a direction which has not been included in the pre-trial timetable, or to vary any direction in that timetable, they must do so as soon as possible.

An outline chart of the typical case management sequence for cases in the Commercial Court is reproduced in **Appendix 1** to this book.

3.5.3   The case memorandum and List of Common Ground and Issues

Once a defence (and any reply) has been served, the parties' lawyers should agree a case memorandum and a List of Common Ground and Issues.

According to para D4.2 of the Guide, the case memorandum should contain:

(a)   a short and uncontroversial description of what the case is about;

(b)   a very short and uncontroversial summary of the material procedural history of the case.

The List of Common Ground and Issues should include the main issues of fact and law in the case. The list should identify the principal issues in a structured manner, such as by reference to headings or chapters. The beginning section of the document should specify what is Common Ground between the parties.

The claimant's solicitors will normally be responsible for the preparation of both documents.

After the case management conference, the parties must cooperate in ensuring that both these documents are kept up to date.

3.5.4 The case management bundle

The claimant's solicitors must prepare a case management bundle before the case management conference. It should contain the claim form, all statements of case, the case memorandum, the List of Common Ground and Issues, the case management information sheets and the pre-trial timetable if one has already been established, all principal orders made in the case, and any written agreement relating to disclosure of documents. A finalised single joint Disclosure Review Document (see **3.6**) should be filed by the claimant not later than five days before the case management conference.

The claimant's solicitors must lodge the bundle with the court at least seven days before the case management conference. They must then update the court's bundle as follows:

(a)   within 10 days of the case management conference, add the pre-trial timetable and any other order made at the case management conference, along with a revised case memorandum;

(b)   within 10 days of the making of any significant order, add a copy of that order or revise the case memorandum;

(c)   within 14 days of the service of any amended statement of case, replace the original statement with the new statement and revise the case memorandum and the List of Common Ground and Issues;

(d)   if the case memorandum or List of Common Ground and Issues is revised for any other reason, do so within 10 days.

3.5.5 The case management conference

By para 10.2 of PD 58, the claimant must apply for a case management conference (CMC) within 14 days of the date when all defendants who intend to file and serve a defence have done so, although any party may apply for a CMC earlier than then if they wish to do so.

If the claimant does not apply within the 14-day time limit, any other party may apply for a CMC. If none of the parties has applied for a CMC within 28 days, the Listing Office at the court will inform the judge in charge of the list, and a date for the CMC will then be fixed without further reference to the parties.

The court also has the power to fix a CMC at any time on its own initiative. If it does, it must give the parties at least seven days' notice, unless there are compelling reasons for a shorter period of notice.

The CMC will normally take place on the first available date six weeks after all defendants who intend to serve a defence have done so. This allows time for the preparation and service of any reply.

If any party wishes to postpone the conference (eg because of the late service of a reply), they should apply to the court in writing. There will not be an oral hearing of the application unless any other party requests one or the court feels that such a hearing would be helpful.

At the conference, each party should be represented by a solicitor with conduct of the case and an advocate retained in the case. There is no need for any of the clients to attend unless the court orders to the contrary.

Each party must file and serve a completed case management information sheet at least seven days before the conference. This information sheet takes the place of the directions questionnaire used in mainstream litigation. An example of a case management information sheet appears in **Appendix 2** of this book.

According to para D7.9 of the Guide, the judge will, at the hearing of the conference:

(a)   discuss the issues in the case by reference to the draft List of Common Ground and Issues, and approve a List of Common Ground and Issues;

(b)   discuss the requirements of the case (including disclosure), with the advocates retained in the case;

(c)   fix the entire pre-trial timetable or, if that is not practicable, fix as much of the pre-trial timetable as possible;

(d)   give a direction for the trial date to be fixed promptly after the hearing, unless there is good reason to defer the fixing of the trial to a later stage in the case. That includes setting a time estimate for the trial;

(e)   consider with the parties their proposals for the use of information technology in the case, including its use at trial. In deciding whether and to what extent IT should be in the case, including at trial, the Court will have regard to the financial resources of the parties and where those resources are unequal it will consider whether it is appropriate that one or more but not all of the parties should initially bear the cost subject to the Court's ultimate orders as to the overall costs of the case following judgment. Unless the Court can be satisfied that no unfairness would result from a party being excluded, or a party requests that it be excluded, all parties must have access to and an ability to use any IT systems proposed to be used in the case, including at trial;

(f)   consider with the parties the question of document translation, if there is likely to be a significant volume of documentary material not in English;

(g)   in appropriate cases make an NDR order;

(h)   in appropriate cases, consider whether the case should be retained in or be transferred out of the Commercial Court, and if retained whether it is suitable for the Shorter Trials Scheme or the Flexible Trials Scheme in the interests of reducing the length and cost of trial;

(i)   expect to be informed, if known, whether there are or are likely to be other cases raising the same or similar issues, so that the potential for coordinated case management, if appropriate, can be considered.

3.5.6   Security for costs

Where the defendant (or defendant to a counterclaim) intends to apply for security for costs, they should do so no later than the case management conference. Guidance is provided by Appendix 10 to the Guide. This states that any delay which is prejudicial to the claimant or to the administration of justice will probably cause the application to fail. Similarly, if the court forms the view that the application is motivated by a desire to harass the claimant, it is likely to be refused.

The Commercial Court is reluctant to investigate the merits when considering the application. The merits will be taken into account only in cases where it is clear that without any detailed examination of the facts or the law that the claim is certain or almost certain to fail.

As a condition of the grant of security, the defendant may be required to give an undertaking to the court to comply with any subsequent order to compensate the claimant for any loss suffered as a result of giving security. This would be appropriate where no costs order was ultimately made in the defendant's favour.

Where security is granted, this will usually be on the basis that if the claimant fails to comply with the order, it is for the defendant to apply to the court for an order to stay the proceedings or to strike out the particulars of claim. Unless the defendant does so, the case will continue in accordance with the pre-trial timetable. The aim is to prevent any unnecessary delay in the proceedings pending a decision by the court about the claimant's default.

3.5.7   Negotiated dispute resolution

The Guide refers to ADR as NDR (negotiated dispute resolution). The court will consider applications for an adjournment of the case at the case management conference stage to enable the parties to negotiate a settlement or to use some form of NDR. The parties can use the case management information sheet to indicate that such an adjournment may be appropriate.

The Guide then goes on to say at D7.11(b):

> In an appropriate case, an NDR order may be made without a stay of proceedings. The parties should consider carefully whether it may be possible to provide for NDR in the pre-trial timetable without affecting the date of trial.

If the court does adjourn the case and all parties want an extension to the adjournment, one of the parties should write to the court before the end of the adjournment period confirming that all parties consent to the further adjournment. The letter should also explain what steps are being taken to settle the case and identify any mediator or other third party who is seeking to help the parties to settle the case. As under CPR 1998, any further adjournment is likely to be for no more than four weeks, but the court can then grant further adjournments if it sees fit.

Section G of the Guide deals specifically with NDR. Paragraph G1.2 states:

> Legal representatives in all cases should consider with their clients and the other parties concerned the possibility of attempting to resolve the dispute or particular issues by NDR and should ensure that their clients are fully informed as to the most cost effective means of resolving their dispute.

In an appropriate case the judge may consider making an NDR order in the terms set out in Appendix 3 to the Guide.

The Commercial Court also provides parties with the option of taking advantage of its early neutral evaluation (ENE) service. If all parties agree, the court will provide a without prejudice, non-binding ENE of the dispute or of particular issues. The judge who conducts the ENE will take no further part in the case unless the parties agree otherwise. Details of this service are set out in para G.2 of the Guide.

3.5.8 The pre-trial timetable

This will include a progress monitoring date (see **3.5.10** below) and a direction that the parties attend upon the Clerk to the Commercial Court to obtain a fixed date for trial.

A standard form of pre-trial timetable is set out in Appendix 4 to the Guide, which is reproduced in **Appendix 3** at the end of this book.

The parties can agree minor variations to the timetable as long as the overall structure is not affected and the variation will not affect the trial date or the progress monitoring date.

If more significant variations to the timetable are needed, the parties should apply to the court for a further case management conference rather than waiting until the progress monitoring date.

3.5.9 Special cases

There are minor variations to the rules on case management conferences for Part 8 and Part 20 claims in paras D.8 and D.9 of the Guide.

3.5.10 Progress monitoring

At the case management conference, the court will fix a progress monitoring date which will usually be after the time for exchanging witness statements and expert reports has expired.

The parties must serve and file a progress monitoring information sheet at least three days before the progress monitoring date. This will tell the court:

(a)   the extent to which they have been able to comply with the pre-trial timetable to date; and

(b)   whether they will be ready for trial on time and, if not, when they will be ready for trial.

A standard form of progress monitoring sheet is set out in Appendix 2 to the Guide and is reproduced in **Appendix 4** of this book.

3.5.11 Reconvening the case management conference

If the progress monitoring information sheets show that one or more of the parties will not, or may not, be ready in time for the trial, the court can reconvene the case management conference. It can rewrite the pre-trial timetable by giving further directions and may make any appropriate orders for costs. It can also stipulate that a statement of case will be automatically struck out unless the party concerned complies with certain directions by certain specified dates.

3.5.12 Pre-trial checklist

Not later than three weeks before the date fixed for trial, each party must send to the Listing Office (with a copy to all other parties) a completed checklist confirming final details for trial (a 'pre-trial checklist') in the form set out in Appendix 2. This is reproduced in **Appendix 5** to this book.

3.5.13 Requests for further information

The court can make orders requiring a party to provide further information under Part 18 of CPR 1998 at the case management conference. Under para D14.1(a) of the Guide, the parties must communicate directly with each other in an attempt to reach agreement before any application is made to the court. If an application is then made, it will not be listed for hearing unless the applicant has confirmed in writing that the requirements of para D14.1(a) have been complied with.

3.5.14 The trial date

The normal practice of the Commercial Court is to fix the trial date immediately after the pre-trial timetable has been set at the case management conference. The Guide recognises that there may be some cases where, through matters outside the court's control, the trial may be delayed by a few days. If this might 'cause particular inconvenience', the Clerk to the Commercial Court should be given plenty of notice so that they can take steps to avoid the problem.

3.5.15 Provisional estimates of the length of the trial

As in all courts, accurate estimates of the likely length of the trial are essential to the efficient running of the court. Provisional estimates of the minimum and maximum duration of the trial will be made at the case management conference and will become part of the pre-trial timetable. These will then be confirmed or revised by the advocates when the pre-trial checklist is filed. It is the duty of all advocates who are to appear at the trial to seek agreement, if possible, on the estimated minimum and maximum lengths of trial. As soon as one of the advocates realises that the provisional or confirmed estimate may be inaccurate, they must contact the other advocates with a view to agreeing a revised estimate which can be filed with the court.

3.5.16 The pre-trial review

The Guide, in para D17.1, states that the court will order a pre-trial review in any case in which it considers it appropriate to do so. This will usually be some two to eight weeks before the trial begins and should be attended by the advocates who will appear at the trial.

The claimant's advocate should prepare a timetable for the trial in consultation with the other advocates, and they should indicate any areas of disagreement about this timetable. The judge will finalise the timetable at the pre-trial review.

3.6 DISCLOSURE

Generally, CPR 1998, PD 57AD provides for disclosure in the Business and Property Courts. This is significantly different from disclosure in mainstream litigation under CPR 1998, Part 31. Further details about this can be found in **Chapter 10**.

3.7 INTERIM APPLICATIONS

3.7.1 General

Although Section F of the Guide confirms that Part 23 of CPR 1998 applies to proceedings in the Commercial Court along with its supplementary Practice Direction, it does exclude certain parts of the Practice Direction and impose qualifications on other parts of the Practice Direction. This book merely deals with the main differences between the Guide and PD 23. In practice, it is important to consult the exact wording of the Guide and PD 23.

Except for orders made by the court on its own initiative (rather than on application by a party), orders are not drawn up by the court but by the parties. The party who made the application is responsible for drafting the order, which is usually required to be signed by all the parties or (more usually) their legal representatives and lodged at court for sealing within three days of the relevant decision. The draft order should be lodged in hard copy together with a further copy in Word format. The parties are expected to cooperate to ensure that the draft order is prepared promptly and accurately reflects the decision of the court.

On most occasions, where the parties are able to agree the terms of the order they wish to make, they need not attend a hearing but may submit a draft consent order for approval. The exceptions are the case management conference and pre-trial review, where the consent order procedure cannot be used. Although the parties are encouraged to agree the directions they wish the court to make prior to these hearings, they must attend even if agreement is reached.

3.7.2 Service

In accordance with the usual procedure in the Commercial Court, application notices must be served by the parties. The court will not effect service.

3.7.3 Hearings

Although most applications will be heard in public, this does not apply to applications for freezing injunctions or search orders, neither does it apply to most arbitration applications (see CPR 1998, r 62.10(3)(b)).

Although PD 23 refers to applications being heard by telephone or by a video conference, para F1.7 of the Guide indicates that regard should now also be had in particular to guidance issued from time to time as to the Court's approach to remote or hybrid hearings.

3.7.4 Expedited applications

Where an urgent application has to be made, but the case is not one which justifies an application without notice, the Commercial Court is able to offer an expedited application with an earlier hearing than would otherwise be the case. The Clerk should be asked to make expedited arrangements, but all other parties must be notified of this request.

3.7.5 Ordinary applications

The Guide defines ordinary applications as 'applications on notice expected to involve an oral hearing lasting half a day or less'. Such applications will normally be listed for hearing on a Friday. The timetable for such applications will be that:

(a)   the supporting evidence should be served with the application;

(b)   the respondent should serve their evidence within 14 days;

(c)   the applicant should serve any evidence in reply within 7 days (PD 58, para 13.1).

In the Commercial Court, the evidence may take the form of either a witness statement or an affidavit (unless an affidavit is specifically required).

This timetable can be abridged by agreement of the parties or by order of the court.

The applicant should lodge an application bundle by 1 pm one clear day before the date of the hearing (ie if the application is to be heard on a Friday it must be lodged by 1 pm on Wednesday). The application bundle must include copies of the following documents:

(a) the application notice;

(b) the draft order sought;

(c) statements of case;

(d) any relevant previous order;

(e) witness statements and affidavits in support of/opposition to the application together with any exhibits.

Skeleton arguments must be lodged and served by 1 pm on the day before the hearing (ie in the case of a hearing on a Friday, by 1 pm on Thursday).

Failure to lodge documents on time may result in the court refusing to hear the application.

3.7.6 Heavy applications

Hearings which are likely to last longer than half a day are regarded as 'heavy applications'. Because there is likely to be a lot more evidence in such applications, which may involve more documents and more extensive issues than ordinary applications, the timetable is extended. Evidence in support of the application should still be lodged with the application, but:

(a) the respondent has 28 days to serve their evidence; and

(b) the applicant has 14 days in which to serve any evidence in reply (PD 58, para 13.2).

Such applications will not usually be dealt with on a Friday. If, for example, the application is to be heard on a Thursday, the applicant must lodge an application bundle with the court by 4 pm two clear days before the hearing (ie by 4 pm on Monday).

The applicant's skeleton argument should be served and lodged with the application bundle. The respondent's skeleton argument should be served and lodged within the next 24 hours (ie in our example, by 4 pm on Tuesday). Guidelines on the preparation of such arguments are set out in Appendix 5 to the Guide. An example of a skeleton argument can be found in **Appendix 7** of this book.

The parties must also inform the court of the reading time (by the judge) required in order to enable the judge to dispose of the application within the time allowed for the hearing.

In heavy applications and others where the reading time is likely to exceed one hour, each party must lodge with the Listing Office, not later than 1 pm, two clear days before the hearing of the application, a reading list (identifying those documents the judge needs to read before the hearing) with an estimate of the likely reading time.

In all other applications, this must be lodged not later than 1 pm on the day before the hearing.

It will usually be useful to include a chronology or timetable of events; a cast list (referred to in the Guide as *dramatis personae*) explaining who the principal people in the case are; and indices identifying the relevant pages for each piece of evidence. Further guidance can be found in Appendix 6 to the Guide.

Failure to lodge the appropriate documents at the appropriate time may result in the court refusing to hear the application.

3.7.7 Time estimates and time limits

Paragraph F5.5 of the Guide indicates the normal maximum time for certain types of application (eg applications for summary judgment should not normally exceed four hours). A longer time estimate will be accepted by the court only if the advocate in question makes a written application to the judge in charge of the Commercial List explaining why extra time is needed.

Time estimates can assume that the judge will have read the skeleton arguments and the documents in the reading list before the hearing. The time estimate for an ordinary application should allow for judgment to be given. In a heavy application, the judge is likely to reserve judgment to a later date.

3.8 EXPERT EVIDENCE

3.8.1 Single joint experts

Although CPR 1998 emphasise the need to use single joint experts where appropriate, and the Guide recognises the need to avoid unnecessary expenditure on expert witnesses, para H2.6 of the Guide goes on to say:

> In many cases it will be appropriate for each party to be given permission to call one expert in each field requiring expert evidence.

3.8.2 The expert's duty to the court

Appendix 8 to the Guide sets out useful guidance to experts about their duty to the court. It is set out in full in **Appendix 8** of this book. It is the solicitor's responsibility to ensure that Appendix 8 is drawn to the attention of their party's expert(s) as early as possible.

3.8.3 Request for directions

If an expert wishes to file a written request to the court for directions as to how they should fulfil their duties as an expert, they must normally give the party who instructed them seven days' notice of their intention to make such an application, and four days' notice of their intention to make such an application to all other parties. This ensures that one or other party can approach the court first if the request prepared by the expert would result in the expert informing the court about, or about matters connected with, communications or potential communications between the parties that are without prejudice or privileged.

3.8.4 Sequential exchange

When fixing the pre-trial timetable, the court will consider whether experts' reports should be exchanged sequentially rather than simultaneously. This would be appropriate where, for example, it would be difficult for the defendant's expert to comment fully without sight of the claimant's expert evidence. A simultaneous exchange in such circumstances is likely to result in the defendant applying for permission for their expert to file a supplemental report, and sequential exchange may be more cost- and time-effective. The claimant, on the other hand, may perceive an order for sequential exchange as giving the defendant an unfair advantage.

3.9 THE TRIAL

3.9.1 The documents

Appendix 7 to the Guide sets out the requirements for the trial bundle. The trial bundle should normally be agreed with the other parties at least 14 days before the trial date and lodged with the court at least seven days before the trial date. It is for the claimant's representatives to compile and lodge the bundle.

3.9.2 Information technology

By para J.2 of the Guide:

> J2.1 Parties and their legal representatives should seek to minimise the use of paper at trial. In any event, no hard copy trial bundle, only electronic trial bundles, should be lodged for use by the Court unless specifically requested.
>
> J2.2 Parties are strongly encouraged to consider the use of information technology at trial beyond just the use of electronic rather than paper bundles. The Court will expect proposals to be made, or an explanation given why it is not proposed to make any wider use of IT at trial, at the pre-trial

review, if there is one, and in the parties' pre-trial checklists. This will not be necessary if directions for the use of IT in the case, including at trial, have been made at an earlier stage (see D2.3(e)) and there is no proposal to alter those directions.

J2.3   Where IT is to be used in presenting the case at trial the same system must be used by all parties and must be made available to the Court.

3.9.3   Trial documentation

A single reading list approved by all advocates must be lodged by 1 pm on the earlier of either the day before the reading period for the trial (set out in the CMC order or as subsequently amended by pre-trial order/checklist or otherwise) commences or two clear days before the start of the trial. At the same time, the claimant should also lodge a trial timetable, prepared by the advocate for the claimant after consultation with the advocates for all other parties. This will provide for oral submissions, witness evidence and expert evidence over the course of the trial.

Each party must prepare written skeleton arguments. The claimant should serve and lodge their skeleton argument by the same deadline as for the reading list, and the defendant should do the same not later than 1 pm on the following day. In 'heavier' cases, the parties should try to serve and lodge their skeleton arguments earlier than the normal deadlines. Indeed, the court may impose an earlier deadline in the pre-trial timetable or at any pre-trial review.

When the claimant provides their skeleton argument, they should also provide a chronology and consider whether it will be helpful to supply indices and a list of dramatis personae.

As soon as possible after skeleton arguments have been exchanged, the claimant must provide the Listing Office with a bundle of the authorities referred to in the skeleton arguments.

3.9.4   Trial and costs

The trial will proceed in much the same way as in any other court, but in the more substantial cases, once the court has heard all the evidence, it will adjourn to enable the advocates to prepare written closing submissions before making their oral closing submissions.

The rules governing the award and assessment of costs are the same as in other courts.

3.10   POST-TRIAL MATTERS

Even after the case has been tried, any application to continue, vary or set aside interim remedies or undertakings must be made to a commercial judge. Paragraphs 1.2 and 1.4 of PD 25 – Interim Injunctions, which enable such applications to be made to a Master, do not apply in the Commercial Court. Enforcement, on the other hand, will automatically be referred to a Master of the King's Bench Division or a district judge (PD 58, para 1.2(2)).

3.11   THE CIRCUIT COMMERCIAL COURTS

These regional equivalents of the Commercial Court (see **3.1**) are part of the Business and Property Courts of England and Wales and generally follow the practice and procedure of the Commercial Court Guide, save to the extent that Part 58 and PD 58 differ from Part 59 (Circuit Commercial Courts) and PD 59. By r 59.1(2) a claim may only be started in a Circuit Commercial Court if it relates to a commercial or business matter in a broad sense and is not required to proceed in another specialist list of the Business and Property Courts. There is a Circuit Commercial Court Guide providing detailed guidance on how to conduct a claim in the court. It is similar to, but considerably shorter than, the Commercial Court Guide. Provisions as to case management in the Circuit Commercial Court are similar, though not identical, to those in the Commercial Court.

As with the Commercial Court, all interim matters are dealt with by a Circuit Commercial Court judge, rather than by a District Judge or Master. The Guide contains the Circuit

Commercial Court Case Management Information Sheet, which has to be filed by all parties at least seven days before the Case Management Conference (CMC). It also contains a set of specimen directions for use at the CMC, the pre-trial checklist and a useful table of cross-references to the equivalent provisions in both CPR 1998 and the Commercial Court Guide.

3.12 SUMMARY

The Commercial Court provides a specialised service for business organisations for cases normally worth a minimum of £200,000. It sits in London and many of its cases have an international element.

Specialist Commercial Court judges deal with all interim applications as well as trials.

Procedure in the Commercial Court is governed by CPR 1998, Part 58 and PD 58, together with the Commercial Court Guide.

The regional equivalents of the Commercial Court are the Circuit Commercial Courts sitting in Birmingham, Bristol, Cardiff, Leeds, Liverpool, Manchester and Newcastle.

THE CHANCERY DIVISION

LEARNING OUTCOMES

After reading this chapter you will understand:

- which types of proceedings are suitable for the Chancery Division
- use of Part 8 claim forms.

4.1 INTRODUCTION

Whilst most High Court civil claims are commenced in the King's Bench Division, certain types of case are better suited to the Chancery Division. Chancery business involves specialist knowledge of, for example, land law and trusts, intellectual property, insolvency and company law, and although procedure in the Chancery Division will generally follow CPR 1998, litigants will continue to commence proceedings in the Chancery Division to take advantage of the specialist skills of the Chancery judges, should the case come to trial.

There is a Chancery Guide (published in July 2022 and updated in June 2023) which notifies areas where practice in the Chancery Division will depart from the normal CPR 1998. These differences are by no means as significant as in the Commercial Court and, for the purposes of this book, readers can assume that practice in the Chancery Division will follow CPR 1998. In practice, however, it will be necessary to check the details of the Chancery Guide for any proceedings commenced in the Chancery Division.

Certain types of 'commercial' actions will be started in the Chancery Division rather than in the Commercial Court. These include disputes involving land, probate, trusts and intellectual property. If the claim is a 'commercial claim' as defined by r 58.1(2), the procedure adopted in the Chancery Division will generally be that used in the Commercial Court, save that the case management of the case will be handled by a Master (or district judge) rather than by a High Court judge.

The Chancery Division and its specialist lists (**see 1.2**) are now all part of the Business and Property Courts of England and Wales. As such, PD 57AD disclosure rules apply in the Chancery Division from 1 January 2019 – for further details see **Chapter 10**.

4.1.1 Allocation of business

Although the Chancery Division deals with land, trusts, probate actions and other property disputes, the Senior Courts Act 1981, Sch 1, para 1 also allocates some other commercial matters to the Chancery Division. These include the following proceedings which should be commenced in the Chancery Division:

(a)   bankruptcy;

(b)   dissolution of partnerships and taking partnership or other accounts;

(c)   patents, trade marks, registered designs and copyright;

(d)   matters affecting the affairs of a company.

4.1.2 Personnel

The head of the Chancery Division is the Chancellor of the High Court ('the Chancellor'). There are currently 18 High Court judges attached to the Division.

4.1.3 Procedure

There are special procedures for certain types of actions (eg probate actions are governed by CPR 1998, Part 57, and possession claims by CPR 1998, Part 55). This book does not deal with these specialist Rules.

Further, as mentioned in **4.1**, the Chancery Division has its own guide to practice in this Division, just as there is the Guide to Commercial Court Practice. The Chancery Guide sets out, for example, the steps taken before a hearing, including the preparation of bundles of documents, skeleton arguments, witness statements and expert evidence, and the use of pre-trial reviews and checklists.

4.2 ALTERNATIVE PROCEDURE FOR CLAIMS

Whilst most civil claims are commenced with a Part 7 claim form, that standard procedure is not appropriate for cases where the principal issues are legal or interpretative rather than factual. Part 8 of CPR 1998 sets out an alternative procedure for such claims, which will always be allocated to the multi-track. That procedure is dealt with in this chapter because it is more likely to be used in the sort of cases which are dealt with in the Chancery Division. It may, however, be used by any claimant if the claim is 'unlikely to involve a substantial dispute of fact' (r 8.1(2)). There is a summary of the procedure at **Appendix 9** to this book.

The claimant will file a claim form indicating that the claim is being made under Part 8. The claim form must indicate what questions the claimant wants the court to decide, the remedy the claimant is seeking and the legal basis for the claim (r 8.2(b)). At the same time, the claimant must file their written evidence. The court will then serve the claim form and the claimant's evidence on the defendant.

A defendant who wishes to contest the claimant's application should file an acknowledgement of service. If they fail to do so, the claimant will not be able to enter a default judgment. However, although the defendant may attend the hearing of the claim, they will not be able to take part in the hearing without the court's permission.

A defendant who acknowledges service must state whether or not they contest the claim, and any remedy they are seeking. At the same time, the defendant must file and serve any written evidence they intend to rely on. The claimant then has 14 days in which to file and serve further written evidence.

No further evidence is allowed without permission of the court. The court does have a discretion to require or permit additional oral evidence and/or to require the maker of a statement to be cross-examined on that statement.

A defendant who wishes to raise an additional claim under Part 20 in a Part 8 case will always need the permission of the court to do so. If the court grants permission it will give directions regarding the conduct of the additional claim.

A defendant who believes that the Part 8 procedure is not appropriate should state their objections and the reasons for them when they file their acknowledgement of service. The court will then have to give directions as to the future management of the case, and these could include an order that the claim continue as if the Part 8 procedure had not been used.

4.3 SUMMARY

The Chancery Division deals with cases involving specialist knowledge of areas of the law such as land law, trusts, intellectual property, insolvency and company law.

Procedure is governed by the Chancery Guide as well as the CPR 1998.

Most cases in the Chancery Division are commenced with a Part 8 claim form as the principal issues in Chancery cases are legal or interpretive rather than factual.

THE TECHNOLOGY AND CONSTRUCTION COURT

LEARNING OUTCOMES

After reading this chapter you will understand:

- which types of proceedings are suitable for the TCC
- the procedure in the TCC
- the use of Scott Schedules.

5.1 INTRODUCTION

The Technology and Construction Court (TCC) is a specialist court which deals with cases which are technically complex or for which a trial by a judge of the TCC is for any other reason desirable. Cases involving the construction industry are the most common cases in the TCC, but many cases involving complex documentary or expert evidence are appropriate for the court. The types of actions normally dealt with in the TCC include:

(a) building or other construction disputes, including claims for the enforcement of the decisions of adjudicators under the Housing Grants, Construction and Regeneration Act 1996;

(b) engineering disputes;

(c) claims by and against engineers, architects, surveyors, accountants and other specialised advisers relating to the services they provide;

(d) claims by and against local authorities relating to their statutory duties concerning the development of land or the construction of buildings;

(e) claims relating to the design, supply and installation of computers, computer software and related network systems;

(f) claims relating to the quality of goods sold or hired, and work done, materials supplied or services rendered;

(g) claims between landlord and tenant for breach of a repairing covenant;

(h) claims between neighbours, owners and occupiers of land in trespass, nuisance, etc;

(i)   claims relating to the environment (for example, pollution cases);

(j)   claims arising out of fires;

(k)   claims involving taking of accounts where these are complicated;

(l)   challenges to decisions of arbitrators in construction and engineering disputes including applications for permission to appeal and appeals;

(m)   energy disputes, including claims concerning oil and gas pipelines and facilities, onshore and offshore windfarms, waste to energy plants and other renewables; and

(n)   public procurement claims.

The TCC is similar to the Commercial Court in that CPR 1998 apply to proceedings in the court, but subject to the provisions of Part 60 and its Practice Direction. As with the Commercial Court, the TCC has its own Guide. The current edition of the Guide was published in October 2022. This chapter will identify some of the differences in procedure in the TCC from the mainstream courts.

The website of the Technology and Construction Solicitors Association (www.tecsa.org.uk) is a very useful source of information on the TCC.

As it is part of the Business and Property Courts of England and Wales, PD 57AD disclosure rules apply – for further details see **Chapter 10**.

5.2 PRE-ACTION MATTERS

Many cases which are suitable for the TCC are covered by the Pre-Action Protocol for Construction and Engineering Disputes (reproduced in **Appendix 10** to this book). Where the dispute involves a claim against architects, engineers or quantity surveyors, this Protocol prevails over the Pre-Action Protocol for Professional Negligence.

If the Protocol applies, the TCC will expect all parties to have complied with its provisions. Even if a dispute is not covered by the Protocol, for example a claim relating to computers, the court would normally expect its provisions to be followed.

Paragraph 2.3 of the TCC Guide sets out six situations where the Protocol does not have to be followed. These are where the claim:

(a)   is to enforce the decision of an adjudicator;

(b)   is to seek an urgent declaration or injunction in relation to adjudication (whether ongoing or concluded);

(c)   includes a claim for interim injunctive relief;

(d)   will be subject of a claim for summary judgment pursuant to Part 24 of CPR 1998;

(e)   relates to the same or substantially the same issues as have been the subject of a recent adjudication or some other formal alternative dispute resolution procedure;

(f)   relates to a public procurement dispute.

Apart from these exceptions, failure to comply with the Protocol can result in the usual costs sanctions (TCC Guide, para 2.6).

5.3 COMMENCEMENT

Many TCC claims are dealt with in the High Court. In London, as part of the Business and Property Courts of England and Wales, the TCC is based at the Rolls Building, Fetter Lane, London EC4A 1HD. There, the TCC has its own judges who deal only with TCC work. In the High Court outside London, TCC claims can be issued in any District Registry. However, para 3.3 of the Practice Direction – Technology and Construction Court Claims – states that wherever possible such claims should be issued in one of the following District Registries, in which a TCC judge will usually be available: Birmingham, Bristol, Cardiff, Chester, Exeter,

Leeds, Liverpool, Manchester, Newcastle upon Tyne and Nottingham. There are full-time TCC judges in Birmingham, Leeds and Manchester.

5.4 TRANSFER

If, in a case started in the usual way, either party considers that the matter is now more suitable for the TCC, they may apply for a transfer to that court. The court can also order a transfer of its own motion if the parties consent or have been given an opportunity to object.

The court may also transfer TCC proceedings back into the High Court mainstream, if it considers that the case may be tried more appropriately in that court.

5.5 CASE MANAGEMENT

As with the Commercial Court, all TCC claims are treated as being allocated to the multi-track and CPR 1998, Part 26 does not apply (r 60.6). However, CPR 1998, Part 29 and its PD do apply to the case management of TCC claims, except where varied by or inconsistent with the Practice Direction to Part 60.

When a TCC claim is issued, or a case is transferred to the TCC, the court will assign the claim to a TCC judge who will have the primary responsibility for the case management of that claim. Again, this is similar to the position in the Commercial Court. Normally, all applications in the case will be heard by the assigned TCC judge.

Paragraph 8 of the Practice Direction to Part 60 deals with the case management conference (CMC). Much more detailed guidance is given in Section 5 of the TCC Guide. The court will fix a CMC within 14 days of the earliest of:

(a)   the filing of an acknowledgement of service;
(b)   the filing of a defence;
(c)   the date of an order transferring the claim to a TCC.

When the court notifies the parties of the date and time of the CMC, it will send them a case management information sheet and a case management directions form. (These forms are set out in Appendices A and B to the Practice Direction.) All parties must file and serve completed copies of these forms at least two days before the CMC. As usual, the parties are encouraged to agree directions. Failure to file or serve the forms can lead to sanctions.

The directions given at the CMC will normally include the fixing of dates for:

(a)   any further CMCs;
(b)   a pre-trial review;
(c)   the trial of any preliminary issues that the court orders to be tried;
(d)   the trial.

When the court fixes the date for a pre-trial review it will send each party a pre-trial review questionnaire. (This form is set out in Appendix C to the Practice Direction.) All parties must file and serve a completed copy of this form at least two days before the pre-trial review. Again, the parties are encouraged to agree directions, and failure to file or serve the form may lead to sanctions.

At the pre-trial review the court will give such directions for the conduct of the trial as it sees fit.

The provisions about pre-trial checklists and listing in CPR 1998, Part 29 and its Practice Direction do not apply to TCC claims.

Whenever possible the trial will be heard by the assigned TCC judge.

5.6   EXPERT EVIDENCE

Section 13 of the TCC Guide deals with the use of expert evidence in the TCC. The Guide reflects the problems regarding expert evidence that may arise in TCC cases. Paragraph 13.3.1 refers to the 'unresolved tension arising from the need for parties to instruct and rely on expert opinions from an early pre-action stage and the need for the court to seek, wherever possible, to reduce the costs of expert evidence by dispensing with it altogether or by encouraging the appointment of jointly instructed experts'.

As in the Commercial Court (see **3.8.1**) the TCC Guide reflects the fact that single joint experts are not usually appropriate for the principal liability disputes in large cases, or in cases where considerable sums have been spent on an expert in the pre-action stage (para 13.4.2). The Guide goes on to say that single joint experts are generally inappropriate where the issue involves questions of risk assessment or professional competence.

At para 13.4.3, however, the Guide states that single joint experts may often be appropriate:

(a)   in low value cases, where technical evidence is required but the cost of adversarial expert evidence may be prohibitive;

(b)   where the topic with which the single joint expert's report deals is a separate and self-contained part of the case, such as the valuation of particular heads of claim;

(c)   where there is a subsidiary issue, which requires particular expertise of a relatively uncontroversial nature to resolve;

(d)   where testing or analysis is required, and this can conveniently be done by one laboratory or firm on behalf of all parties.

5.7   SCOTT SCHEDULES

Apart from the usual statements of case in an action, it will be common for the judge to order additional statements of case in the form of a 'Scott Schedule'. (GA Scott, who was a judge in the 1920s, devised this document, although it is no longer peculiar to the TCC.) An example of a Scott Schedule appears in **Appendix 11** to this book. Paragraph 5.6 of the Guide explains when the use of a Scott Schedule is appropriate.

A Scott Schedule sets out the issues in tabular form so that they are clearly stated in one source rather than being scattered through the statements of case. Such a Schedule is especially appropriate where there are a large number of disputed issues or the case is very detailed. There is no fixed form which has to be followed. In the example in **Appendix 11**, column 1 gives the item's number for ease of reference at the trial. Column 2 gives the claimant's allegations on each issue, and their estimate of the loss they have suffered on each point appears in column 3. Columns 4 and 5 are for the defendant's side of the story. The defendant gives their specific response to the claimant's allegations. The defendant also gives, on a without prejudice basis, their estimate of the actual loss suffered by the claimant should the court accept the claimant's allegation. The final column is left blank. The judge uses it for their findings at the trial.

Where there are a number of parties there will be additional columns so that the court can see a summary of each party's views on every issue affecting them. The Schedule is normally settled by counsel.

The order requiring a Scott Schedule is normally made at the case management conference. The claimant is usually required to draw it up. The order specifies when the Schedule must be delivered to the other parties who will have to complete their parts of the Schedule and return it to the claimant within a specified time. If a party gives insufficient information in the Schedule, they can be ordered to give further information.

The claimant must lodge the court copy with the court clerk well in advance of the trial so that it can be read by the judge. Each party needs a copy for counsel, a copy for the solicitor, and a copy for each expert witness.

5.8 PREPARATION FOR TRIAL

5.8.1 The documents

A case proceeding in the TCC will often have a large number of documents and, as always, it will be necessary to produce an agreed bundle. It will usually be helpful to have separate bundles for the statements of case, correspondence, contracts, etc. If the parties cannot agree on whether a particular document is relevant, they can prepare a supplementary bundle of each party's additional documents. It is usually easier, however, to have just one bundle containing every document any party wants to have included.

The documents should be arranged chronologically and given consecutive page numbers. In addition to the court bundle, each lawyer and the witness who is giving evidence will need a copy of the bundle. If there are a large number of documents, the court clerk should be consulted about what should be filed in advance. It is likely that the judge in such cases will read the statements of case and any Scott Schedule in advance, but will expect counsel to take them through the remainder of the documents at the trial.

5.8.2 The pre-trial review

Before the pre-trial review, every party must complete a pre-trial review questionnaire. This takes the place of the pre-trial checklist used in mainstream litigation. The judge is likely to ask the claimant's counsel to circulate a list of issues beforehand, together with proposals for the conduct of the trial, so that the other parties can comment. At the pre-trial review, the judge will check that their directions have been complied with and settle the arrangements for the preparation of the bundles and the trial (eg whether facilities are needed to show evidence on video or by computer graphics). Counsel who are going to attend the trial should also attend the pre-trial review.

5.9 THE TRIAL

The trial will proceed in substantially the same way as any trial elsewhere in the High Court. In longer cases and the more difficult short cases, the judge will often want to inspect the subject matter of the action, accompanied by an expert appointed by each party. The parties do not have to pay the expenses of this inspection unless it takes place abroad.

5.10 ALTERNATIVE DISPUTE RESOLUTION

Section 7 of the TCC Guide gives guidance on the use of ADR in TCC cases. As with other courts, the TCC will encourage the parties to make use of any appropriate form of ADR. At the first CMC, the TCC will want to be addressed on the parties' views as to the likely efficacy of ADR, the appropriate timing of ADR, and the advantages and disadvantages of a short stay of proceedings to allow ADR to take place.

5.11 SUMMARY

The TCC will deal with many transactions of a business nature, especially where there is a need for an exhaustive investigation of matters of technical detail.

Cases can be commenced in the TCC or transferred to that court at a later date.

Scott Schedules will frequently be used in the TCC.

Injunctions: The Law

LEARNING OUTCOMES

After reading this chapter you will understand:

- the types of injunction available
- the background law relating to the grant of an interim injunction
- the importance of the claimant's undertaking as to damages
- the importance of the *American Cyanamid* guidelines in interim prohibitory injunctions
- exceptions to the *American Cyanamid* guidelines
- the role of undertakings
- how to vary or set aside an interim injunction.

6.1 INTRODUCTION

This chapter explains the various types of injunction the courts can grant. It discusses the factors the court takes into account in deciding whether or not to grant an injunction pending trial (an interim injunction) or at the trial (a final injunction). It also explains why the claimant may have to compensate the defendant for any harm caused by the injunction if the injunction is varied or set aside later on in the case. Lastly, it explains how the defendant may avoid an injunction by giving a promise (known as an undertaking) to the court.

Injunctions are common in commercial cases because they can be used to protect confidential and commercially sensitive information, and to guard against the dissipation of assets. They are generally available only to claimants.

6.2 TYPES OF INJUNCTION

An injunction is a court order, breach of which is punishable as a contempt of court.

A party may seek an injunction at any time after proceedings have been commenced (and in exceptional cases, even before proceedings have been commenced). Such injunctions, made before trial, are known as interim injunctions. They remain in force until the case comes to trial (or until further order). At the trial, the court will decide whether or not to make a final or perpetual injunction. Both interim and final injunctions can take various forms.

There are three types of interim and final injunction, which all have a different effect. The normal type of injunction is a prohibitory or negative injunction. It prevents the defendant from taking certain steps (eg soliciting customers of the claimant). There are also mandatory injunctions which require the defendant to do something (eg to remove an obstruction to the claimant's light) and quia timet injunctions which require the defendant to take steps to prevent harm occurring (eg to provide support for the claimant's adjoining land in order to prevent subsidence).

Interim injunctions are normally obtained on notice (ie the defendant is given notice of the injunction hearing). They last until the trial of the claimant's action unless they are set aside earlier by the court (eg because of a change of circumstances). However, by r 25.3(1) of CPR 1998, the court may grant an interim remedy on an application made without notice if it appears to the court that there are good reasons for not giving notice (eg there is insufficient time to give notice, or giving notice would enable the defendant to harm the claimant in some way, such as destroying evidence which would support the claimant's case).

An injunction without notice takes one of two forms. It may fix a date for a further hearing, with all parties present, in which case it lasts until the date specified for that hearing. At the hearing, the defendant may argue that the injunction should not be granted. If the defendant succeeds, the injunction will be set aside. Alternatively, rather than fixing a hearing date, an injunction without notice may simply tell the defendant that they can apply, if they wish (on notice), for the order to be varied or set aside. In the meantime, the injunction remains in force until trial or further order.

6.3 GENERAL PRINCIPLES

The general principles which usually apply to all injunctions are that:

(a)   it must be just and convenient to grant the injunction;

(b)   they are a discretionary remedy; and

(c)   damages must be an inadequate remedy.

These principles are discussed in more detail at **6.3.2–6.3.4**. In the case of mandatory and quia timet injunctions, there are certain other factors considered by the courts, and these are set out at **6.3.5** and **6.3.6**. In addition, the requirements and guidelines which normally apply to applications for an interim injunction are discussed at **6.4–6.7**.

First, however, it is necessary to consider the court's general jurisdiction to grant an injunction.

6.3.1 The court's powers

Under s 37 of the Senior Courts Act 1981 an injunction can be granted 'in all cases in which it appears to the court to be just and convenient to do so'. It may be granted either unconditionally or on such terms and conditions as the court thinks fit.

Although the County Court generally cannot grant specialised injunctions called freezing injunctions or search orders (see **Chapters 8** and **9**), s 38 of the County Courts Act 1984 gives the County Court the same power to grant any other injunctions as that possessed by the High Court.

6.3.2 Just and convenient

Generally, an injunction has not been granted unless the claimant could show that they have a substantive cause of action in English law. The House of Lords stated in *South Carolina Insurance Co v Assurantie Maatschappij 'De Zeven Provincien' NV* [1987] AC 24 that the claimant must show that the defendant is either:

(a)   threatening to invade (or has invaded) the claimant's legal or equitable rights; or

(b)   threatening to behave (or has behaved) in an unconscionable manner.

However, since the *South Carolina Insurance Co* judgment, the courts have moved away from this strict categorisation, particularly in light of the development of the freezing injunction (see **Chapter 8**). The correct question to ask now is: what does the 'just and convenient' test in s 37 require? This was answered in *Convoy Collateral Ltd v Broad Idea International Ltd* [2021] UKPC 24, where the Privy Council identified two requirements before an injunction can be granted: first, an interest of the claimant which merits protection, and, second, a legal or equitable principle which justifies exercising the power to order the defendant to do or not do something.

6.3.2.1   Criminal offences

Sometimes a person chooses to break the criminal law because the profits they can make by so doing exceed the penalties which may be imposed by the criminal courts. In such cases the only effective way of enforcing the law is to obtain an injunction. If the defendant breaks the injunction, they can be punished by imprisonment or by severe financial penalties.

A private individual cannot usually obtain an injunction to enforce the criminal law. Usually, the Attorney-General seeks the injunction, although some laws (eg planning law) are enforced by local authorities acting under s 222 of the Local Government Act 1972.

An individual can get an injunction restraining criminal acts only if they can show that:

(a)   the offence was created to protect a particular class of people; and

(b)   they are a member of that class; and

(c)   they have suffered special damage as a result of the defendant's crimes.

For example, in *Ex parte Island Records Ltd* [1978] Ch 122, a record company obtained an injunction preventing 'bootleggers' from making and selling pirate copies of its records contrary to the Dramatic and Musical Performers Protection Act 1958 (now repealed).

6.3.3   Injunctions are a discretionary remedy

A claimant may have a good claim in law but still fail to get an injunction (eg because the matter is too trivial). This is because, as an injunction is an equitable remedy, it is discretionary and the claimant must comply with the usual 'equitable maxims'. Matters which might persuade the court to refuse an injunction include the following.

6.3.3.1   They who come to equity must come with clean hands

In *Hubbard v Vosper* [1972] 2 QB 84, the Court of Appeal refused to grant an injunction preventing the publication of information criticising a religious cult because, according to Megaw LJ, the claimants had been 'protecting their secrets by deplorable means'. If the claimant has behaved dishonestly or spitefully, they may be refused an injunction.

On the other hand, the defendant's behaviour and motivation is also a factor. If the defendant has been harming the claimant out of malice, this may persuade the court to grant an injunction in a borderline case.

6.3.3.2   Acquiescence

If the claimant knew that the defendant was infringing their rights and failed to object, they may be refused an injunction because they led the defendant to believe that they did not object to the defendant's behaviour. In *Sayers v Collyer* (1885) 28 Ch D 103, the defendant was selling beer in breach of a restrictive covenant. The claimant owned the land with the benefit of that covenant. The claimant sought to enforce the covenant but failed when it was proved that they had, for the past three years, been a regular customer of the defendant.

Delay of itself does not amount to acquiescence. The claim for an injunction will only fail if the delay has led the defendant to believe that they had not done any wrong; that, as a result of that belief, the defendant has acted to their detriment and that it would now be unfair to allow the claimant to obtain an injunction (*Jones v Stones* [1999] 1 WLR 1739).

In *Church of Scientology of California v Miller* (1987) *The Times*, 23 October, the claimants sought an injunction to restrain publication of confidential information. They had known for some time of the defendant's plans. The defendant's preparations for publication were well advanced. An injunction was refused because, although it would have been appropriate earlier, it would now cause excessive damage and inconvenience.

6.3.4   No injunction will be granted if damages would be an adequate remedy

Under s 50 of the Senior Courts Act 1981, the court can award damages instead of (as well as in addition to) an injunction, whether or not the claimant applied for damages in their statement of case. An injunction will be granted where:

(a)   there is serious harm which is likely to continue; or

(b)   the harm is irreparable or cannot be quantified in financial terms; or

(c)   the defendant does not have the means to pay damages.

Damages were awarded instead of an injunction in *Proctor v Bayley* (1889) 42 Ch D 390 (the harm was over and unlikely to recur) and *Lyme Valley Squash Club Ltd v Newcastle-under-Lyme Borough Council* [1985] 2 All ER 405 (the harm to the claimant was only slight).

Cases where damages were not sufficient to prevent the grant of an injunction include *Evans Marshall & Co v Bertola SA* [1973] 1 WLR 349 (the alleged breach of contract would disrupt the claimant's business); *League Against Cruel Sports Ltd v Scott* [1986] QB 240 (the defendant had repeated their conduct on several occasions); and *Radley Gowns Ltd v Costas Spyrou (t/a Touch of Class and Fiesta Girl)* [1975] FSR 455 (limited lifespan of new styles and damage to goodwill). Damages are rarely seen as adequate compensation where the claimant is seeking to enforce a valid restrictive covenant relating to land.

6.3.5   Mandatory injunctions

A mandatory injunction must specify exactly what the defendant has to do and the time within which they must do it. Such orders are granted much less frequently than prohibitory injunctions. They will be granted only if the claimant will suffer serious harm if an injunction is not granted. The court will not require the defendant to incur expenditure which is disproportionate to the harm the claimant will otherwise suffer.

The approach of the courts can be illustrated by comparing two cases. In *Wrotham Park Estate Co v Parkside Homes Ltd* [1974] 2 All ER 321, the defendant had built houses in breach of a restrictive covenant. The claimant sought an injunction ordering the defendant to demolish the houses. The court refused the order as this would have involved 'an unpardonable waste of much needed houses'.

On the other hand, in *Pugh v Howells* (1984) 48 P & CR 298, the defendant built an extension to their property which interfered with the claimant's right to light. The claimant had warned the defendant that they would seek an injunction. The defendant's own surveyor had advised against the extension. The court ordered the defendant to demolish the extension.

6.3.6   Quia timet injunctions

Quia timet injunctions are a particular type of prohibitory injunction and, as stated by Lord Upjohn in *Redland Bricks Ltd v Morris* [1970] AC 652 at 655, are applicable to the following types of cases:

(a)   where the respondent has as yet done no hurt to the applicant but is threatening and intending (as the applicant alleges) to do works which will cause irreparable harm to them or their property if carried to completion;

(b)   where the applicant has been fully recompensed, both at law and in equity, for the damage they have suffered, but where the applicant alleges that the earlier action of the respondent may lead to future causes of action (eg where the respondent has withdrawn support from their neighbour's land, or where they have so acted in depositing their soil from their mining operation as to constitute a menace to the applicant's land).

A quia timet injunction will be granted to restrain an apprehended or threatened injury only where the injury is certain or imminent, or where mischief of an overwhelming nature is likely to be done.

Often a quia timet injunction is sought against persons unknown. For example, in *University of Brighton v Persons Unknown Occupying Land* [2023] EWHC 1485 (KB), the court had previously granted an interim injunction against persons unknown who had occupied the claimant's premises. Having recovered possession of the premises, the claimant sought a final quia timet injunction to restrain or prevent future acts of trespass by persons unknown. The court indicated that there must be a sufficiently real and imminent risk of a tort being committed to justify quia timet relief, as well as a strong probability that, unless restrained, the defendant will do something which will cause the claimant irreparable harm – that is to say, harm which, if it occurs, cannot be reversed or restrained by an immediate interim injunction and cannot be adequately compensated by an award for damages.

6.3.7   Special cases

In some types of cases, the courts apply special criteria before granting an injunction.

6.3.7.1   Banking

An injunction will not be granted to interfere with a banker's irrevocable letter of credit unless there is clear evidence of fraud: *Bolivinter Oil SA v Chase Manhattan Bank NA* [1984] 1 WLR 392.

6.3.7.2   Employment

By s 236 of the Trade Union and Labour Relations (Consolidation) Act 1992, a court cannot grant an order for specific performance of a contract of employment or an injunction to prevent a breach of such a contract where to do so would compel an employee to do any work or attend a place in order to do work. The courts are also reluctant to enforce restrictive covenants in a contract of employment by granting an interim injunction. They prefer to deal with the matter by ordering an early trial.

The courts also rarely grant injunctions requiring an employer to perform a contract of employment.

6.4   THE CLAIMANT'S UNDERTAKING AS TO DAMAGES

The court decides whether to grant an interim injunction based on the evidence presented at the interim hearing. It therefore grants such an injunction before there is an opportunity to investigate liability fully. At the final trial of the case, the defendant may win and the interim injunction may have caused loss to the defendant in the meantime. If so, the defendant needs compensation for any loss they have suffered as a result of the injunction. Therefore, the court will usually grant an interim injunction only if the claimant gives an undertaking to compensate the defendant for any harm caused by the injunction if it is discharged at a later date. The normal wording of the undertaking is:

> If the Court later finds that this Order has caused loss to the Respondent, and decides that the Respondent should be compensated for that loss, the Applicant will comply with any Order the Court may make.

This undertaking is often referred to as the 'claimant's cross-undertaking'.

The claimant's ability to meet their potential liability under this undertaking is taken into account in deciding whether or not to grant an injunction. The claimant will usually have to give evidence of their financial circumstances, for example, in the case of a business, by producing recent accounts. Further, the court can order the claimant to pay money into court or to provide some other form of security to show that the undertaking is not worthless. However, the claimant will not be deprived of an injunction simply because they are short of money. In *Allen v Jambo Holdings Ltd* [1980] 2 All ER 502, the Court of Appeal held that even a legally-aided claimant can obtain an injunction in appropriate cases, in spite of the fact that their undertaking as to damages is of little value.

The cross-undertaking is not required where the injunction is sought to enforce the law by an agency such as a department of State (*Hoffman-La Roche & Co AG v Secretary of State for Trade and Industry* [1975] AC 295) or a local authority (*Kirklees Metropolitan Borough Council v Wickes Building Supplies Ltd* [1993] AC 227) or the Securities and Investments Board (*Securities and Investments Board v Lloyd-Wright* [1993] 4 All ER 210).

If the defendant subsequently wins the case at trial or establishes that the injunction should not have been granted, they can enforce the claimant's undertaking as to damages by applying for a court inquiry, by a Master or District Judge, into the damage caused to the defendant by the injunction. The defendant will have to prove their loss. If they can, the claimant will have to compensate them even though the claimant acted in good faith throughout. It is possible for exemplary damages to be awarded if the claimant was not acting in good faith.

Even defendants who were not subject to the injunction may be able to claim damages against the claimant under this undertaking (*Berkeley Administration Inc v McClelland* (1996) *The Times*, 13 August).

EXAMPLE

A has commenced proceedings against B and C, alleging that B has infringed A's copyright by producing copies of A's work, and that C is also guilty of infringing A's copyright by selling B's copies. A obtains an interim injunction preventing B from producing any alleged copies of A's work. When the action comes to trial, B proves that they were not infringing A's copyright. B can claim damages for B's loss of profits arising from B's inability to make their products during the period between the injunction and the trial. C can claim damages from A for the loss of profits arising from C's inability to sell B's products during the same period, even though A had not sought an injunction against C.

A solicitor should give specific warnings to their client about the potential liability the client may incur as a result of this undertaking when seeking an injunction.

6.5   INTERIM PROHIBITORY INJUNCTIONS AND THE AMERICAN CYANAMID GUIDELINES

As mentioned in **6.4**, when the court hears an application for an interim injunction, it does not know all the facts. As a result, the court is most reluctant to grant interim injunctions which require the defendant to take positive action (ie mandatory injunctions and quia timet injunctions – see **6.7.4**).

The court is more readily prepared to grant interim injunctions which merely restrain the defendant from doing something (prohibitory injunctions). In these circumstances, however, because it does not have all the facts, the court will not usually investigate the merits of the case. Instead, it applies the guidelines laid down by the House of Lords in *American Cyanamid Co v Ethicon Ltd* [1975] AC 396. Broadly, these guidelines divide into the following parts:

(a)   whether there is a serious question to be tried;

(b)   whether damages are an adequate remedy for either side;

(c)   whether the balance of convenience lies in favour of granting or refusing the injunction; and

(d)   whether there are any special factors.

These are considered below.

6.5.1   Serious question to be tried

Although the court does not generally investigate the full merits of the case in deciding whether or not to grant an interim prohibitory injunction, the claimant does have to establish that there is a serious question to be tried before they can get such an injunction.

This does not mean that the claimant has to prove that they are more likely to win than to lose. Nevertheless, the claimant has to show that they have real prospects of success. If the claimant cannot do this, an injunction will not be made.

Thus, if it is clear that the claimant has no right to an injunction under the general principles discussed above (see **6.3.2** and **6.3.3**), they will not get the injunction. Nevertheless, if the claimant does establish that there is a serious question to be tried, the defendant must then show that there is an arguable defence. If the defendant does not, then, subject to damages not being an adequate remedy for the claimant, the court can grant an injunction without further ado. If, however, both parties have arguable cases, the court will have to consider the second factor, the adequacy of damages as a remedy for either side.

6.5.2   Adequacy of damages

The court will usually consider whether it would be possible to compensate either party financially for the consequences of its decision. So adequacy of damages as compensation must be considered from both the claimant's and the defendant's points of view.

If damages would be an adequate remedy for the claimant in any event, the claimant will not get a final injunction (see **6.3.4**) and the court will refuse to grant an interim injunction.

If damages would not be adequate compensation for the claimant if the court were to refuse the injunction, the court will usually go on to consider the impact of the claimant's undertaking as to damages (see **6.4**). If it is clear that the claimant will be able to provide adequate financial compensation to the defendant for any harm caused by the injunction, 'there would be no reason upon this ground to refuse an [interim] injunction' (Lord Diplock in *American Cyanamid*). Therefore, in practice, the court is more likely to grant an interim prohibitory injunction if it is satisfied that it would later be possible to compensate the defendant for any harm caused by the injunction, by ordering the claimant to pay damages. However, in many cases damages will not be an adequate remedy for either side, and the court then has to consider the third factor, the balance of convenience.

6.5.3   Balance of convenience

The court will now consider what course of action will cause the least damage to the parties, ie where the balance of convenience lies. If granting an injunction would clearly cause less harm to the defendant than the harm the claimant would suffer from the refusal of an injunction, the court will grant the injunction. If, on the other hand, refusing the injunction would cause little harm to the claimant but granting it would cause great harm to the defendant, the court will refuse the injunction. Most injunction applications are determined on the balance of convenience.

> **EXAMPLE**
>
> A is seeking an injunction against B. If the injunction is granted, B will go out of business. If the injunction is refused, both parties will stay in business, although A will suffer financial losses. The consequences for B of granting the injunction are much more serious than the consequences for A if an injunction is refused. The court would usually decline to grant an injunction to A.

Where all other factors are equal, the court will prefer to uphold the status quo (*Garden Cottage Foods Ltd v Milk Marketing Board* [1984] AC 130). If the claimant delayed in applying for the injunction, the status quo is the position as it was just before the application was issued. If there was no delay, the status quo is the position as it was before the start of the conduct which is the subject matter of the application. However, where there has been an alleged breach of a restrictive covenant, the status quo will be the position prior to the alleged breach (*Unigate Dairies Ltd v Bruce* (1988) *The Times*, 2 March).

> **EXAMPLE**
>
> Until recently, B was employed by A in a senior management post. B has resigned and set up in competition with A. A alleges that B is about to harm A by using trade secrets B acquired while working for A and is seeking an injunction restraining B from making use of the alleged confidential information. If the matter cannot be resolved by an award of damages (including damages paid by A under the cross-undertaking), the court is likely to preserve the 'status quo' by granting an injunction unless A has delayed seeking an injunction until B is well established in business, when the court will uphold the 'status quo' by refusing an injunction.

A couple of cases may help to illustrate the court's approach in deciding the balance of convenience. In *Dalgety Spillers Foods Ltd v Food Brokers Ltd* [1994] FSR 504, the defendants had plans to market a range of food products in competition with the claimants' established range of food products. They were aware that the claimants might try to prevent this by a passing off action and that the claimants might seek an injunction restraining them from marketing this particular product. The defendants therefore wrote to the claimants in October 1992 advising the claimants of their plans. The claimants acknowledged this letter but took no further action. The defendants put their products on the market in September 1993. The claimants then issued a claim form alleging 'passing off' and applied for an injunction. The court refused the injunction because the claimants' failure to respond to the original letter had caused the defendants to expend time, trouble and cost which they might not have incurred if the claimants had given an earlier indication of their objections.

In *News Group Newspapers Ltd v Mirror Group Newspapers Ltd* [1989] FSR 126, the defendants had advertised their newspaper by using the 'masthead' of the *Sun* which was a newspaper published by the claimants. The claimants sought an injunction to prevent this and succeeded because the injunction would cause little or no harm to the defendants, whereas the claimants could suffer significant harm if the defendants were allowed to continue what they were doing.

Finally, although the whole object of the *American Cyanamid* guidelines is to avoid a detailed investigation of the facts at this stage, if the above approach does not produce a solution, the court can be influenced by the fact that one party seems clearly to have the stronger case. Under this guideline, the court will take into account the relative strengths of a party's case only if there is no significant difference in the harm each party will suffer if the application goes against them, and the witness statements clearly show that one party has a disproportionately stronger case.

6.5.4 Special factors

When setting out the *American Cyanamid* guidelines, Lord Diplock stated:

> I would reiterate that, in addition to those to which I have referred, there may be many other special factors to be taken into consideration in the particular circumstances of individual cases.

There is no definition of what may amount to special factors, but case law since *American Cyanamid* gives various examples, such as injunctions to thwart winding-up petitions and defamation. Other special cases are considered at **6.7.5**.

6.5.5 Approach of the courts in practice

Cases since *American Cyanamid* have stressed that the guidelines 'must never be used as a rule of thumb, let alone as a straitjacket' (Kerr LJ in *Cambridge Nutrition Ltd v BBC* [1990] 3 All ER 523). The courts are mindful that this is a flexible remedy and it is a matter of discretion, taking into account all the facts. In his judgment in *Series 5 Software v Clarke* [1996] 1 All ER 853, Laddie J discussed whether the courts are just paying 'lip-service' to *American Cyanamid* as, in practice, they still seem to consider the strengths of the parties' cases when reaching their decision. It was Laddie J's view that the House of Lords in *American Cyanamid* was trying to stop mini-trials, with detailed analysis of evidence at the interim injunction stage. However, this did not prevent the courts from looking at the strengths of a party's case at this stage, and this certainly seemed to be the practice prior to *American Cyanamid*. In *Series 5 Software*, Laddie J acknowledged that the courts should not try to solve complex issues of law and fact at this interim stage. Nevertheless, he suggested that if it is apparent from the material available that one party's case is stronger than another, this should not be ignored.

In *Talaris (Sweden) AB v Network Controls International Limited* [2008] EWHC 2930 (TCC) the court considered to what extent its case management powers, and in particular its ability to order a speedy trial of the underlying issues, might affect the balance of convenience. The court held that the fact that it would be possible for the issues to be finally resolved within six to seven weeks (as the issues in dispute were narrow, and limited evidence would be required) was a factor that led the court to exercise its discretion to grant an injunction to remain in force until such trial.

6.6 INTERIM INJUNCTIONS CHECKLIST

1. Do the *American Cyanamid* guidelines apply?
2. Is the court satisfied that there is a serious question to be tried?
3. Would damages be an adequate remedy for the claimant?
4. How far are damages (under the claimant's cross-undertaking) an adequate remedy for the defendant?
5. Where does the balance of convenience lie?
   - Whether the claimant or the defendant will suffer the *greater harm* if the decision goes against them, eg consider:
     - Whether either will suffer irreparable harm, eg to reputation?
     - What is the course of action which would cause the least harm?
   - If the balance of the relative harm does not clearly favour one party, the court will uphold the *status quo*.
     - If the claimant delayed in applying for the injunction, the status quo is the position as it was just before the application was issued.
     - If there was no delay, the status quo is the position as it was before the start of the conduct which is the subject matter of the application.
6. Can the court make a decision after considering the above? If not, does one party clearly have the stronger case?

7.   If an injunction is granted, consider an early trial.

8.   Reach a conclusion.

6.7   INJUNCTIONS WHERE AMERICAN CYANAMID DOES NOT APPLY

In some special cases, set out below, the courts have varied or not applied the *American Cyanamid* guidelines.

6.7.1   There is unlikely to be a trial

The *American Cyanamid* approach assumes that the case will proceed to trial and that the claimant will either win their case and get a final injunction, or will lose and the defendant will be compensated for the harm caused by the earlier interim injunction. There are many cases, however, where the result of the interim application will be decisive and the action will never go to trial. The case of *Fulwell v Bragg* (1983) *The Times*, 6 January is an example. A firm of solicitors had expelled one of its partners. They considered that their expulsion was improper and wanted to persuade former clients of the firm to take their business away from the firm and to deal with them. The expelled partner sought an order requiring the firm to allow them to do this. It was common ground that, whether an injunction was granted or refused, the matter would end there. The court, therefore, felt obliged to do what it could to investigate the merits of both parties' claims.

This illustrates that where there is unlikely to be a trial, the *American Cyanamid* guidelines do not apply and the claimant must show that they are likely to succeed at trial before an injunction will be granted.

6.7.2   Applications to prevent court proceedings

If a claimant wants to prevent someone from bringing proceedings in this country, they will have to show that those proceedings will be an abuse of process (*Bryanstone Finance Ltd v De Vries (No 2)* [1976] Ch 63).

If a claimant wants an order preventing someone from taking legal proceedings in another country, they must establish:

(a)   that there are equivalent proceedings which could be taken in this country; and

(b)   that the English proceedings would be much less vexatious and oppressive than the foreign proceedings (*Arab Monetary Fund v Hashim (No 6)* (1992) *The Times*, 24 July).

As stated in *Bankers Trust Co v PT Jakarta International Hotels & Development* [1999] 1 All ER 785:

> Similarly the courts will enforce an arbitration agreement governed by English law by granting an injunction restraining the respondent from bringing foreign proceedings in breach of that agreement.

6.7.3   Public interest

The courts will usually grant an injunction preventing publication of confidential information if it is in the public interest that confidentiality should be preserved. They do recognise, however, that there are cases where the public interest requires the truth to be revealed. Two examples of cases where an injunction against publication was refused on this ground are *Lion Laboratories Ltd v Evans* [1985] QB 526 (former employee seeking to disclose information about the reliability of a breath-test machine) and *In re a Company's Application* [1989] Ch 477 (reports of alleged infringements of the tax laws and the Financial Services Act 1986). In such public interest cases, the courts are not afraid to investigate the merits of the case before deciding whether to grant an injunction.

6.7.4   Mandatory injunctions

It is very difficult to get a mandatory interim injunction since the court usually requires clear evidence that the claimant is likely to succeed at trial and the *American Cyanamid* guidelines do not apply. Thus, in *Jakeman v South West Thames Regional Health Authority* [1990] IRLR 62, an employee failed to obtain an interim order for the payment of allegedly withheld wages.

However, the presumption against granting interim mandatory injunctions may be overridden if refusal of an injunction would clearly cause undue hardship. For example, in *Films Rover International Ltd v Cannon Film Sales Ltd* [1986] 3 All ER 772, the defendant was the claimant's only supplier and the claimant would go out of business if an injunction was not granted. In *Nikitenko v Leboeuf Lamb Greene & MacRea* (1996) *The Times*, 26 January, the court ordered the defendant to disclose documents to the claimant even though it was not sure that the claimant was entitled to see those documents. It did so because disclosure was unlikely to harm the defendant, whereas if the claimant was entitled to see the documents it was vital that they did so then. The case is, however, exceptional. The balance of convenience is generally not a relevant issue when considering an interim mandatory injunction.

Mandatory injunctions should not be confused with orders pursuant to s 99 of the Copyright, Designs and Patents Act 1988 for delivery up of copies or articles where the claimant alleges breach of copyright.

6.7.5 Other cases

6.7.5.1 Freezing injunctions and search orders

The *American Cyanamid* principles are not appropriate for freezing injunctions and search orders. These are dealt with in **Chapters 8** and **9**.

6.7.5.2 Land

The court will always grant an injunction to restrain breach of an enforceable restrictive covenant relating to land. As the defendant has already promised not to behave in a particular way, the court will enforce their promise (*Hampstead & Suburban Properties Ltd v Diomedous* [1969] 1 Ch 248). Similarly, if the defendant is clearly trespassing on the claimant's land, the claimant will usually be entitled to an injunction to restrain the trespass even if the trespass did not harm them.

6.7.5.3 Trade disputes

Section 221(2) of the Trade Union and Labour Relations (Consolidation) Act 1992 specifically states that where an injunction is sought against a defendant who claims that they are acting 'in contemplation or furtherance of a trade dispute' (as defined by the Act), the court must 'have regard to the likelihood of [the defendant's] succeeding at the trial'. The defendant may raise the defence of immunity from certain tort liabilities or peaceful picketing under ss 219 and 220 of the 1992 Act respectively. If the defence is likely to succeed at the trial, an injunction will be refused unless this would be disastrous for the claimant or other people. In such a case the defendant will have to show that their defence is almost certain to succeed before an injunction will be refused (*NWL Ltd v Woods* [1979] 3 All ER 614).

6.8 INJUNCTIONS WITHOUT NOTICE

Orders are made without notice if the matter is so urgent that the claimant does not have time to tell the defendant that they intend to seek an injunction. They are also made if secrecy is needed because, if the defendant learns of the claimant's plans, the defendant will try to cause irreparable harm to the claimant before the claimant gets an injunction.

> **EXAMPLE**
>
> B has just been sacked by A. B is about to set up in business in competition with A. A has evidence that B is going to use confidential information belonging to A to compete with A. In addition, A also has evidence that B will conceal or destroy any confidential papers if B knows that A is taking court proceedings. A would be entitled to apply for an injunction without notice restraining B from using such information.

6.8.1   The duty of full and frank disclosure

To proceed without notice, the claimant must also show that they have a strong enough case to justify the court not hearing the defendant's case. This is a departure from the rules of natural justice that all parties should be heard. Therefore, in the interests of fairness, the claimant must disclose all relevant facts, including any matters favourable to the defendant. This is often called the duty of full and frank disclosure or to make a full and fair disclosure of all the material facts (*Kensington Income Tax Commissioners* (1917) 1 KB 486). The material facts are those which it is material for the judge to know when dealing with the application. Materiality is to be decided by the court and not by the assessment of the applicant or their legal advisers (*Thermax Ltd v Schott Industrial Glass Ltd* (1981) FSR 289). The applicant must make proper inquiries before making the application (*Bank Mellat v Nikpour* (1985) FSR 87). The duty of disclosure therefore applies not only to material facts known to the applicant but also to any additional facts which they would have known had they made proper inquiries. The extent of those inquiries which will be held to be proper, and therefore necessary, depends on all the circumstances of the case including (a) the nature of the case which the applicant is making when they make the application, (b) the order for which the application is made and the probable effect of the order on the defendant, and (c) the legitimate urgency and the time available for inquiries (*Brink's-Mat Ltd v Elcombe* [1988] 3 All ER 188).

In *Siporex Trade SA v Comdel Commodities Ltd* [1986] 2 Lloyd's Rep 428 at [437], Bingham J said that the applicant:

> must show the utmost good faith and disclose his case fully and fairly ... He must identify the crucial points for and against the application, and not rely on general statements and the mere exhibiting of numerous documents. He must investigate the nature of the cause of action asserted and the facts relied on before applying and identify any likely defences.

In the *Pugachev* case [2014] EWHC 4336 (Ch) at [171], Mann J said:

> The obligation to anticipate defences in pursuit of the obligation to make full and frank disclosure is very important. An Applicant for without notice relief has actively to consider what points of defence might be taken by the defendant and put them before the court. That is a fundamental requirement, and safeguard.

Failure to do this will invariably result in the injunction being set aside with orders for costs against the claimant who may also have to pay damages to the defendant for any harm caused by the injunction (see **8.9.1**).

6.9   UNDERTAKINGS IN PLACE OF AN INJUNCTION

A defendant who:

(a)   denies the claimant's allegations; or

(b)   is prepared to wait until the trial before challenging them; or

(c)   concedes that the claimant is likely to succeed,

may save costs by giving an undertaking to the court to avoid the need for an injunction. This will usually be in the same terms as the injunction the claimant is seeking. Such an undertaking has the same effect as an injunction and non-compliance is punishable as a contempt of court.

Sometimes the defendant is not prepared to give an undertaking until the court has found in the claimant's favour at an interim hearing. The defendant will then offer an undertaking (which may be 'without prejudice to an appeal') so that, at any subsequent hearing, the defendant is not at a psychological disadvantage in being regarded by the judge as a person who has had to be restrained by an injunction.

6.10 VARYING AND SETTING ASIDE INJUNCTIONS

As mentioned at **6.2**, an interim injunction on notice lasts 'until trial or further order'. It will usually contain a clause giving either party liberty to apply to vary or set aside the order. Even if it does not expressly do so, either party can apply to vary or set aside the order if circumstances change. The defendant is more likely to apply for this than the claimant. For example, the defendant may do this because the burden of the injunction has become too onerous, as in *Jordan v Norfolk County Council* [1994] 1 WLR 1353. In that case, the defendant council had caused damage to the claimant's land by an admitted trespass. The claimant obtained an injunction requiring the defendant to make good that damage. Everyone assumed that this would cost about £12,000. The defendant then learned that the cost of complying with the order would be over £250,000. The claimant's land was worth only £25,000. The court varied the injunction.

A defendant may combine an application to set aside the injunction with an application to dismiss the claimant's action for want of prosecution. This is appropriate if the claimant does not proceed with their case with all proper speed. For instance, the claimant may try to delay proceedings because the claimant realises there is a risk that they will be unsuccessful at trial and fail to obtain a permanent injunction. By delaying, the claimant ensures that they benefit from the interim injunction for as long as possible prior to trial.

A defendant may also apply to vary or set aside an undertaking. However, it is more difficult to do this because the defendant gave the original undertaking voluntarily. In *Chanel Ltd v F W Woolworth* [1981] 1 WLR 485, the Court of Appeal held that the defendants could vary their undertaking only if there had been a significant change of circumstances or they had become aware of new facts which they could not possibly have known about when they gave their undertaking.

As regards orders without notice, these can also be varied or set aside by the defendant, either on the return date fixed by the order, or on the defendant's application at any time (see **6.2**). Non-disclosure of material facts by the claimant is often the principal ground for setting aside an order without notice. Thus, on an application to set aside an interim prohibitory injunction on this ground, the court will again apply the *American Cyanamid* guidelines and decide whether, in the light of the defendant's new evidence, the injunction should have been granted in the first place. Non-disclosure is discussed in more detail at **8.9**.

Whenever an injunction is set aside, the defendant may have a claim for damages under the claimant's undertaking as to damages. As explained in *Cheltenham and Gloucester Building Society v Ricketts* [1993] 4 All ER 276, unless it is obvious what loss the defendant has suffered (or it is obvious that no loss has been suffered), there will have to be a separate hearing to investigate the amount of the defendant's loss. This will usually be at or after the trial of the claimant's main action.

6.11 HUMAN RIGHTS

As with civil litigation generally, it is likely that Article 6(1) of the European Convention for the Protection of Human Rights and Fundamental Freedoms (Rome, 4 November 1950) ('the European Convention on Human Rights') will be most relevant to commercial litigation:

> In the determination of his civil rights and obligations or of any criminal charge against him, everyone is entitled to a fair and public hearing within a reasonable time by an independent and impartial tribunal established by law. ...

The reference to 'everyone' in Article 6(1) includes companies as well as individuals.

It may be considered that an injunction granted without the defendant having any notice of the application does not comply with Article 6(1). On the other hand, there are circumstances where it might defeat the whole purpose of the injunction if notice were given to the other party, and therefore less harm is done by making the order in the absence of one party (see **Chapters 8** and **9**). The absent party does, of course, have some protection in relation to the disclosure requirements imposed on the applicant and the possible sanctions which may be levied by the court (see **6.8**).

6.12 SUMMARY

The court can grant injunctions to maintain the status quo pending the final trial of the claimant's action against the defendant. Such injunctions (known as interim injunctions) will be granted only where it is just and equitable to do so. There are guidelines (known as the *American Cyanamid* guidelines) which help the court to decide whether or not to grant such interim prohibitory injunctions. Under these guidelines, the court will balance the risk of injustice by considering whether it would be more convenient to grant or to refuse an injunction at this stage of the case. The court can always vary or set aside an injunction at a later date. If it does, the claimant will usually have to compensate the defendant for any harm suffered by the defendant as a result of the injunction.

Although the *American Cyanamid* guidelines represent the usual approach of the court in deciding whether or not to grant an interim injunction, there are cases (see **6.7**) where the court adopts a different approach.

A defendant can avoid being subject to an injunction by giving an undertaking to the court.

The court may also grant a final injunction at the trial of the claimant's action. In such cases (as opposed to interim injunctions), it will consider the merits of the case in detail.

INTERIM INJUNCTIONS: THE PROCEDURE

LEARNING OUTCOMES

After reading this chapter you will understand:

- how Part 25 of CPR 1998 applies to interim injunctions
- how to obtain an in interim injunction
- how to serve an interim injunction
- how to enforce an interim injunction.

7.1 INTRODUCTION

This chapter deals with the procedure for obtaining interim injunctions. It also explains how to enforce injunctions and undertakings in the courts.

The general procedure for applying for interim remedies is covered by Parts 23 and 25 of CPR 1998. This chapter will outline that general procedure as interpreted by PD 25A to CPR 1998 – Interim Injunctions (PD 25A). Although it will usually be the claimant who is seeking the injunction, it is also possible for defendants to apply for injunctions. The Rules and PD 25A therefore refer to the person seeking the injunction as the applicant and to the other party as the respondent. That is the terminology we shall use in this chapter and the following two chapters.

7.2 THE PROCEDURE FOR OBTAINING INJUNCTIONS

Final or permanent injunctions are granted when the applicant's action comes to trial and generally cause few procedural problems. This chapter deals solely with the procedure for obtaining interim injunctions.

7.2.1 When an injunction can be granted

Interim remedies are governed by Part 25 of CPR 1998, and r 25.1 confirms that an interim injunction is one of the remedies to which Part 25 applies. The court can grant an interim injunction whether or not the applicant has made a claim for a final injunction (r 25.1(4)).

Normally, an interim remedy will be sought at some time between the court issuing the claim form and the trial. However, r 25.2 confirms that, subject to any practice direction or other rule, the court can grant any interim remedy before the start of proceedings, but only if the matter is urgent or 'it is otherwise necessary to do so in the interests of justice' (r 25.2(2)(b)). Thus, if the applicant can, for example, satisfy the court that the respondent will attempt to destroy evidence as soon as they know that they are being sued, the court will grant an interim injunction enabling the applicant to preserve the evidence before the claim form is issued by the court.

Under r 25.2(3), a court which grants an interim injunction before the claim has been commenced 'may give directions requiring a claim to be commenced'. This will normally involve the applicant undertaking to issue a claim form immediately. By para 5.1(5) of PD 25A, this will usually be on the same or the next working day. The courts have, in the past, imposed heavy penalties on applicants and their solicitors for failing to comply with this undertaking. They have even discharged the original injunction, as in *Siporex Trade SA v Comdel Commodities Ltd* [1986] 2 Lloyd's Rep 428.

The court's directions will probably also require the applicant's solicitor to inform the issuing department of the court of the urgency of the situation and to ensure that the claim form is issued on the day it is filed. Practice Direction 25A does say that, where possible, this claim form should be served with the injunction.

Where an injunction is granted before the claim form has been issued, the title to the action should describe the parties as 'the Claimant and Defendant in a Intended Action'.

The court requires the solicitors acting for an applicant who has obtained an injunction before a claim form has been issued to continue to show a sense of urgency in their conduct of the case. If the applicant does not pursue their claim once they have obtained their injunction, the court could use its case management powers under Part 3 to dismiss this case.

Rule 25.2(1) also confirms that there is power to grant an injunction after the court has granted a final judgment (eg for the payment of damages). This would normally be sought in aid of attempts to enforce the judgment.

A defendant who intends to apply for an injunction, as part of their counterclaim, can do so after filing either an acknowledgement of service or a defence (r 25.2(2)(c)).

7.2.2   The normal procedure

The application for the injunction will, if the main action is also proceeding in this country, be made to the court which is currently dealing with the main action (or, if proceedings have not yet been commenced, to the court where the main action will be commenced).

Generally, the application must be made by an application notice, although r 23.3(2)(b) allows the court to dispense with this requirement. The cases where this will be done will usually be very urgent cases where the respondent is not being given advance notice of the application (see **7.2.3**).

Under r 23.6 the application notice must state:

(a)   what order the applicant is seeking; and

(b)   briefly, why the applicant is seeking the order.

Paragraph 2 of PD 25A says that the notice must also state the date, time and place of this hearing.

Rule 22.1(3) states that, if the applicant wishes to rely on anything in the application notice as evidence, it must be verified by a statement of truth.

Rule 25.3(2) says that an application for an interim remedy must be supported by evidence unless the court orders otherwise. This will usually be in the form of a witness statement including all material facts of which the court should be made aware.

Rule 23.7(1) requires the application notice to be served as soon as practicable after it has been issued and, in any event, at least three days before the hearing of the application. The court may, however, allow a shorter period of notice, or even dispense with service if this will help achieve the overriding objective.

The application must, when it is served, be accompanied by any supporting witness statements and copies of any draft order the applicant is seeking. Rule 23.7(2) says that the supporting witness statements must be filed with the court along with the application notice.

Under r 23.11, the court has power to proceed if the applicant or the respondent fails to attend the hearing. If the applicant fails to attend, the court will almost certainly dismiss the application. If the respondent fails to attend, the court will grant the application, but only if it is satisfied that the respondent had sufficient notice of the application to be able to attend. It will be easier to satisfy the court on this point if the papers were served on the respondent in person.

If the court does make an order on an application for an interim injunction in the absence of one of the parties, it may re-list the application under r 23.11(2). This would be appropriate if, for example, a party were able to show that they were unable, through no fault of their own, to attend the original hearing.

Practice Direction 25A does not contain a standard form of interim injunction. It merely states that the injunction must contain an undertaking as to damages (see **6.4**) and that, if the injunction is granted in the presence of all respondents, or at a hearing of which they all had notice, it may (and usually will) state that it is effective until trial or further order. A suggested specimen interim injunction is set out in **Appendix 12** to this book. Whenever possible, the applicant should file a draft injunction electronically.

Some general points to note about the contents of the standard form order, as set out in **Appendix 12**, are:

(a)   The injunction usually lasts until after final judgment. Nevertheless, the respondent may apply to court at any time to vary or set aside the order, provided they give the necessary prior notice to the applicant. The respondent may wish to make this application if circumstances change prior to trial.

(b)   The respondent is injuncted from doing something themselves 'or in any other way'. The wording of the order makes it clear that not only is the respondent prevented from performing the prohibited acts, but they cannot use others to do them on their behalf.

(c)   Schedule 2 to the order contains the standard undertaking as to damages given by the applicant (see **6.4**).

(d)   The front of the order must also include a penal notice, in a prominent position, warning of the consequences of disobeying the order. The standard wording of the notice is:

If you the within named **AB DISOBEY** this order you may be held to be in contempt of court and **LIABLE TO IMPRISONMENT OR FINED OR YOUR ASSETS SEIZED.**

The standard form order also begins with a warning to the respondent of the effect of breaking the order, but this is not a substitute for a penal notice in the above form. If the injunction does not contain such a penal notice, it generally cannot be enforced if broken by the respondent.

7.2.2.1   Costs

If an interim injunction is granted on the balance of convenience, the court should usually reserve the costs of the application to the trial judge (*Richardson v Desquenne et Giral UK Ltd* (1999) LTL, 23 November). However, this is not an absolute rule, and it could be right to depart from the general approach if, on the balance of convenience, it was so clearly a case in favour of the claimant that the defendant should have a costs order against them for not conceding to the application. If a defendant waits until just prior to the hearing of the application before deciding not to contest it, the defendant runs the risk of being ordered to pay the costs of the hearing (*Picnic at Ascot Inc v Derigs* [2001] FSR 2).

7.2.3   Applications made without notice

Rule 25.3(1) states that the court may grant an interim remedy without notice to the respondent if the court thinks that there are good reasons for not giving notice but, by para (3), the evidence in support of the application must explain why notice has not been given. No application can be made without notice unless this is permitted by a rule, or a Practice Direction or a court order. The usual reasons for seeking an interim injunction without notice will be either:

(a)   that the matter is too urgent to allow for notice to be given; or

(b)   that the respondent would take steps to harm the applicant if they were forewarned of the application.

Sometimes there will have been insufficient time for the application to be made in writing. In such cases, the application may be made orally, but the court will require undertakings from the applicant or their solicitor to file and serve written evidence forthwith. Paragraph 4.3 of PD 25A states that if a claim form has been issued:

(1)   the application notice, evidence in support and a draft order (as in 2.4 above) should be filed with the court two hours before the hearing wherever possible,

(2)   if an application is made before the application notice has been issued, a draft order (as in 2.4 above) should be provided at the hearing, and the application notice and evidence in support must be filed with the court on the same or next working day or as ordered by the court, and

(3)   except in cases where secrecy is essential, the applicant should take steps to notify the respondent informally of the application.

The procedure where no claim form has yet been issued is described at **7.2.1**.

The evidence in support of the application should state:

(a)   the facts giving rise to the applicant's action;

(b)   the facts justifying an interim injunction;

(c)   the facts justifying an application without notice to the respondent;

(d)   any answer which is likely to be raised by the respondent;

(e)   any facts known to the applicant which might make a without notice remedy inappropriate; and

(f)   the precise order being sought.

The applicant therefore must inform the court of any points they believe the respondent would have made if they had had the opportunity to be heard. Indeed, this duty extends to facts of which the applicant would have known if they had made proper enquiries (see **6.8.1**). If the court subsequently considers that the applicant had not made proper enquiries or full disclosure, it will invariably set aside the injunction. This will expose the applicant to a damages claim under their cross-undertaking.

When the court grants an application for an injunction made without notice, the applicant will have to serve the injunction on the respondent. At the same time, unless the court directs otherwise, the applicant must serve the application and the supporting evidence on all respondents against whom the order was sought (even if it was not made in respect of all of those respondents).

The applicant should also provide full notes of the hearing (*Interoute Telecommunications (UK) Ltd v Fashion Group Ltd* (1999) *The Times*, 10 November).

When the order has been served on the respondent, they can apply to the court to set aside or vary the injunction. The respondent will normally have to do so within seven days of the order being served on them. The order will contain a statement reminding the respondent of this right and the time limit (r 23.9(3)).

The usual ground for applying to set aside an injunction made without notice is likely to be that the applicant did not disclose all relevant information to the court. This is dealt with in more detail at **8.9.1**.

7.2.3.1 Applications outside normal court hours

Cases of extreme urgency may be dealt with by telephone. The detail is set out in para 4.5 of PD 25A:

(a) the judge is likely to require a draft order to be supplied electronically to them;

(b) the application notice and supporting evidence must be filed in court on the same day (or the next working day if so ordered) together with two copies of the order for sealing;

(c) the applicant must be legally represented.

If the court office is closed, the claimant's solicitor will first have to contact the court's security officer. They will put the claimant's solicitor in contact with the duty judge's clerk who will then, if they consider it appropriate, give the claimant's solicitor a telephone number for the duty judge.

7.2.3.2 Costs

A judge who hears an application for an injunction without notice is unlikely to make any final order for the payment of costs. They are likely to leave the issue of costs open until the return date.

7.2.3.3 Contents of the order without notice

An injunction made without notice will, in addition to the usual undertaking as to damages, contain the following undertakings:

(a) an undertaking by the applicant to serve the application notice, supporting evidence, and the injunction on the respondent as soon as practicable;

(b) (where relevant) an undertaking to file the application notice and pay the court fee on the same day or the next working day; and

(c) (where relevant) an undertaking to issue the claim form and pay the court fee on the same day or the next working day (unless the court gives other directions for the commencement of the claim).

It will also contain a return date, which is a hearing where the respondent will have the opportunity to argue that the injunction should be set aside.

A suggested form of injunction without notice is set out in **Appendix 13** to this book.

7.3 SERVICE

The rules relating to service and enforcement of injunctions are contained in Part 81 of CPR 1998, which states that an injunction must be served personally on the defendant before the claimant can take any steps to enforce it. It also states that a mandatory injunction must be served on the defendant before the time stated in the injunction for compliance with the order has expired.

On a practical note, as personal service is required, it is important to have a process server on standby so that the injunction may be served as soon as it has been granted.

Rule 6.16 of CPR 1998 gives the court power to dispense with service, and r 6.15 enables the court to authorise service by some alternative method if the usual methods are impracticable.

The court is only likely to exercise these powers in injunction cases when the defendant is trying to evade service.

By r 81.8 of CPR 1998, the court may enforce a purely prohibitory injunction before it has been served if the respondent was present when the injunction was granted or has subsequently been informed of its terms (eg by telephone).

7.4 ENFORCEMENT

7.4.1 Methods of enforcement

Injunctions are enforced strictly. Even if the respondent believed that their actions did not break the injunction, they will be in contempt of court if the court rules that they have broken the injunction (*In re Mileage Conference Group of the Tyre Manufacturers' Conference Ltd's Agreement* [1966] 1 WLR 1137).

If the respondent does not comply with the injunction then, under Part 81 of CPR 1998, the two principal methods of enforcing an injunction are sequestration (seizure of property) and committal to prison. Alternatively, the court may:

(a)   impose a fine; or

(b)   take security to be of good behaviour; or

(c)   under CPR 1998, r 70.2A, order that the acts required to remedy the breach be done by some person appointed by the court, at the respondent's expense.

The court's role is to ensure future compliance. Punishment is a secondary consideration. As a result, the first enforcement order is often suspended. It will affect the respondent only if they break the injunction again.

Sequestration is usually used where the respondent is a limited company or an unincorporated association like a trade union (although it may also be used against the property of any director or officer of such an organisation if they were party to the breach). If the court grants leave for a writ of sequestration to be issued, it appoints four commissioners to handle the respondent's finances and to extract a financial penalty for breaking the injunction. The amount of the penalty is fixed by the court. Companies may be vicariously liable for the acts of their employees (*Re Supply of Ready Mixed Concrete (No 2)* [1994] 3 WLR 1249).

Individual respondents can be committed to prison for contempt of court. This penalty is also used against the individual officers of a defendant company who were responsible for the breach (*Attorney-General for Tuvalu v Philatelic Distribution Corp Ltd* [1990] 2 All ER 216).

Many of the authorities on committal proceedings are matrimonial cases. The principles are, however, the same for all types of cases.

7.4.2 The penal notice

If there is no penal notice on the injunction it cannot be enforced. The notice must be prominently displayed on the front of the order and must be pointed out to the respondent when the order is served. The process server should explain the consequences of failing to comply with the order.

7.4.3 Third parties

Anyone who knowingly assists the respondent to break the injunction is also in contempt of court (*Acrow (Automation) Ltd v Rex Chainbelt Inc* [1971] 3 All ER 1175).

It is also a criminal contempt of court for a person who knows of an interim injunction to act in a way which will affect the applicant's prospects of making that injunction permanent. In *Attorney-General v Times Newspapers Ltd* [1992] 1 AC 191, the Government had obtained an interim injunction against some newspapers preventing the publication of extracts from a book which had allegedly been written in breach of confidence. Other newspapers then published other extracts from the same book. This meant that it would be more difficult for the Government to succeed at the trial in making the injunction permanent. The House of Lords confirmed that these later publications were a contempt of court.

7.4.4 Procedure for committal

Rule 81.10 of CPR 1998 sets out the procedure for committal. The applicant usually applies by an application notice in the existing proceedings. This must fully describe the alleged breaches (*Chiltern District Council v Keane* [1985] 2 All ER 118). It must be supported by an affidavit explaining how the respondent is alleged to have broken the injunction.

Both documents have to be served personally on the respondent at least three working days before the committal hearing. If the papers have not been served then, unless the court has dispensed with service (see the next paragraph), the court will not hear the application, even though the applicant can prove that the respondent knew of the application.

By r 81.5(1) of CPR 1998, the court has power to dispense with service. The court exercises its power to do this only in exceptional circumstances. An example is *Wright v Jess* [1987] 2 All ER 1067. In that case, the court dispensed with service of the committal papers and committed the respondent for contempt where they had been committed for contempt on three previous occasions. An attempt had been made to serve the present papers on them and they had broken the injunction again on the day of the committal hearing.

The application is heard in public unless, for example, the original proceedings related to a secret process, discovery or invention. Even if the application is heard in private, the decision to commit must be announced in public.

The applicant has to prove the breach beyond reasonable doubt. The parties can give oral evidence, but the applicant will not normally be allowed to give evidence of matters which have happened since their affidavit or witness statement was served.

The application may be dealt with in the respondent's absence on proof that they had received the committal papers. If the court does decide to adjourn because it is not satisfied that the respondent had received the committal papers, notice of the new hearing date must be served on the respondent personally.

Note that r 81.10 provides a mechanism by which a contemnor who has purged their contempt can be released before they have served the entirety of their prison sentence. However, it does not provide an alternative route for challenging the correctness of the court's earlier decision on the contempt application. The proper route for any such challenge is an appeal (*Jaldhi Mideast DMCC v Al Ghurair Resources LLC* [2023] EWHC 1889 (Comm)).

The committal order, if made, must be in the correct form and state what breaches have been proved. If the committal order does not do this, it is invalid and will be quashed on appeal. Technical defects which do not cause prejudice or injustice will not affect the validity of the order (*Nicholls v Nicholls* [1997] 1 WLR 314). The order must specify a fixed term of imprisonment not exceeding two years (Contempt of Court Act 1981, s 14). If a committal order is made (even in the respondent's absence), the court tipstaff is directed to arrest the respondent.

In *Delaney v Delaney* [1996] 2 WLR 74, the Court of Appeal quashed a decision to commit a respondent to prison for an unspecified period of time while the judge decided what the sentence would ultimately be.

If the applicant does not follow the rules exactly, their application to commit the respondent for contempt may fail or the committal order may be quashed on appeal. The applicant can, however, make a fresh application to commit based on the same facts as the original application (*Jelson (Estates) Ltd v Harvey* [1984] 1 All ER 12), but only if the application to commit was dismissed on a technicality as opposed to on the merits.

Where the defendant is an individual and orders making findings of contempt and for committal have been made against the defendant at separate hearings, if the challenge to the finding of contempt is made after the order for committal has been made, as part of the appeal against sentence, can both orders be appealed without permission? Yes, held the Court of Appeal in *Deutsche Bank AG v Sebastian Holdings Inc and another* [2023] EWCA Civ 191.

7.4.5 Procedure for sequestration

The procedure for sequestration is set out in r 83.14A of CPR 1998. The applicant applies to a judge by an application notice for permission to issue a writ of sequestration. The application must be served personally on the respondent unless the judge dispenses with service. The application notice will state the grounds of the application. It is supported by an affidavit explaining why sequestration is needed.

7.4.6 Enforcement of undertakings

An undertaking given in lieu of an injunction should be indorsed with a penal notice and a copy should be served on the defendant (*Hussain v Hussain* [1986] Fam 134).

An undertaking to the court is enforceable in the same way as an injunction. Further, in *Midlands Marts Ltd v Hobday* [1989] 3 All ER 246, the court treated the respondent's undertaking as a contract, and instead of committing the respondent, it awarded the applicant damages.

7.5 SUMMARY

The normal procedure for obtaining an interim injunction is to give notice of the application to the respondent. In exceptional circumstances, however, the application may be made without notice to the respondent. An applicant who intends to apply without notice to the respondent must make a thorough investigation of the facts of the case before they make their application. The applicant must then disclose all relevant facts to the court. The consequences of failing to do either of these things are explained in more detail in the following chapter (see **8.9**).

Solicitors seeking injunctions need to be fully familiar with the relevant rules and the Practice Directions referred to in this chapter.

An injunction may be enforced by committal proceedings only if it contains a penal notice. The applicant's solicitor has to serve the injunction before any enforcement steps can be taken. However, if the injunction is purely prohibitory, it may still be possible to enforce it if the applicant can prove that the respondent knew of the injunction.

Anyone seeking to enforce an injunction must follow the rules to the letter. An application to commit may fail if there has been any procedural irregularity.

Undertakings can be enforced in the same way as injunctions.

CHAPTER 8

FREEZING INJUNCTIONS

LEARNING OUTCOMES

After reading this chapter you will understand:

- the nature of a freezing injunction
- the grounds for applying for a freezing injunction
- the provision of undertakings by the claimant
- the usual terms of a freezing injunction
- the meaning of the privilege against self-incrimination
- how to set aside or vary a freezing injunction
- the availability of worldwide freezing injunctions.

8.1 INTRODUCTION

This chapter explains how it is possible for a claimant to get an order 'freezing' the defendant's assets. Broadly, the claimant can do so where there is a real risk that if the injunction is not granted, the defendant will dispose of their property to avoid enforcement of any judgment subsequently obtained by the claimant. The chapter explains the exceptional circumstances which have to be proved to obtain such an order and the undertakings the claimant will have to give. Further, it details various provisions in the order which are designed to protect the interests of all parties to the action and anyone who is in possession of the defendant's property when the order is made.

The power of the court to make freezing injunctions was first established by the Court of Appeal in the case of *Mareva Compania Naviera SA v International Bulk Carriers SA, The Mareva* [1980] 1 All ER 213, which was actually decided in 1976. For a generation, such injunctions were referred to by lawyers as *Mareva* injunctions. But CPR 1998 introduced the term 'freezing injunction' because that was easier for the general public to understand. Readers of cases decided before 1999 will, however, come across the term '*Mareva* injunction' frequently.

This jurisdiction has thrown up various problems about the privilege against self-incrimination and the claimant's disclosure obligations when seeking an injunction without notice. This chapter deals with these problems, which may also occur in any application for an injunction or a search order. The relevant sections (**8.7** and **8.9**) should therefore also be borne in mind when considering the materials dealt with in **Chapters 6**, **7** and **9** of this book.

Lastly, there are various problems involved in seeking a freezing injunction where there is a foreign element in the case, and this is dealt with in **8.10** below.

8.2 THE NATURE OF THE REMEDY

A freezing injunction is an order which prevents the defendant from disposing of their property pending the trial of the claimant's action against them. It is usually restricted to the defendant's property within the jurisdiction and limited in value to the likely amount of the judgment.

Such injunctions are not granted lightly. The effect of the order on the defendant is very harsh. The court will grant it only if there is clear evidence that the defendant would otherwise dispose of their property to prevent the claimant enforcing any later judgment. The court will not make the order simply to protect the claimant against the risk that the defendant might subsequently become insolvent.

As it is usually necessary to obtain the injunction urgently and secretly, it is normal to apply without notice. The claimant must give the usual undertaking as to damages (see **6.4**). If the injunction is subsequently discharged, the defendant will be able to claim substantial damages as a result of this undertaking. Therefore, solicitors should warn clients who want a freezing injunction of the risks involved.

A freezing injunction also affects third parties who have possession or control of the defendant's property (eg the defendant's bank). They are told that the order has been made and they have to 'police' the order on the claimant's behalf. If they allow the defendant to break the terms of the order, they are at risk of being in contempt of court themselves (see **7.4.3**).

8.2.1 Related remedies

Sometimes, a freezing injunction is not the complete solution to the claimant's problems. The court does have additional powers which the claimant can use. If the defendant is a shareholder in a company, the court can make orders preventing them from using their shares, or the voting rights they give them, in a way which might harm the claimant, as in *Standard Chartered Bank v Walker* [1992] 1 WLR 561. If the defendant has already disposed of property, s 423 of the Insolvency Act 1986 enables the court, in certain circumstances, to set aside that disposition in aid of the freezing injunction, as was done in *Moon v Franklin* [1996] BPIR 196.

8.2.2 Innocent third parties

The claimant may consider that the freezing injunction will be completely effective only if other people involved with the defendant are covered by the order, even though these other people are innocent of any fraud. The courts have confirmed in *TSB Private Bank International SA v Chabra* [1992] 1 WLR 231 that this can be done. However, they have also said that freezing injunctions should not usually be used against banks as defendants (*Polly Peck International plc v Nadir (No 2)* [1992] 4 All ER 769) or in respect of routine banking transactions (*Lewis and Peat (Produce) v Almatu Properties* (1992) *The Times*, 14 May).

This can cause problems for such co-defendants. If it becomes public knowledge that they are subject to a freezing injunction, public confidence in their business may be affected. If the claimant is aware of potential damage to such a defendant's business reputation, the claimant should ask for the application for the freezing injunction to be held in private (*Polly Peck v Nadir* (1991) *The Times*, 11 November).

8.3 THE GROUNDS FOR THE INJUNCTION

The claimant must satisfy the court on two points. First, the claimant must show that they have a good arguable case against the defendant. Secondly, the claimant must show that the defendant has property within the jurisdiction and that there is a real risk that if no order is made the defendant will dispose of their property in order to frustrate the enforcement of any judgment.

8.3.1 The strength of the claimant's case

As is the case for all interim injunctions, the claimant must have a good arguable claim.

> 92. In applying for a freezing injunction, the relevance of a cause of action, where there is one, is evidential: in showing that there is a sufficient basis for anticipating that a judgment will be obtained to justify the exercise of the court's power to freeze assets against which such a judgment, when obtained, can be enforced. That is the rationale for requiring the applicant to show a good arguable case; but there is no reason why the good arguable case need be that the applicant is entitled to substantive relief from the court which is asked to grant a freezing injunction. What in principle matters is that the applicant has a good arguable case for being granted substantive relief in the form of a judgment that will be enforceable by the court from which a freezing injunction is sought. (per Lord Leggatt in *Convoy Collateral Ltd v Broad Idea International Ltd* [2021] UKPC 24 and see further **6.3.2**)

Since the application is made without notice, the claimant is subject to the usual obligations to make detailed investigations before seeking the order and to make full and frank disclosure of all relevant facts (both for and against their case) when seeking the order (see **6.8**). Failure to do so will inevitably result in the defendant applying to have the order set aside for non-disclosure. The defendant will also seek costs and substantial damages under the claimant's undertaking as to damages. The claimant's obligation to make full disclosure extends to facts discovered after the making of the order. If there is any material change in the facts, the claimant must inform the court so that it may decide whether to continue the injunction (see *Commercial Bank of the Near East plc v A, B, C & D* [1989] 2 Lloyd's Rep 319 and *O'Regan v Iambic Productions Ltd* (1989) 139 New LJ 1378).

8.3.2 The risk that the property will disappear

The claimant must show that the defendant has property within the jurisdiction and that the defendant may deal with that property in a way that will hinder the enforcement of any judgment the claimant subsequently obtains. The courts will not allow the claimant to use a freezing injunction to rewrite the insolvency laws and jump the queue ahead of other legitimate creditors of the defendant. Neither will they allow the claimant to use it as a means of putting unfair pressure on a defendant to settle a disputed debt.

There usually needs to be clear evidence that the defendant is a 'debt dodger' and that the removal of assets will be done with a corrupt or dishonest purpose. This might take the form of evidence of their dishonesty vis-à-vis the claimant or other creditors. Other relevant factors will include the ease with which assets could be moved out of the claimant's reach and any subsequent difficulties in enforcement. In the case of foreign defendants the courts will take account of the fact that, if a defendant is able to remove their property from the jurisdiction, it may be very difficult for the claimant to enforce a later judgment. In such cases, evidence about the general trading reputation of businesses from the defendant's country, and information about the difficulties of enforcing English judgments in that country, is very helpful.

8.4 OBTAINING THE INJUNCTION

The claimant applies, without giving notice, with supporting affidavit evidence (a witness statement will not suffice). The application is often made before a claim form has been issued and is often supported by draft evidence only. Subject to **8.5**, the procedure is the same as for any injunction made without giving notice (see **7.2.3**). The application can also be made at any time during the proceedings, or indeed after judgment has been obtained.

Under CPR 1998, PD 25A, para 1.1, only High Court judges and other 'duly authorised' judges may grant a freezing injunction before the claimant has obtained judgment. Outside London, a party who wishes to apply for a freezing injunction should commence proceedings in the High Court, irrespective of the value of their claim. In reality, the cost of obtaining a freezing injunction will usually make it an inappropriate remedy in a low-value claim.

8.5 THE CLAIMANT'S UNDERTAKINGS

The standard form order used for a freezing injunction is set out in CPR 1998, PD 25A. It states that the claimant should normally give the following undertakings:

SCHEDULE B
UNDERTAKINGS GIVEN TO THE COURT BY THE APPLICANT

(1) If the court later finds that this order has caused loss to the Respondent, and decides that the Respondent should be compensated for that loss, the Applicant will comply with any order the court may make.

[(2) The Applicant will—

(a) on or before [date] cause a written guarantee in the sum of £ to be issued from a bank with a place of business within England or Wales, in respect of any order the court may make pursuant to paragraph (1) above; and

(b) immediately upon issue of the guarantee, cause a copy of it to be served on the Respondent.]

(3) As soon as practicable the Applicant will issue and serve a claim form [in the form of the draft produced to the court] [claiming the appropriate relief].

(4) The Applicant will [swear and file an affidavit] [cause an affidavit to be sworn and filed] [substantially in the terms of the draft affidavit produced to the court] [confirming the substance of what was said to the court by the Applicant's counsel/solicitors].

(5) The Applicant will serve upon the Respondent [together with this order] [as soon as practicable]—

(i) copies of the affidavits and exhibits containing the evidence relied upon by the Applicant, and any other documents provided to the court on the making of the application;

(ii) the claim form; and

(iii) an application notice for continuation of the order.

[(6) Anyone notified of this order will be given a copy of it by the Applicant's legal representatives.]

(7) The Applicant will pay the reasonable costs of anyone other than the Respondent which have been incurred as a result of this order including the costs of finding out whether that person holds any of the Respondent's assets and if the court later finds that this order has caused such person loss, and decides that such person should be compensated for that loss, the Applicant will comply with any order the court may make.

(8) If this order ceases to have effect (for example, if the Respondent provides security or the Applicant does not provide a bank guarantee as provided for above) the Applicant will immediately take all reasonable steps to inform in writing anyone to whom he has given notice of this order, or who he has reasonable grounds for supposing may act upon this order, that it has ceased to have effect.

[(9) The Applicant will not without the permission of the court use any information obtained as a result of this order for the purpose of any civil or criminal proceedings, either in England and Wales or in any other jurisdiction, other than this claim.]

[(10) The Applicant will not without the permission of the court seek to enforce this order in any country outside England and Wales [or seek an order of a similar nature including orders conferring a charge or other security against the Respondent or the Respondent's assets].]

The first undertaking is the usual undertaking as to damages. However, the claimant also has to undertake to provide a written bank guarantee for a fixed sum of money. This is to provide security for their liability under the undertaking as to damages. The claimant has to serve a copy of the guarantee on the defendant and the freezing injunction will automatically lapse if the claimant does not provide the guarantee within the time specified in their undertaking.

The claimant also undertakes to serve the claim form on the defendant along with the order. The words in square brackets will be included where, as is often the case, the order has been obtained before issuing the claim form. This undertaking effectively means that the injunction cannot be served until a claim form has been issued. If that is not possible, the claimant's lawyers must try to persuade the court to accept a variation of the standard undertaking.

The fourth undertaking will be needed wherever the claimant has not had time to complete all the usual formalities regarding evidence before applying for an injunction. As undertaking (5) shows, the evidence is served with the injunction along with an application notice for continuation of the order.

As the third parties who have possession or control of the defendant's property are required to police the order, they will obviously need copies of it. The sixth undertaking deals with this.

In undertaking (7), the claimant promises to reimburse the third parties (eg, the bank with whom the defendant holds an account) for the expenses they incur in complying with the injunction. In practice, the third parties will usually pass on these costs to their customer (the defendant). If the defendant cannot meet these costs, the claimant will have to meet the bill which will cover both legal and administrative costs.

The claimant has to undertake to inform all third parties affected by the injunction if it lapses, for example because the claimant fails to provide the bank guarantee or the defendant provides security (see **8.6.3**).

8.6 THE TERMS OF THE ORDER

Practice Direction 25A contains a suggested form of freezing injunction. This is reproduced in **Appendix 14** to this book. It will need to be amended and added to, depending on the facts of the individual case. However, an injunction omitting important terms may be set aside (*Bank of Scotland v A Ltd* (2000) *The Times*, 18 July). The order must also contain the usual penal notice.

Clause 2 of the order informs the defendant that they have the right to apply to vary or discharge the order. Clause 3 of the order refers to the fact that there will be a further hearing known as the return date. This will usually be about a week after the granting of the order, and the defendant can make any application for variation or discharge on that day.

8.6.1 Freezing the assets

Clauses 5–8 of the order deal with this.

Clause 5 prevents the defendant from dealing with the assets in any way, up to a certain value, which should be the approximate value of the claim. If the defendant has assets worth more than the amount specified in the order, the defendant remains free to use the surplus. Clause 6 gives a wide meaning to 'the defendant's assets'. They include jointly-owned assets, for example a bank account in joint names, and any asset over which the defendant has the power, directly or indirectly, to dispose of or deal with as if it were their own. The defendant is to be regarded as having such power if a third party holds or controls the asset in accordance with the defendant's direct or indirect instructions.

If a defendant holds assets as a bare trustee, so that they have no beneficial interest in them, then such assets will not come within the scope of a standard form freezing injunction. However, in *Federal Bank of the Middle East v Hadkinson* [2000] 1 WLR 1695 the Court of Appeal held that orders made in more specific terms might cover bank accounts in which a defendant had no beneficial interest but which were in their name and under their control.

The meaning of 'assets' in the context of a freezing order was considered by the Supreme Court in *JSC BTA Bank v Ablyazov* [2015] UKSC 64. In this case the claimant (one of Kazakhstan's national banks) had obtained a number of judgments against the respondent (its former chairman and majority shareholder) amounting to $4.4 billion, none of which had been paid. A freezing order had been obtained on 12 November 2009.

Paragraph 4 read as follows:

> Until judgment or further order ... the respondent must not, except with the prior written consent of the Bank's solicitors –
>
> a.   Remove from England and Wales any of his assets which are in England and Wales ... up to the value of £451,130,000 ...
>
> b.   In any way dispose of, deal with or diminish the value of his assets in England and Wales up to the value of ... £451,130,000 ...
>
> c.   In any way dispose of, deal with or diminish the value of any of his assets outside England and Wales unless the total unencumbered value ... of all his assets in England and Wales ... exceeds £451,130,000 ...

Paragraph 5 of the freezing order read as follows

> Paragraph 4 applies to all the respondents' assets whether or not they are in their own and whether they are solely and jointly owned and whether or not the respondent asserts a beneficial interest in them. For the purpose of this Order the respondents' assets include any asset which they have power, directly or indirectly, to dispose of, or deal with as if it were their own. The respondents are to be regarded as having such power if a third party holds or controls the assets in accordance with their direct or indirect instructions.

The wording of para 5 is in accordance with the version in Appendix 5 of the Commercial Court Guide. This is a slightly wider definition of assets than in the standard order in CPR 1998, Part 25 as it includes the phrase 'and whether or not the Respondent is interested in them legally, beneficially or otherwise'.

Paragraph 9 of the freezing order set out the exceptions to the order:

> a.   Paragraph 4 of this Order does not prohibit the respondent from spending up to £10,000 a week ... towards his individual ordinary living expenses ... nor does it prohibit the respondent from spending a reasonable amount on legal advice and representation. But before spending any money on legal advice and representation the respondent must notify the Bank's legal representatives in writing where the money to be spent is to be taken from.
>
> b.   This Order does not prohibit the respondent from dealing with or disposing of any of his assets in the ordinary and proper course of any business conducted by him personally.

The respondent had entered into a total of four binding and effective loan facility agreements dated 1 September 2009, 1 April 2010, 17 August 2010 and 1 December 2010 with two British Virgin Islands companies. Each agreement provided a loan facility of £10,000,000. Under the terms of each agreement the respondent could direct the lender to transfer funds to a third party.

The loan agreements were fully drawn down and various payments made to third parties, including $16 million to the respondent's former solicitors.

The Supreme Court had to determine three issues in relation to the construction of the freezing order.

(1)   Whether the respondent's right to draw down under certain loan agreements is an 'asset' within the meaning of the freezing order.

(2)   If so, whether the exercise of that right by directing the lender to pay the sum to a third party constitutes 'disposing of' or 'dealing with' or 'diminishing the value' of an 'asset'.

(3)   Whether the proceeds of the loan agreements were 'assets' within the meaning of the extended definition in para 5 of the freezing order on the basis that the respondent had

power 'directly or indirectly to dispose of, or deal with [the proceeds] as if they were his own'.

The Supreme Court allowed the claimant's appeal on issue (3). The proceeds of loan agreements entered into by the respondent after the order had been made were 'assets' within the meaning of the extended definition in para 5 as the respondent did have power directly or indirectly to dispose or deal with them as if they were their own.

In clause 7 of the order the claimant should provide details of any information they have about the defendant's assets, such as the address of any property owned by the defendant or details of any relevant bank account.

TDK Tape Distributor (UK) Ltd v Videochoice Ltd [1985] 3 All ER 345 confirms that the order is not limited to property owned by the defendant when the order was made. The order operates like a floating charge, in the sense that any property the defendant subsequently acquires is still subject to the terms of the order (although it does not give the claimant priority as a creditor – see **8.3.2**). Indeed, *Bank Mellat v Kazmi* [1989] 1 QB 541 decided that a defendant subject to a freezing injunction would be in breach of the order if they forgave payment of a debt due to them.

If the case does go to trial and the claimant wins, the claimant will want to continue the injunction until they have been able to enforce their judgment. *Orwell Steel (Erection and Fabrication) Ltd v Ashphalt and Tarmac (UK) Ltd* [1984] 1 WLR 1097 confirms that the trial judge has jurisdiction to continue the order in this way after judgment (see also r 25.2(1)(b) of CPR 1998).

8.6.2 Disclosure

Clause 9 of the order requires the defendant to inform the claimant's solicitor immediately of all their assets within the jurisdiction, giving their value and location. By clause 10, this information must be confirmed in an affidavit.

Nevertheless, clause 9 also informs the defendant that, in cases where the privilege against self-incrimination applies, the defendant may be entitled to refuse to provide information on the ground that it may incriminate them (see **8.7**).

In cases where the defendant serves evidence and the claimant thinks it is incomplete, the claimant can obtain an order permitting them to cross-examine the defendant about its contents. Orders for cross-examination will, however, be made only in exceptional circumstances (see *Yukong Line Ltd of Korea v Rendsburg Investment Corp of Liberia* [1996] 2 Lloyd's Rep 604). If information is needed from a third party, a separate order will be needed (see *Arab Monetary Fund v Hasgood (No 5)* [1992] 2 All ER 911).

8.6.3 Exceptions to the order

Although clause 5 of the order prevents the defendant from dealing with their assets, a defendant still needs money to meet their day-to-day living expenses. The exceptions to the order set out in clause 11 deal with this by allowing the defendant to withdraw a specified weekly sum to meet these expenses and other recurrent bills. According to *PCW (Underwriting Agencies) Ltd v Dixon* [1983] 2 All ER 158, the amount should be a reasonable sum based on the defendant's usual lifestyle. The exceptions also allow a specified weekly amount for business expenses and payment of legal costs. In return, the defendant has to tell the claimant's solicitors where they are getting the money from. But does the respondent have to disclose the amount being spent on legal costs? No, held the High Court in *CRO v REC and another* [2023] EWHC 189 (Comm).

Paragraph 3 of the exceptions enables the parties to agree in writing that the defendant can incur additional expenditure. If the parties cannot agree, the defendant can ask the court for permission to incur the additional expenditure.

The last exception gives the defendant the opportunity to bring the injunction to an end by providing security for the amount applied for by the claimant, for example by a payment into court.

8.6.4   Costs

Clause 12 states that the costs of the application to obtain the freezing injunction are reserved to the judge who deals with the case on the return date.

But should the costs of an application for a freezing order, including a contested inter partes application, be reserved to the trial judge? There are conflicting answers. Yes – see *Al Assam v Tsouvelekakis* [2022] EWHC 2137 (Ch); no – see *Harrington & Charles Trading Ltd and others v Mehta and others* [2023] EWHC 609 (Ch).

8.6.5   Variation or setting aside of the order

Clause 13 of the order states that a defendant or third party affected by the order may apply to court to vary or set aside the injunction, having first informed the claimant's solicitors. For the procedure and grounds for variation and setting aside, see **8.9**.

8.6.6   Third parties

Clause 16 of the order warns that anyone who has been informed of the order will be in contempt of court if they help the defendant to break the order.

However, although the third party may be liable for contempt, they are not liable to the applicant for damages if they allow the defendant to break the order.

In *HM Commissioners of Customs and Excise v Barclays Bank plc* [2006] UKHL 28, Customs and Excise obtained freezing injunctions against Brightstar Systems Ltd and Doveblue Ltd, granted on 26 and 30 January 2001 respectively. The value of the assets restrained was £1,800,000 in the Doveblue case. Both companies held accounts with Barclays. The following sequence of events then took place.

12.33 pm, 20 January 2001	Brightstar order served on Barclays by fax
2.30 pm, 29 January 2001	Barclays allow Brightstar to withdraw £1,240,570
11.38 am, 30 January 2001	Doveblue order served on Barclays by fax
2 pm, 30 June 2001	Barclays allow Doveblue to withdraw £1,064,289

Subsequently, Customs and Excise obtained judgments against both companies who failed to pay.

Customs and Excise then brought proceedings against Barclays, claiming damages on the basis that Barclays, once served with the freezing injunctions, owed it a duty of care and had acted negligently in permitting the withdrawals to be made.

The House of Lords decided that the bank owed no such duty of care and was therefore not liable.

Where, as is usually the case, a bank is one of the third parties affected by the injunction, clause 17 of the order will allow the bank to take any money due to it from the defendant and to meet any existing liabilities under any cheque or credit card which it has issued to the defendant.

The order will allow the defendant to withdraw money for living, business and legal expenses (see **8.6.3**). There is obviously a risk that they may abuse this by purporting to withdraw money for such expenses when they are, in fact, dissipating their assets to prevent the claimant enforcing any later judgment. Clause 18 of the order makes it clear that, as far as banks are concerned, this is a matter between the claimant and the defendant, and that the bank will not be blamed for any such abuse by the defendant if they appeared to be acting under one of the permitted exceptions to the order. Other third parties are obliged to ensure that the defendant is using the money for a proper purpose.

8.7 THE PRIVILEGE AGAINST SELF-INCRIMINATION

In freezing cases and in some other injunction applications, the claimant may accuse the defendant of conduct which would amount to a criminal offence. In such cases, the defendant will try to claim the privilege against self-incrimination. If the defendant succeeds, they can refuse to disclose information about their assets by claiming that this could lead to their prosecution. The defendant may therefore use this as a reason for not disclosing all or part of their assets in the affidavit which they are required to swear under clause 10 of the standard form injunction order (see **8.6.2**). (The defendant will at the same time protest that they are innocent of any crime. The defendant will say that, if the claimant chooses to make such accusations, they cannot then ask the defendant to provide the evidence for those accusations.) This privilege was considered by the Court of Appeal in *Den Norske Bank ASA v Antonatos* [1998] 3 All ER 74. It held that the privilege applies to any information which might be used as evidence at a criminal trial, or which might influence a decision whether or not to prosecute. The person claiming privilege does not need to show that the information would increase the risk of them being prosecuted.

A successful claim to privilege often prevents the claimant from obtaining the information the claimant needs to make the injunction effective. Section 72 of the Senior Courts Act 1981 removes the privilege where it relates to intellectual property and passing-off cases, and s 31 of the Theft Act 1968 prevents claims to privilege in civil cases regarding offences under that Act. Section 13 of the Fraud Act 2006 similarly removes the right to claim privilege in 'proceedings relating to property' where the risk of incrimination relates to offences under the Fraud Act or 'related offences', including conspiracy to defraud. 'Proceedings relating to property' was given a wide meaning in the case of *Kensington International Ltd v Republic of Congo and Others* [2007] EWCA Civ 1128.

Even where the claim for privilege still exists, the House of Lords, in *AT & T Istel Ltd v Tully* [1993] AC 45, decided that it would be possible to override such a privilege claim if the Crown Prosecution Service (CPS) promised that the information disclosed by the defendant would not be used in any subsequent prosecution. In such cases, the claimant would get the information they needed. If the CPS was not able to give such a promise (or had not been asked for such a promise), the courts would not make any order overriding the defendant's claim to privilege (*Johnstone v United Norwest Co-operative Ltd* (1994) *The Times*, 24 February).

In practice, where the defendant claims privilege, the claimant's best course of action is to apply for an order under r 31.19(5) of CPR 1998 asking the court to decide whether the claim to privilege (which must be made in writing and state the grounds on which privilege is claimed – r 31.19(3)) should be upheld. The court may then require the defendant to disclose the documents in question to the court so that the court can decide whether the claim to privilege is justified (r 31.19(6)). If the court agrees that it is justified, there is nothing more the claimant can do. If the court decides that there is no claim to privilege, it will order the defendant to disclose the documents to the claimant.

8.8 AFTER THE ORDER HAS BEEN MADE

8.8.1 Service

As soon as possible after the hearing, the claimant must serve the relevant documents on the defendant and any third parties, such as banks holding assets on behalf of the defendant. It may be advisable to serve the relevant documents on the defendant's bank before the defendant, to ensure that the account is frozen by the bank before the defendant knows what has happened. The documents which must be served are the freezing injunction, the application notice and a copy of the affidavit in support with any exhibits. As with all injunctions, the defendant must be served personally. If the defendant disobeys the order, the defendant may not be the only person liable to contempt proceedings. As already mentioned at **8.2**, the third party who allowed the defendant to do so may also be liable.

8.8.2 Land

Where the defendant owns land, the claimant will want to give notice to potential buyers and mortgagees that the land is subject to a freezing injunction. If the land has registered title, the claimant does this by applying for a restriction under s 42(1) of the Land Registration Act 2002. There is no equivalent protection if the title is unregistered. This is because *Stockler v Fourways Estates Ltd* [1983] 3 All ER 501 decided that a freezing injunction does not give the claimant rights over the defendant's land which can be protected by registration as a land charge.

If the title is unregistered, there are still practical steps the claimant can take. The claimant can, for example, contact local estate agents, inform them of the order, and ask them to let the claimant know if the property is put on the market.

8.8.3 The main action

The defendant's property is now subject to this oppressive order. If the defendant cannot set it aside, it will continue to affect them until the case comes for trial. The courts have said on many occasions that this places the claimant under a duty to press ahead with the claim quickly so that the issues between the parties can be swiftly resolved. If the claimant does not do so, an early application to strike out their statement of case is a real possibility.

8.9 SETTING ASIDE AND VARIATION

8.9.1 The defendant seeks to set aside the order

The principal ground for setting aside the injunction is that it should not have been made in the first place. This normally involves allegations that the claimant did not disclose all the material facts when they made the application. The defendant will argue that if the court had been aware of the full facts it would not have been satisfied that the grounds for the making of the freezing injunction were made out – ie the claimant does not have a good arguable case and/or there is no real risk of dissipation of the defendant's assets in order to avoid enforcement of any judgment.

In such cases, the court considers two matters: are the new facts material to the issues; and was the non-disclosure deliberate?

Where the court considers that it would not have granted the injunction if it had known the full facts, it will inevitably set aside the injunction. It will do this even if the claimant had acted in all good faith and was totally unaware of the new facts. The courts will normally take the view that the claimant did not make proper investigations before they applied for the order. The claimant will therefore have to pay costs (possibly on an indemnity basis – see, for example, *Piroozzadeh v Persons Unknown and others* [2023] EWHC 1024 (Ch)) and damages for the loss caused by the injunction.

Nevertheless, sometimes there will be cases where the court considers that it would still have granted the injunction, even if it had known the full facts. It will still want to know why those facts were not available at the first hearing. The court does not like being misled, neither does it like to have its time wasted by incompetence.

If the court considers that there was a deliberate attempt to mislead it by concealing information (or that there was incompetence), it can do the following:

(a)   it can penalise the claimant in costs;

(b)   it can set aside the original injunction and replace it with a new one. This gives the defendant the opportunity to claim damages for the harm the first injunction caused, whilst maintaining the security of the injunction should the claimant eventually win the case;

(c)   in extreme cases, it can set aside the injunction completely on the basis that, while the claimant would usually be entitled to an injunction, their deliberate attempt to mislead the court disqualifies them from such protection.

The general principles were set out by Carr J (as she then was) in *Alexander Tugushev v Vitaly Orlov* [2019] EWHC 2031 (Comm) at [7]:

> ... If material non-disclosure is established, the court will be astute to ensure that a claimant who obtains injunctive relief without full disclosure is deprived of any advantage he may thereby have derived;

> ... Immediate discharge (without renewal) is likely to be the court's starting point, at least when the failure is substantial or deliberate.

> ... The court will discharge the order even if the order would still have been made had the relevant matter(s) been brought to its attention at the without notice hearing. This is a penal approach and intentionally so, by way of deterrent to ensure that applicants in future abide by their duties;

> The court nevertheless has a discretion to continue the injunction (or impose a fresh injunction) despite a failure to disclose. Although the discretion should be exercised sparingly, the overriding consideration will always be the interests of justice. Such consideration will include examination of i) the importance of the facts not disclosed to the issues before the judge ii) the need to encourage proper compliance with the duty of full and frank disclosure and to deter non-compliance iii) whether or not and to what extent the failure was culpable iv) the injustice to a claimant which may occur if an order is discharged leaving a defendant free to dissipate assets, although a strong case on the merits will never be a good excuse for a failure to disclose material facts;

> The interests of justice may sometimes require that a freezing order be continued and that a failure of disclosure can be marked in some other way, for example by a suitable costs order. The court thus has at its disposal a range of options in the event of non-disclosure.

Although non-disclosure is the principal reason for setting aside freezing injunctions, it is not the only one. Sometimes they are set aside because of procedural irregularities by the claimant (eg failure to comply with one of their undertakings, such as issuing a claim form). Alternatively, property affected by the injunction may not belong to the defendant. In the latter case, even if the property belongs to the defendant's spouse, it must still be freed from the order if the spouse is not a party to the claimant's action. However, if the issue of ownership is unclear the courts may, as in *SCF Finance v Masri* [1985] 2 All ER 747, decide to leave the order in place for the time being and resolve the question of ownership when the main action comes up for trial. Inordinate delay by the claimant in pursuing the action may also be a ground for setting aside.

Courts usually prefer to deal with applications to set aside an injunction at the trial of the claimant's action. However, often such an approach is not appropriate for 'freezing' cases, as the defendant then has to 'suffer the oppression' of the injunction in the meantime (*Ali & Fahd Shobokshi Group Ltd v Moneim* [1989] 2 All ER 404). Where the freezing injunction is set aside, the judge should always consider whether it is appropriate to assess damages at once and direct immediate payment by the claimant, rather than wait until trial (*Practice Direction (Mareva Injunctions and Anton Piller Orders)* [1994] 1 WLR 1233).

8.9.2   The defendant seeks to vary the order

Even if the defendant is not in a position to apply to set aside the injunction, the defendant may want to have it varied, for example to increase the amount they can withdraw for living expenses or to pay out other monies contrary to the claimant's wishes. The defendant may argue that the injunction in its current format is oppressive.

To save costs, and to comply with the overriding objective, the parties should try to agree any variation. If they cannot agree, the defendant will have to apply to the court.

The court will normally require evidence from the defendant dealing with their financial position so that it can see that the variation is necessary. Courts have required evidence that the expenditure cannot be financed from other sources such as foreign property or, in the case of a corporate defendant, from some associated company.

The court will also want to be satisfied that the expenditure is necessary. If it thinks that the application is an attempt to circumvent the order it will refuse it. However, if the expenditure is genuine and would have been incurred were it not for the existence of the freezing injunction, then it will be authorised. This will happen even though the defendant then has insufficient money to meet the amount of the claimant's claim.

8.9.3 Third parties

Third parties can apply to have the injunction varied or set aside if it is causing them undue difficulty. Thus, in *Galaxia Maritime SA v Mineralimportexport, The Eleftherios* [1982] 1 WLR 539 the defendant's property had already been loaded on board ship by the time the order was made. The shipowner was unable to set sail as a result of the order (apparently unloading the defendant's property did not solve the problem) so the order was discharged because it was imposing an excessive burden on the shipowner.

8.9.4 Other creditors

If the defendant will not seek to vary the injunction to pay other creditors, those creditors may (at least if they have established rights over the defendant's property) be able to take the initiative. Thus, debenture holders succeeded in varying an injunction so that they could exercise their rights over the defendant's property in *Cretanor Maritime Co Ltd v Irish Maritime Management Ltd, The Cretan Harmony* [1978] 1 WLR 966. Further, solicitors with money in client accounts were able to obtain permission to use that money to meet bills they had sent to the defendant in *Prekookeanska Plovidba v LNT Lines Srl* [1988] 3 All ER 897 (see also *Cala Cristal SA v Emran Al-Borno* (1994) *The Times*, 6 May).

8.10 CASES WITH A FOREIGN ELEMENT

Subject to the normal problems which arise when suing a defendant out of the jurisdiction (see **Chapter 16**), the court can, under s 37(3) of the Senior Courts Act 1981, grant an injunction against a defendant wherever they live and whatever their nationality. However, there may be problems where the defendant's property is out of the jurisdiction.

8.10.1 The location of the property

Usually, English courts will only make orders (including orders for disclosure) relating to property within the jurisdiction. This principle applies before and after judgment has been obtained. However, in *Derby & Co Ltd v Weldon* [1990] Ch 48, the Court of Appeal agreed that, in exceptional cases, the English courts could make 'worldwide' freezing orders ('WFOs'). It laid down three conditions:

(a)   that a large amount of money (eg several million pounds) must be involved;

(b)   that there must be insufficient property within the jurisdiction to meet the amount sought by the claimant; and

(c)   that the risk of property being concealed, etc, must be exceptionally high.

These conditions will exist only in very few cases.

Even if these conditions are met, there is no point is making an order in this country if it is going to be ignored by the courts in the country where the property is located. Evidence on the issue of enforcement will be needed, although in *Derby & Co Ltd v Weldon (No 6)* [1990] 1

WLR 1139, the Court of Appeal said that, in appropriate cases, the defendant could be ordered to transfer the property to a country which would recognise and enforce the English court's order. If the defendant did not comply, they could be debarred from taking any further part in the English proceedings.

Where a WFO order has been made, however, the English courts will not give the claimant a blank cheque. The claimant normally has to give undertakings that they will seek leave of the English courts before seeking to enforce the order out of the jurisdiction or commencing fresh proceedings in another country arising out of the same facts.

Whilst the Court of Appeal in *Derby & Co Ltd v Weldon* gave little guidance as to the circumstances in which the court would exercise its discretion to grant permission to enforce a WFO, in *Dadourian Group Int v Simms & Others* [2006] EWCA Civ 399, the Court of Appeal took the opportunity to lay down such guidelines, as follows:

> Guideline 1: The principle applying to the grant of permission to enforce a WFO abroad is that the grant of that permission should be just and convenient for the purpose of ensuring the effectiveness of the WFO, and in addition that it is not oppressive to the parties to the English proceedings or to third parties who may be joined to the foreign proceedings.

> Guideline 2: All the relevant circumstances and options need to be considered. In particular consideration should be given to granting relief on terms, for example terms as to the extension to third parties of the undertaking to compensate for costs incurred as a result of the WFO and as to the type of proceedings that may be commenced abroad. Consideration should also be given to the proportionality of the steps proposed to be taken abroad, and in addition to the form of any order.

> Guideline 3: The interests of the applicant should be balanced against the interests of the other parties to the proceedings and any new party likely to be joined to the foreign proceedings.

> Guideline 4: Permission should not normally be given in terms that would enable the applicant to obtain relief in the foreign proceedings which is superior to the relief given by the WFO.

> Guideline 5: The evidence in support of the application for permission should contain all the information (so far as it can reasonably be obtained in the time available) necessary to enable the judge to reach an informed decision, including evidence as to the applicable law and practice in the foreign court, evidence as to the nature of the proposed proceedings to be commenced and evidence as to the assets believed to be located in the jurisdiction of the foreign court and the names of the parties by whom such assets are held.

> Guideline 6: The standard of proof as to the existence of assets that are both within the WFO and within the jurisdiction of the foreign court is a real prospect, that is the applicant must show that there is a real prospect that such assets are located within the jurisdiction of the foreign court in question.

> Guideline 7: There must be evidence of a risk of dissipation of the assets in question.

> Guideline 8: Normally the application should be made on notice to the respondent, but in cases of urgency, where it is just to do so, the permission may be given without notice to the party against whom relief will be sought in the foreign proceedings but that party should have the earliest practicable opportunity of having the matter reconsidered by the court at a hearing of which he is given notice.

The English courts are also concerned that WFOs should not oppress third parties who have possession or control of the defendant's property in foreign countries. The order will therefore contain a proviso which states that the third parties are not at risk of English committal proceedings.

Practice Direction 25A contains the full text of the claimant's undertakings, the proviso for third parties, and the other terms of the standard form freezing injunction prohibiting the disposal of assets worldwide.

If the claimant has obtained final judgment, the court may order a defendant to disclose their assets outside the jurisdiction, even though the conditions for granting a WFO are not satisfied (*Gidrxslme Shipping Co Ltd v Tantomar Transporters Maritimos Ltd, The Naftilos* [1995] 1 WLR 299).

8.11 SUMMARY

A freezing injunction is an exceptional remedy which enables the claimant to prevent the defendant from dealing with some of their property until the claimant's action comes to trial. The court may grant this injunction only where the claimant can demonstrate that:

(a)   they have a good arguable case after full disclosure; and

(b)   the defendant has property within the jurisdiction and intends to deal with the property so as to frustrate the enforcement of the claimant's judgment.

The claimant will apply without notice for the injunction. The claimant will have to give undertakings to protect the position of the defendant and the third parties who have possession of the defendant's property.

The injunction prevents the defendant from dealing with their property up to a specified value, and will usually require them to disclose what assets they have and where they are. It will also, among other things, allow the defendant to spend a certain amount of money for ordinary living expenses, legal costs and paying their business debts.

If the claimant is accusing the defendant of criminal behaviour, the defendant may be able to rely on the privilege against self-incrimination to avoid revealing information about their assets.

If the claimant has failed to reveal information relevant to the case, the injunction may be set aside and the claimant could then have to pay compensation to the defendant under the usual undertaking as to damages.

The court may in very exceptional circumstances grant freezing injunctions where the bulk of the defendant's property is outside the jurisdiction.

CHAPTER 9

SEARCH ORDERS

LEARNING OUTCOMES

After reading this chapter you will understand:

- the nature of a search order
- the grounds for applying for a search order
- the role of the supervising solicitor
- how to serve and execute a search order
- the position of the respondent to a search order
- the undertakings required to be given by the applicant and supervising solicitor
- how to advise a respondent faced with the execution of a search order.

9.1 INTRODUCTION

This chapter explains how a claimant can get an order which requests the defendant to allow the claimant to enter and search the defendant's premises for property belonging to the claimant, or for evidence that the defendant has been harming the claimant. If the defendant does not comply, they may be committed to prison for contempt of court.

This chapter also explains the facts which the claimant must prove to get such an order and the dangers to the claimant in seeking such an order. The obligations created by the order are set out at **9.6**, which refers to the standard form search order contained in PD 25A, set out in **Appendix 15** to this book. It also deals with the undertakings which the claimant and other people involved in the execution of the order have to give to the court.

The chapter concludes with some tips on the advice which the defendant's solicitor should give to their client, and some practical points which might be of relevance to one or other of the parties.

9.2 THE NATURE OF THE ORDER

The court's power to grant a search order was established by the Court of Appeal in *Anton Piller KG v Manufacturing Processes Ltd* [1976] Ch 55. In the same way as freezing injunctions used to be called *Mareva* injunctions (see **8.1**), search orders used to be called *Anton Piller* orders, and readers should bear this in mind when reading pre-1999 cases. The court now has statutory authority to make such an order pursuant to s 7 of the Civil Procedure Act 1997.

A search order requires the defendant to allow the claimant's named representatives to enter and search the defendant's premises specified in the order. The claimant, however, is not permitted to use force to enter the defendant's premises.

The order is used to recover property belonging to the claimant which the defendant is using to harm the claimant. Thus, if a former employee of the claimant has wrongfully taken customer and price lists from the claimant and is using them to compete against the claimant, a search order can be used to recover the stolen lists.

Search orders are also used to obtain evidence of wrongdoing. For example, if a competitor is infringing the claimant's copyright, a search order can be used to search the defendant's premises for evidence of infringing copies, the addresses of suppliers and customers, and details of the profits made by the infringement.

The order has also been used in aid of enforcement (*Distributori Automatica Italia SpA v Holford General Trading Co Ltd* [1985] 1 WLR 1066).

A search order is often made at the same time as a freezing injunction. It may be combined with orders for disclosure and/or further information. It is even possible to obtain an order which prevents the defendant from leaving the country for a short period of time so that the defendant remains available to comply with the search order.

As with freezing injunctions (see **8.4**) the application should be made in the High Court.

9.3   ENTITLEMENT TO THE ORDER

A search order is a fundamental interference with the defendant's civil liberties. As such, it is granted only in the most extreme cases when the order is needed to ensure that justice is done. The claimant has to show three things:

(a)   an extremely strong prima facie case;

(b)   that they will suffer, or continue to suffer, very serious harm if the order is not made;

(c)   that the defendant has incriminating material in their possession and there is a real possibility that the defendant may destroy or dispose of that material.

The court must then be satisfied that the harm likely to be caused to the defendant and the defendant's business is not excessive or out of proportion to the legitimate object of the order.

To apply for a search order, the claimant will have to prepare the following documents:

(a)   application notice;

(b)   affidavit in support;

(c)   draft order;

(d)   draft claim form, if not already issued;

(e)   a second application notice for a return date if this is not dealt with on the search order application notice. (If the search order is granted, the court will fix a return date about one week after the initial hearing to enable the defendant to make representations about the order.)

In view of the draconian nature of the order, the comments in **Chapter 8** (on freezing injunctions) about the need for detailed inquiries and full disclosure also apply here. The supporting affidavit must disclose very fully the reasons for seeking the order, including the probability that relevant material would disappear if the order was not made. It must also state the address of the premises to be searched and state whether it is a private or business address.

A search order will not be made where there is any doubt about the court's jurisdiction unless the defendant has been given the opportunity to be heard on the question of jurisdiction (*Altertext Inc v Advanced Data Communications Ltd* [1985] 1 All ER 395). Since such a hearing would defeat the whole point of seeking a search order, it may be preferable in such cases to take proceedings in the defendant's local court. This helps ensure that jurisdiction is not challenged.

9.4   PITFALLS AND SAFEGUARDS

Universal Thermosensors Ltd v Hibben [1992] 3 All ER 257 and *Columbia Picture Industries Inc v Robinson* [1987] Ch 38 are essential reading for solicitors involved in a search order case. They both give detailed guidance on obtaining and executing a search order.

The claimant will have to give the usual undertaking as to damages (see **5.4**), and this will cover oppressive execution of the order, and damages for innocent third parties who have been harmed by the order. The *Columbia Picture* case shows that aggravated damages may be awarded against a claimant who fails to make proper disclosure or who executes an order oppressively.

It is also very easy for the solicitors involved with a search order to make mistakes. Such mistakes can put them in contempt of court, as in *VDU Installations Ltd v Integrated Computer Systems & Cybernetics* [1989] 1 FSR 378.

The standard form order in PD 25A contains provisions which may help the claimant and their solicitors to avoid such problems.

9.4.1   The supervising solicitor

The standard form order provides that it should be executed by the claimant's solicitor under the guidance of a supervising solicitor who must be experienced in the operation of search orders. The supervising solicitor will be an independent solicitor from some other firm, whose role is to help the defendant understand what is happening and to ensure that nothing unfair happens. The supervising solicitor will have to prepare a report afterwards, which they will send to the claimant's solicitor, who will then provide copies for the defendant and the court. The Law Society keeps a list of supervising solicitors (as does the London Solicitors Litigation Association). The claimant's solicitors should file an affidavit, identifying the supervising solicitor's experience in executing search orders.

The order must be served personally by the supervising solicitor.

9.4.2   Dealing with the items the claimant is searching for

The order will specify the items which are the subject of the search (Schedule B to the order). Only items which are clearly covered by the terms of the order may be removed. *Columbia Picture* confirms that the claimant cannot take away everything which might be relevant in order to inspect it at their leisure. The applicant's solicitor undertakes to answer forthwith any query made by the defendant as to whether any particular document or article is within the scope of the order.

What happens to the removed items depends on who owns them. If they indisputably belong to the applicant, they can do what they like with them. Usually, however, the position is not that clear-cut.

Often the documents which are taken as evidence belong to the defendant. The applicant's solicitor undertakes to return those originals within two working days. During that time, they will take copies. Occasionally, the applicant may fear that the defendant will be able to use those documents to cause them further harm. It is possible to modify the undertaking to take account of this, but if the documents are also relevant to the defendant's legitimate activities, they must be allowed some form of access to them.

The applicant will want to use the items seized as evidence against the defendant in this action. The applicant may also want to use them as evidence of wrongdoing by other people, either by joining them as defendants to the present action or by commencing fresh proceedings against them.

The defendant may also be under investigation by the police, HM Revenue and Customs or the Serious Fraud Office. They will be very interested in any information the applicant has about the defendant. The undertaking given by the applicant's solicitor to keep all such items in safe custody, however, means that they cannot allow anyone else to see or use the items without the permission of the court. Such permission is rarely granted (*EMI Records Ltd v Spillane* [1986] 1 WLR 967; *General Nutrition v Pradip Pattni* [1984] FSR 403).

9.5 THE TERMS OF THE ORDER

The standard search order from PD 25A is set out in **Appendix 15** to this book. The following text explains the main provisions of the search order.

A search order made upon an application which materially departs from the requirements of the Practice Direction and the standard form of order may be set aside (*Gadget Shop Ltd v Bug.Com Ltd* (2000) *The Times*, 28 June).

9.5.1 The penal notice

The penal notice, addressed to the respondent, stipulates that if the respondent disobeys the order, the respondent may be held in contempt of court and subjected to imprisonment or fine or seizure of assets. Anyone who knows of the order and helps or permits the respondent to breach its terms will be likewise in contempt and subject to the same range of penalties.

The penal notice, in the case of a corporate body, applies to directors and officers of that body. Partnerships and limited liability partnerships fall within this provision (*Olympic Council of Asia v Novans Jets LLP and others* [2023] EWHC 276 (Comm)).

In *Ocado Group PLC and another v McKeeve* [2021] EWCA Civ 145 and [2022] EWHC 2079 (Ch), the Court of Appeal allowed an appeal against the refusal of permission to apply for committal of a solicitor who had instructed their clients' information technology manager to destroy an electronic data storage device which was subject to a search order. The Chancery Court subsequently found the solicitor liable for criminal contempt.

9.5.2 The applicant's rights

The applicant is entitled to ask for the respondent's cooperation but cannot compel it. The applicant cannot use force if the respondent will not comply with the order. In such circumstances, the only remedy is to apply to have the respondent committed for contempt of court.

Paragraph 6 of the order is the 'business' part of the order, ordering that entry and search of premises, and vehicles on and around the premises, be allowed. It is addressed to the respondent. Subject to what is said at **9.7**, they must allow access immediately.

This part of the order also permits a search of any premises of the respondent not mentioned in the order but discovered as a result of executing the order. In addition, it extends the power to search the respondent's vehicles to those around the premises, as well as those on the premises. However, the power is expressly limited to those vehicles on or around the respondent's premises which are under the respondent's control.

It may be necessary to include the respondent's home in the premises to be searched. If the respondent is not there, their spouse can be required to comply with the order. If the order is to be executed on a woman on her own in a private house, the supervising solicitor serving the order must be a woman or be accompanied by one (see the footnote to the part of the order headed 'The Search').

Although the order is served by solicitors, they will need help to execute the order. Usually, they will not have the technical expertise to identify the matters covered by the order. Paragraph 6 therefore allows them to be accompanied by a specified number of representatives of the applicant, who will help them to identify the relevant materials. Sometimes, search orders are used in bad faith by applicants who simply want to gain access to the respondent's trade secrets. Because of this risk, the applicant should inform the court if any representative of the applicant will be present when the order is carried out (see **9.5.3**).

Given the likelihood that much of the material in question will be stored on computer, one of the team of searchers should be skilled in operating computers to ensure that information on the computer is not withheld by the respondent.

The order must specify the premises to be searched and the items which the applicant is looking for. These are listed in Schedules A and B to the order respectively.

9.5.3 Serving and executing the order

The order must be served by the supervising solicitor, who must also supervise the execution of the order. The supervising solicitor has to explain the order to the respondent in ordinary language. This is very important. When the solicitor arrives at the respondent's premises and announces that they have a court order which entitles them to enter and search the property, they are likely to be met with a reaction of blank disbelief. The respondent's initial reaction will almost certainly be to refuse admission. If the solicitor simply turns away and applies to have the respondent committed for contempt of court, the application will probably fail. Any attempt to deal with the respondent's refusal to comply with the order is likely to involve a detailed investigation of the conduct of the supervising solicitor in carrying out the order. The court will need to be satisfied that every attempt was made to explain the following matters to the respondent:

(a)   that the supervising solicitor is acting under a court order;

(b)   that the respondent can be punished by imprisonment if they do not obey the order;

(c)   that it can be in the respondent's own interests to cooperate if they are innocent of any wrongdoing;

(d)   that the respondent is entitled to take legal advice from their own solicitor before complying with the order.

As mentioned above, it is the supervising solicitor's obligation to explain the respondent's right to legal advice. The respondent may want to exercise this right, so that their own solicitor is present when the order is executed. Alternatively, they may wish to discuss with their solicitor whether there are grounds for applying to court at once to set aside or vary the order before it is executed (see **9.7**). Whilst considering these possible courses of action, the respondent may ask the supervising solicitor to delay the search for up to two hours or such period as the latter may permit.

The respondent's right to take legal advice is, however, qualified. If the respondent wants to take legal advice, they must do so immediately. This clearly implies that the order should be executed at a time when it will be possible for the respondent to take legal advice. In *Universal Thermosensors Ltd v Hibben* (at **9.4**), the court specifically said that the order should be executed during normal working hours, and the standard form order says that normally it should be served on a weekday morning after 9.30 am. This causes no problems where the premises to be searched are business premises. It creates great difficulty if the applicant also wants to search the respondent's home. If the respondent is not going to be at home during office hours, the guidance of the judge should be sought when the order is obtained. There are a number of possible solutions available to the judge. They may be prepared to allow the order to be executed when someone other than the respondent is on the premises. Otherwise, they might allow the applicant's solicitor to arrive, for example, at breakfast time when the respondent will not have to wait very long before they can take legal advice. Another possibility is that they might stipulate that the independent supervising solicitor should act as the respondent's legal adviser. Alternatively, they could require the applicant's solicitor to give advance notice to the respondent's solicitor of the proposed time for executing the order, so that the respondent's solicitor can be available to give advice at that time.

Initially, the respondent will probably seek legal advice over the telephone. The rules on solicitor/client confidentiality mean that the other solicitor cannot be present while the respondent is talking to their own lawyer. However, before this takes place the supervising solicitor should ensure that the respondent is genuinely speaking to a lawyer and is not taking the opportunity to warn any accomplices or to tamper with the evidence.

Before allowing entry to anyone but the supervising solicitor, the respondent also has the right to gather together any documents covered by legal professional privilege or the privilege against self-incrimination in cases where that privilege applies. The respondent should hand these documents to the supervising solicitor who will form a view on whether or not the documents are privileged. If the supervising solicitor thinks that the documents are privileged, or of doubtful status, they will exclude them from the search and retain any documents of doubtful status until the court has had an opportunity of ruling on the matter. However, if the supervising solicitor considers that the documents are not privileged, but the respondent still withholds them from the applicant, the respondent runs the risk of being in contempt of court.

In *C plc and W v P (Secretary of State for the Home Office and the Attorney General intervening)* [2006] EWHC 1226 (Ch) proceedings were brought for breach of confidence and copyright infringement. A search order was made and during the search computer images of children were discovered. The respondent wished to rely on the privilege against self-incrimination. The court held that, in the circumstances, the offensive material could be passed on to the police.

As mentioned above, if the respondent wants to delay permitting entry while they exercise the above rights, take legal advice, or apply to court to vary or set aside the order (see **9.5.7**), they only have to allow access to the supervising solicitor in the meantime. Nonetheless, they must keep the supervising solicitor informed of what they are doing, and they can refuse to allow the search to begin only for a short period whilst they exercise their rights. According to para 10 of the order, this delay in execution should not exceed two hours unless the supervising solicitor is prepared to agree to a longer period.

The respondent may fear (sometimes with good reason) that the applicant will use the search order as an opportunity to find out about the respondent's business and trade secrets. The respondent will therefore want to refuse entry to the applicant in person or their employees. The footnote to the part of the order entitled 'The Search' stipulates that none of the persons accompanying the applicant's solicitor should be capable of gaining personally or commercially from the search unless their presence is essential. However, there will be cases where the applicant's lawyers need the expertise of the applicant or their employees to identify the material they are looking for. In that case, the order may name one representative of the applicant to whom the respondent cannot deny access.

The respondent is usually entitled to a list of all the items which have been removed. They should be given an opportunity to check and sign the list before the items are removed from their premises. Items should not usually be removed in the respondent's absence. In both instances, however, the supervising solicitor can permit non-compliance if full compliance is impractical.

9.5.4 The respondent's position

The respondent is required to cooperate with the executing solicitors. The respondent cannot merely allow them to search. Paragraph 18 of the order requires the respondent to show them where the items referred to in the order are. If they are in locked cupboards, they must unlock those cupboards. If the information is stored on a computer, they must allow effective access to that computer, subject to the applicant's party having the necessary expertise to use the computer without damaging it. By para 16, the respondent is required to hand over the items covered by the order. The respondent can be required to confirm all the information supplied, or required to be supplied, under the order.

Paragraph 18 also requires the respondent to reveal the identities and whereabouts of their suppliers and customers, and the location of the items sought by the applicant which have not already been handed over under para 16. The respondent is also required to confirm that this information is accurate.

The respondent also has entitlements, however, and these are dealt with in a separate part of the order. This makes it clear that the respondent is entitled to have the order explained to them by the supervising solicitor in everyday language.

Paragraphs 10 and 11 of this section of the order explain that the respondent may be entitled to refuse disclosure of documents protected by the privilege against self-incrimination (in cases where that privilege applies, see **8.7**) or by legal professional privilege. The order then explains the respondent's rights to legal advice and the circumstances in which they may delay complying with the order (see **9.7**).

9.5.5 Prohibited acts by the respondent

Paragraph 20 prevents the respondent from telling anybody except their lawyers about the proceedings or the search order. Although it seems harsh, it is designed to ensure that the respondent does not warn accomplices, of whom the applicant is unaware, of what is happening. The clause is of limited duration and should last only for as long as is necessary for the applicant to study the items removed under the order and to find out whether they need to take action against any other people who are harming them by their illegal activities. This will usually be until the return date.

In para 21 the respondent is also prohibited from destroying, tampering with, cancelling or disposing of the listed items, unless permitted by the order.

9.5.6 The prohibitory injunction

The order will contain a prohibitory injunction preventing the harm the applicant is complaining about. This is contained in para 22. It continues until the trial unless the respondent successfully applies to set aside the order before the trial.

9.5.7 Applications to set aside or vary the order

As with all injunctions, if the respondent wishes to set aside or vary the order, they may apply for this at any time. That application should be served on the applicant giving them proper notice under the procedure described in **Chapter 7**. The respondent can also apply on the return date fixed when the injunction was granted.

If the respondent does apply to set aside the order, the court will mainly be interested in considering the injunction referred to at **9.5.6** on the basis that any harm caused by the search order has already happened and that the issue of compensation for such harm can be left until the final trial of the claim. If, however, the search order is likely to have a deleterious effect on the respondent's business (see **9.7**), it would be possible to apply to set aside that order on the return date.

The respondent may be able to argue that the search order should not have been granted in the first place (ie one or more of the necessary grounds for making the order was not present), or that the applicant failed to execute the order in the correct manner.

The law relating to setting aside and varying injunctions and search orders is the same as the law for setting aside and varying freezing injunctions, and is dealt with at **8.9**.

9.6   THE UNDERTAKINGS

After the usual provisions explaining that the defendant must not arrange for other people to infringe the order on their behalf, Schedules C to E to the standard form search order set out the undertakings required in a search order.

9.6.1   The applicant's undertakings (Schedule C)

These are largely the same as those given in any injunction obtained without notice before proceedings have been issued (see **7.2.3**). Nevertheless, the following aspects are peculiar to a search order. The applicant gives the usual undertaking as to damages, but this also expressly covers the payment of compensation to the respondent if the execution of the order is carried out oppressively (see Schedule C(1)). In para 4, the applicant further undertakes to comply with the rules on confidentiality (see **9.4.2**). These provide that the applicant will not inform anyone else of the proceedings until after the return date unless permitted by the court.

9.6.2   The applicant's solicitor's undertakings (Schedule D)

These include undertaking to retain in safe-keeping all items obtained as a result of the search until the court directs otherwise, and to return to the respondent any original documents which do not belong to the applicant within two working days of their removal in the search.

9.6.3   The supervising solicitor's undertakings (Schedule E)

These relate to the supervising solicitor's duties to:

(a)   explain the effect of the order;

(b)   inform the respondent of their right to legal advice (including their entitlement to legal professional privilege and, where relevant, the privilege against self-incrimination); and

(c)   provide a report on the execution of the order to the applicant's solicitors, the respondent and the court.

9.7   ADVISING THE RESPONDENT

As already discussed, a respondent who does not comply with a search order is in contempt of court. It is no defence that the search order should never have been made in the first place (*Wardle Fabrics v Myristis* [1983] FSR 263). While it was in existence, it was a court order and had to be obeyed. Neither is it a defence that the respondent's associates might cause physical harm to the respondent if they comply with the order (*Coca Cola Co v Gilbey* [1995] 4 All ER 711).

The respondent should usually therefore be advised to obey the order. If the respondent wants their solicitor to be present when the order is executed, the applicant's solicitor should be asked to delay execution until the respondent's solicitor can attend (provided this will not cause unreasonable delay – see **9.5.3**).

Paragraph 10 of the order does contemplate the possibility of refusing to comply with the order pending an immediate application to the court to vary or set aside the order. This has to be read in conjunction with the rest of para 10, which requires the respondent to allow the supervising solicitor to enter the premises. This is to enable the supervising solicitor to assure themselves that the respondent is not just using this as a diversionary tactic while they conceal or destroy evidence.

In practice, there are unlikely to be many cases where the respondent will be in a position to make an immediate application to set aside the order, and they will usually have to comply with it.

If the respondent complies with the order and incriminating evidence is found, they may not be able to rely on the privilege against self-incrimination to withhold evidence (see **8.7**). Usually, in such a case, the respondent has no option but to settle the case on the most favourable terms available.

If the applicant's search is unsuccessful, however, the respondent is in a strong position. The respondent will ultimately be able to apply for the injunction to be set aside and for damages for the harm caused to them by the order (see **8.9**). The respondent may wish to make this application immediately, especially if the order is having an adverse effect on their business. Nevertheless, if, as is often the case, the respondent's grounds for setting aside are that the applicant's original application did not disclose all material facts, the court will have to investigate this allegation. This will take time and the courts prefer not to do this before the trial. In any event, in most cases any harm caused by granting and executing the search order has already finished by the time of any pre-trial hearing. Only in exceptional circumstances will the matter be dealt with prior to the trial (*Dormeuil Frères v Nicolian International (Textiles) Ltd* [1988] 1 WLR 1362). More usually, the court will investigate the matter at the trial of the action, where the appropriate remedy will be damages. However, if in the meantime the applicant delays in bringing their claim to trial, the respondent can apply to strike out the applicant's statement of case and enforce the undertaking as to damages at that stage. *Hytrac Conveyors Ltd v Conveyors International Ltd* [1982] 3 All ER 415 shows that such applications can succeed at a very early stage of the proceedings.

Nevertheless, there are a few cases where it may be appropriate to apply to set aside the order at an early stage. An example is where the applicant is an established business abusing the search order jurisdiction in an attempt to drive out an unwelcome, but legitimate, newly-arrived competitor. In such cases, the search order may starve the respondent of custom, and if it is not set aside quickly, it will put them out of business. In such cases, the court should deal with the application to set aside the order when hearing the respondent's initial application rather than waiting until the trial.

According to *Practice Direction (Mareva Injunctions and Anton Piller Orders)* [1994] 1 WLR 1233, if a search order is set aside before the trial, the judge should always consider whether it is appropriate to assess damages at once and order immediate payment by the applicant (see **8.9**). Another point to note is that even 'guilty' respondents have been able to obtain damages under a search order if the order was executed oppressively, as in *Columbia Picture*. For example, persuading a respondent to agree to the removal of additional documents not covered by the order, could well be regarded as oppressive behaviour.

9.8 PRACTICAL POINTS

If there is a risk of a breach of the peace when the order is executed, the police can be asked to attend. This should rarely be necessary and the judge should be informed of any intention to do this when the order is sought. It is common practice to inform the police of what is happening before executing a search order. However, para 8 of the order makes it clear that the order should not be carried out at the same time as a police search.

If the applicant is suing a large number of people, they will have to coordinate their raids on the different premises with military precision to ensure that the respondents do not tip each other off.

There is an inevitable risk that the solicitor's conduct during the execution of the order will be criticised by the respondent. It is important that there should be no doubt about what happened. Therefore, the solicitor should keep a record of what is happening and should swear an affidavit as to what happened as soon as the search is over. Similarly, the respondent's solicitor should also keep a record of what happens (or, if they cannot be present, advise the client to do so).

9.9 SUMMARY

A search order requires the respondent to allow the applicant's representatives to enter and search the respondent's premises. The applicant will be able to obtain such an order only if they can show the following:

(a)   an extremely strong prima facie case;

(b)   that the applicant has suffered or will suffer very serious harm if the order is not made; and

(c)   that the respondent has incriminating material and there is a real possibility of destruction or disposal of the material.

The order contains safeguards against abuse of the procedure by the applicant, such as the requirement for the order to be executed by an independent supervising solicitor. The terms of the order should be those set out in the standard form contained in PD 25A to CPR 1998.

The respondent's solicitor should usually advise the respondent to comply with the order, even if the result will be that the applicant obtains evidence which supports their case. Non-compliance could result in an order committing the respondent (and their solicitor) to prison for contempt of court. If, however, the order is executed oppressively or unsuccessfully, the respondent may be entitled to substantial damages under the applicant's cross-undertaking as to damages.

CHAPTER 10

HANDLING THE EVIDENCE

> **LEARNING OUTCOMES**
>
> After reading this chapter you will understand:
>
> - how to advise a client in a case requiring large-scale disclosure
> - how to advise a client about initial disclosure
> - the 5 Models of Extended Disclosure
> - how to complete the Disclosure Review Document
> - how to approach the disclosure provided by the other side
> - the role of expert evidence in commercial cases.

10.1 INTRODUCTION

This chapter builds upon CPR 1998 on disclosure, expert evidence, witness statements and further information (see also the Legal Practice Guide, *Civil Litigation*). It also looks at the best tactical use of these procedures and how the overriding objective of CPR 1998 and the court's case management powers affect the ways in which evidence is handled in the build-up to the trial.

Although this chapter discusses evidence in the context of litigation, the topic is equally important in arbitration and other forms of dispute resolution. Each of the procedures described in this chapter can lead to greater knowledge of the strengths and weaknesses of the client's case. With that knowledge, it is possible to review with the client the likely outcome of the case, the cost of proceeding to the next stage and the appropriate strategy and tactics.

PART I – DISCLOSURE AND PRODUCTION

10.2 PRACTICAL POINTS

10.2.1 Practical consequences for the client

Disclosure is a crucial stage in a commercial case. It is often the point at which cases are won or lost because it is the time at which information is exchanged between the parties. Although there are other weapons at the disposal of the parties to obtain information (eg further information or interim applications), disclosure remains central to the action. It is *not* just a matter of listing documents but requires detailed knowledge of the law, in particular regarding which documents are subject to disclosure and/or are privileged. It is an extremely complicated area of the law, which has led to a large amount of case law over the years. The importance of this stage should not be underestimated, either in terms of its importance to the parties or in the obligations imposed on both sides and their lawyers.

Disclosure is, however, also an expensive stage for the parties in commercial cases. There tend to be a vast number of potentially disclosable documents. It takes time to trace them all and to assess whether they are disclosable and, if so, whether they are privileged. It usually takes just as long to read the opponent's list and to inspect their documents. The solicitor should therefore discuss the costs implications with the client. If the case is weak, it may be better to try and settle before disclosure, rather than waste thousands of pounds in legal costs only to discover what was suspected earlier, ie that the client's cause is a lost one.

10.2.2 Disclosure under CPR 1998, PD 57AD

In this section, we will consider PD 57AD which provides for disclosure in the Business and Property Courts (B&PCs). However, note that PD 57AD does not address the following (for which see the Legal Practice Guide, *Civil Litigation*):

(a)   applications for pre-action disclosure and non-party disclosure for which CPR 1998, Part 31 still applies;

(b)   disclosure outside the B&PCs (eg the King's Bench of the High Court and the County Court to which Part 31 still applies); and

(c)   case law defining what amounts to legal professional privilege.

For the purposes of PD 57AD, the term 'document' includes any record of any description containing information.

> 2.5 A 'document' may take any form including but not limited to paper or electronic; it may be held by computer or on portable devices such as memory sticks or mobile phones or within databases; it includes e-mail and other electronic communications such as text messages, webmail, social media and voicemail, audio or visual recordings.
>
> 2.6 In addition to information that is readily accessible from computer systems and other electronic devices and media, the term 'document' extends to information that is stored on servers and back-up systems and electronic information that has been 'deleted'. It also extends to metadata, and other embedded data which is not typically visible on screen or a printout.

10.3 ADVISING THE CLIENT

10.3.1 The overarching principles

Paragraph 2 sets out the following overarching principles of PD 57AD:

> 2.1 Disclosure is important in achieving the fair resolution of civil proceedings. It involves identifying and making available documents that are relevant to the issues in the proceedings.
>
> ...

2.3 The court expects the parties and their representatives to cooperate with each other and to assist the court so that the scope of disclosure, if any, that is required in proceedings can be agreed or determined by the court in the most efficient way possible.

2.4 The court will be concerned to ensure that disclosure is directed to the issues in the proceedings and that the scope of disclosure is not wider than is reasonable and proportionate ... in order fairly to resolve those issues ....

10.3.2 Disclosure duties

Paragraphs 3 and 4 of PD 57AD set out various express duties relevant to disclosure. These disclosure duties are as follows.

10.3.2.1 Client duties

(1) to take reasonable steps to preserve documents in their control that may be relevant to any issue in the proceedings;

(2) [once proceedings have commenced,] to disclose known adverse documents, unless they are privileged ...;

(3) to comply with any order for disclosure made by the court;

(4) to undertake any search for documents in a responsible and conscientious manner to fulfil the stated purpose of the search;

(5) to act honestly in relation to the process of giving disclosure and reviewing documents disclosed by the other party; and

(6) to use reasonable efforts to avoid providing documents to another party that have no relevance to the Issues for Disclosure in the proceedings [so-called 'document dumping'].

The duty to preserve documents is particularly important as the court may order production of original documents (as in *Emirates NBD Bank PJSC and another v Hassan Saadat-Yazdi and others* [2023] EWHC 747 (Comm), where the claimant banks were ordered to produce the originals of purported personal guarantees to the applicant defendants and their forensic expert as the defendants were alleging that the guarantees were forged).

10.3.2.2 Solicitor duties

(1) to take reasonable steps to preserve documents within their control that may be relevant to any issue in the proceedings;

(2) to take reasonable steps to advise and assist [their client] to comply with its Disclosure Duties;

(3) to liaise and cooperate with the legal representatives of the other parties to the proceedings (or the other parties where they do not have legal representatives) so as to promote the reliable, efficient and cost-effective conduct of disclosure, including through the use of technology;

(4) to act honestly in relation to the process of giving disclosure and reviewing documents disclosed by the other party; and

(5) to undertake a review to satisfy themselves that any claim by [the client] to privilege from disclosing a document is properly made and the reason for the claim to privilege is sufficiently explained.

10.3.2.3 Preservation of documents

A key duty for both clients and solicitors is to take steps to preserve documents. Many commercial companies generate significant volumes of documents every day and operate 'document retention' policies setting out how long those documents are retained and stored on their systems, and when they can be deleted. When first instructed, it will be important to check whether your client has any document retention, deletion or destruction policies and advise that they must suspend those policies for the duration of the proceedings.

The duty to preserve documents extends to all documents within the client's or solicitors' control. PD 57AD defines 'control' in the same way as CPR 1998, r 31.8 (a list of definitions used in PD 57AD can be found in Appendix 1 to the Practice Direction). The duty to preserve documents will therefore extend beyond documents which are in the client's physical possession, and will include documents that it has the right to take possession of or the right to inspect. As to the latter, what is required is that the right to possession or inspection is enforceable without the need to obtain the consent of anyone else (*Republic of Mozambique v Credit Suisse International* [2022] EWHC 3054 (Comm)).

The client therefore needs to identify employees, former employees, agents and other third parties who might hold potentially relevant documents not in the client's possession, and notify them in writing not to delete or destroy such documents. The solicitor must obtain the client's written confirmation that these steps (including the suspension of the client's own document retention policies) have been taken.

These duties continue throughout the proceedings and the parties are required to confirm in writing when serving their statements of case that steps have been taken to preserve relevant documents.

10.4   PRE-ACTION PROTOCOLS

Nothing in PD 57AD lessens the need to comply with any relevant specific pre-action protocol that applies or otherwise the Practice Direction – Pre-Action Conduct and Protocols (PD-PAC).

PD-PAC requires the parties to have exchanged sufficient information in order to understand each other's position and try to settle the issues without proceedings (a full list of pre-action objectives is set out in para 3). In order to do so, each party will usually send the other a letter setting out its position and disclosing key documents relevant to the issues in dispute.

Section B3 of the Commercial Court Guide confirms that parties should usually observe PD-PAC (or any other pre-action protocol that might apply), although the parties are not required to engage in elaborate or expensive pre-action procedures and only essential documents should be supplied.

If the parties have failed to comply with PD-PAC and proceedings are commenced, the court may stay those proceedings while steps are taken to comply with PD-PAC and/or sanction the party in default. Those sanctions are set out in para 16 of PD-PAC.

10.5   INITIAL DISCLOSURE

Paragraph 5 of PD 57AD introduces the concept of Initial Disclosure. This involves each party providing to all other parties electronic copies of:

(a)   the key documents on which it has relied in support of the case advanced in its statement of case; and

(b)   the key documents that are necessary to enable the other parties to understand the case they have to meet.

This Initial Disclosure must be provided at the same time as the party serves its statement of case (in the case of a claimant, this refers to its Particulars of Claim and not its Claim Form).

There are two important points to note here:

(1)   Initial Disclosure is limited to providing documents that support your client's case. There is no need to provide 'unhelpful' documents at this stage.

(2)   Initial Disclosure is limited to key documents. There is no guidance in PD 57AD as to what this means, but the courts have been keen to stress that Initial Disclosure is limited to producing 'really very necessary documents' either on which reliance is placed (*State of Qatar v Banque Havilland SA* [2020] EWHC 1248 (Comm) giving the example of a written contract or a key meeting note potentially evidencing the making of a contract or a particular representation) or which enable the other parties to understand the case they have to meet (but not those which are necessary to evaluate and weigh the

prospects of success of that case: *Breitenbach v Canaccord Genuity Financial Planning Ltd* [2020] EWHC 1355 (Ch)).

The Initial Disclosure must be accompanied by an Initial Disclosure List of Documents (unless the parties agree to dispense with this). This should list the documents provided in chronological order, identifying each document with a clear description including the date and, where applicable, any author, sender or recipient (see PD 57AD, Appendix 1, para 1.10). The Initial Disclosure List will commonly be prepared by a junior litigator or trainee and will in practice look very similar to Part 1 of the list of documents prepared for CPR 1998, Part 31 disclosure. (For more detail on Part 31 lists, reference should be made to PD 31A, para 3, Form N265 and the Legal Practice Guide, *Civil Litigation*.)

The Initial Disclosure List must be filed with the court, but the documents themselves should not be.

Initial Disclosure is not required where:

(a)   the parties have agreed in writing to dispense with it (PD 57AD, para 5.3(1)). If so, the parties must record their reasons for doing so and the court may review those reasons at a future CMC. If the court considers that Initial Disclosure is likely to provide significant benefits, it may set aside the parties' agreement (PD 57AD, para 5.8);

(b)   the court orders that it is not required (PD 57AD, para 5.3(2)). This may occur when one party requests that Initial Disclosure is dispensed with, but the other party does not agree;

(c)   a party concludes in good faith that giving Initial Disclosure would involve any party providing more than 1,000 pages of material or 200 documents (whichever is the larger) (PD 57AD, para 5.3(3)). These figures can include any documents already disclosed during the pre-action phase of the litigation. If one party confirms this in writing, then the requirement to give Initial Disclosure ceases for all parties. This exception reinforces that Initial Disclosure is meant to be 'light-touch' and not an excuse to engage in 'document dumping'.

There is no requirement to provide the following documents by way of Initial Disclosure (PD 57AD, para 5.4(3) and (4)):

(a)   documents which have already been provided in compliance with PD-PAC or any other specific pre-action protocol, unless requested to do so;

(b)   documents known to be or have been in the other party's possession, unless requested to do so; and

(c)   adverse ('unhelpful') documents.

There is no obligation at this stage to conduct any search for documents, beyond any search already undertaken for the purpose of the proceedings (PD 57AD, para 5.4(1)). Parties may, however, wish to conduct further searches if they believe other key documents might exist which would support their case.

10.6   EXTENDED DISCLOSURE – THE 5 MODELS

A party wishing to seek disclosure of documents in addition to Initial Disclosure must request Extended Disclosure.

Extended Disclosure may take the form of one or more of the Disclosure Models set out in PD 57AD, para 8. There is no presumption that a party is entitled to Extended Disclosure and, in particular, there is no default Model.

There is a limited exception to the application of these 5 Disclosure Models. In 'Less Complex' claims, Extended Disclosure will be given using only models A, B or D. Less Complex claims are claims which are not particularly complex, of low value (generally, where the value is less than £1 million) and where there is likely to be less in the way of relevant documentation. Less Complex claims are addressed in Appendices 5 to 7 of PD 57AD. They are not considered further here.

10.6.1 Model A (Disclosure confined to known adverse documents)

Model A disclosure is limited to known adverse documents (see **10.6.7**). There is no obligation to search for documents.

10.6.2 Model B (Limited disclosure)

Model B disclosure is confined to key documents on which the party has relied in support of their case and/or which are necessary to enable the other parties to understand the case they have to meet, *plus* known adverse documents. There is no obligation to search for documents.

Note that Model B is very similar to Initial Disclosure, save for two differences:

(1)   there is no limit on the number of documents that could be produced; and

(2)   the party must disclose known adverse documents (see **10.6.7**).

10.6.3 Model C (Disclosure of particular documents or narrow classes of documents)

Model C disclosure comprises:

(a)   searching for and disclosing documents requested by the other parties as set out in the Disclosure Review Document (see **10.7**) and approved by the court; *plus*

(b)   disclosing known adverse documents (see **10.6.7**).

Model C involves requesting that the other side conduct targeted searches for key documents. In many ways, Model C is used in a similar way to specific disclosure under CPR 1998, r 31.12. You will likely use Model C tactically either to:

(i)   request that the other side search for documents that are unhelpful to its case or which are helpful to your client's case; or

(ii)   demonstrate that the other side has no documents that support its case (or portions of that case) and that its case therefore lacks credibility. For instance, if the other side positively asserts something in their statement of case in respect of which you would expect there to be documents, but has not provided any documents by way of Initial Disclosure, you may want to consider requesting sight of those documents by making targeted Model C requests. If no documents are provided in response to those requests, then that would tend to suggest that the other side's case is weak, untruthful or lacks credibility.

10.6.4 Model D (Narrow search-based disclosure)

Model D disclosure comprises:

(a)   searching for and disclosing documents which are likely to support or adversely affect your client's case or that of another party in relation to one or more disputed issues; *plus*

(b)   disclosing known adverse documents (see **10.6.7**).

In many ways, Model D is similar to standard disclosure under CPR 1998, r 31.6 but in respect of only identified specific disputed issues. Rather than requesting that the other party conducts particular searches for particular documents (Model C), Model D requires the party to conduct a reasonable search for documents that relate to specific issues.

This Model refers to 'Narrative Documents'. Please note that this concept is outside the scope of this book.

10.6.5 Model E (Wide search-based disclosure)

Model E disclosure comprises:

(a) (i) searching for and disclosing documents which are likely to support or adversely affect your client's case or that of another party in relation to one or more disputed issues; and/or

(ii) searching for and disclosing documents which may lead to a train of inquiry resulting in the identification of other documents that need to be disclosed; *plus*

(b) disclosing known adverse documents (see **10.6.7**).

Model E is the widest form of disclosure available under PD 57AD and will only be ordered in exceptional cases. In practice, it is often only encountered in cases involving serious allegations of fraud or dishonesty.

This Model refers to 'Narrative Documents'. Please note that this concept is outside the scope of this book.

10.6.6 General principles

An order for Extended Disclosure will only be made if it is reasonable and proportionate to do so (see PD 57AD, para 6.4 for the factors that the court will take into account). Furthermore, the courts will only order 'search-based Extended Disclosure' (being any of Models C, D and/ or E) where it is appropriate to do so to fairly resolve one or more Issues for Disclosure (PD 57AD, para 6.3). We will explore 'Issues for Disclosure' in more detail at **10.7.1**. For now, an Issue for Disclosure means a key issue in dispute that can only be fairly resolved with some reference to contemporaneous documents.

The court may order that Extended Disclosure is given using different Disclosure Models for different Issues for Disclosure (PD 57AD, para 8.3). For example, assume that there are 10 Issues for Disclosure in a case. The court could order that:

(a) the claimant should conduct Model C searches in relation to issues 1, 3 and 6; Model D searches in relation to issues 4, 5 and 8; but only needs to disclose known adverse documents (pursuant to Model A) in relation to the remaining issues; whereas

(b) the defendant should conduct Model C searches in relation to issues 1, 4 and 6; Model D searches in relation to issues, 5, 7 and 8; but only needs to disclose known adverse documents (pursuant to Model A) in relation to the remaining issues.

As can be seen, the Models of Extended Disclosure can be used in a very flexible and targeted way to ensure that the scope of disclosure is no wider than is reasonable and proportionate in order to fairly resolve the disputed issues. However, judges will be cautious that the Disclosure Models do not become used in a way that increases cost through undue complexity. For instance, the greater the number of Model C requests that are made, the more likely it is that the court will instead order that disclosure on the disputed issues is conducted pursuant to Model D. Plus, in the above example, if the claimant needs to look at the same set of documents in relation to all 10 issues, then it is unlikely that the court would require the claimant to search that set of documents using different Models.

In order to work out whether Extended Disclosure should be ordered and, if so, which Model to use, the court will be guided by the completion of the Disclosure Review Document (DRD) (see **10.7**) by the parties in advance of the first CMC.

10.6.7 Known adverse documents

Whatever model of Extended Disclosure is ordered, each party must disclose known adverse documents.

An 'adverse document' is a document that contradicts or materially damages the disclosing party's contention or version of events on an issue in dispute (PD 57AD, para 2.7).

'Known adverse documents' are adverse documents (other than privileged documents) of which a party is actually aware (PD 57AD, para 2.8). The parties do not have to perform additional searches beyond those they have already undertaken for their own purposes, unless they are required to do so under a search-based Extended Disclosure order (being an order which includes either Model C, D and/or E).

How is a partnership, company or any other organisation aware of adverse documents? All persons with accountability or responsibility within the organisation for the events or the circumstances which are the subject of the case, or for the conduct of the proceedings, including those who have since left, must (a) make reasonable and proportionate checks to see if they have or have had control of adverse documents, and (b) undertake reasonable and proportionate steps to locate them (*Castle Water Ltd v Thames Water Utilities Ltd* [2020] EWHC 1374 (TCC)).

The obligation to always disclose known adverse documents was introduced because of fears that parties might simply sit on 'smoking guns' or wilfully pursue positions that were contradicted by the documents. Neither strategy would be consistent with the overriding objective or the 'cards on the table' approach to disclosure. There was also a concern that without the obligation to disclose known adverse documents, parties would be encouraged to push for wider Disclosure Models in an attempt to capture documents that were harmful to an opponent. Requiring the parties to disclose known adverse documents 'come what may' should make the parties more comfortable conducting narrower search-based Extended Disclosure.

Known adverse documents must be disclosed at the same time as other documents where search-based Extended Disclosure is ordered, or otherwise within 60 days of the first CMC.

In either case, the client's employee with responsibility for co-ordinating the disclosure exercise will have to sign a Disclosure Certificate to verify that:

(a)   they have received confirmation from all those people with accountability or responsibility for the events or circumstances that have given rise to the litigation, including those that have since left the organisation, that all known adverse documents have been disclosed; and

(b)   all adverse documents that they themselves are personally aware of have also been disclosed.

A copy of the Disclosure Certificate is at **Appendix 16** to this book.

10.7   THE DISCLOSURE REVIEW DOCUMENT

10.7.1   Practical points

The Disclosure Review Document (DRD) replaces both the disclosure report and the Electronic Documents Questionnaire which are used for disclosure outside the B&PCs (see CPR 1998, r 31.5(3), form N263, PD 31B and the Legal Practice Guide, *Civil Litigation*). The DRD therefore is a key document that may need to be completed in advance of the first CMC.

The DRD is intended to:

(a)   facilitate the exchange of information and provide a framework for discussions around the initial scoping of disclosure;

(b)   help the parties to agree a sensible and cost-effective approach to disclosure and identify areas of disagreement; and

(c)   provide the court with the parties' proposals on disclosure, so the court can make appropriate case management decisions at the CMC.

The DRD only needs to be completed if search-based Extended Disclosure (Model C, D or E) is sought by any party on any issue. There is a copy at **Appendix 6** to this book.

There are three sections of the DRD:

(1)   Section 1A comprises the List of Issues for Disclosure.

(2)   Section 1B allows the parties to list Model C requests for Disclosure.

(3)   Section 2 asks various questions about the documents that each party controls and, in particular, about how each party holds electronic documents and intends to search against those documents.

Sections 1A and 2 must be completed if the parties are seeking an order for Extended Disclosure involving Models D and/or E. All three sections must be completed if the parties are seeking an order for Extended Disclosure involving Model C. The DRD does not need completing if the parties are only seeking Extended Disclosure under Models A and/or B.

10.7.2   Section 1A: the List of Issues for Disclosure

Section 1A aims to provide a concise summary of the parties' proposals in relation to Extended Disclosure by identifying the Issues for Disclosure and the proposed Models for Disclosure in respect of each Issue.

Issues for Disclosure are defined as being 'those *key issues in dispute*, which the parties consider will need to be determined by the court *with some reference to contemporaneous documents* in order for there to be a fair resolution of the proceedings' (PD 57AD, para 7.6, emphasis added).

Some important considerations come out of this definition.

(1)   The List of Issues for Disclosure must focus on issues in dispute. However, it does not extend to every issue which is disputed in the statements of case by denial or non-admission.

(2)   Instead, the Issues for Disclosure must focus on the key issues in dispute the determination of which are likely to have a material impact on the outcome of the case and the resolution of which will depend on contemporaneous documents. There may be many issues in dispute between the parties, but some might revolve around issues of law or witness evidence and so should not be included in the Issues for Disclosure.

(3)   The List of Issues for Disclosure and the List of Common Ground and Issues (drawn up before the first CMC) are intended to be separate documents addressing different purposes. The explanatory notes to the DRD advise that the two documents should 'ultimately be consistent with each other', but it is likely that the List of Issues for Disclosure will be much shorter and more concise than the List of Common Ground and Issues.

The reference here to contemporaneous documents does not mean that only documents contemporaneous with the cause of action must be disclosed. Documents created later will often be disclosable.

> The most obvious example is an admission against the interest of the person making it. If a person admits that he forged a signature, no one is going to suggest that the admission is evidentially worthless because it was not contemporaneous with the forgery. Similarly, a person's behaviour after an event may be important in discerning their state of mind at the time of the event. (per Anderson KC at [27] in *Morina and others v Scherbakova and others (Re Estate of Vladimir Alekseyevich Scherbakov)* [2023] EWHC 440 (Ch))

As well as providing a List of Issues for Disclosure, the parties must set out in section 1A:

(a)   a cross-reference to where each Issue can be found in the statements of case;

(b)   whether each Issue as formulated is agreed (with alternative wording if the Issue as described is not agreed); and

(c)   what Model of Extended Disclosure each party proposes should be adopted in relation to each Issue.

The claimant is responsible for producing the first draft of the List of Issues for Disclosure. Once prepared, the parties must continually liaise with each other to try to reach agreement on the Issues and the Models of Extended Disclosure sought.

Is the List of Issues for Disclosure relevant to giving disclosure of known adverse documents (see **10.6.7**)? No. Whereas the parties must conduct any search-based Extended Disclosure by reference to the Issues for Disclosure set out in section 1A of the DRD, known adverse documents must be disclosed regardless of those Issues. If a known document contradicts or materially damages the party's position in the litigation or supports the position of the opponent, then it must be disclosed. This means the parties cannot 'hide' such documents by drawing up the Issues for Disclosure in a particular way.

10.7.3   Section 1B: Model C requests

Any party proposing Model C Extended Disclosure (requesting that the other party conduct specific searches or produce specific documents) must complete section 1B. There is space in section 1B for the responding party to agree to those requests or reject them with reasons.

The explanatory notes advise as follows:

(a)   The requests should be limited in number, focused in scope and concise so that the responding party is clear as to the particular document or class of documents which it is being asked to search for. Broad and wide-ranging formulations should not be used. For example, avoid a request such as, 'Any or all documents relating to any meetings held between the Claimant and the Defendant.' This should instead be formulated by reference to specific document types, date ranges, custodians and key events such as, 'All minutes of the meeting held on [date] between Janette Lee of the Claimant and Anne Freeman of the Defendant prepared by Anne Freeman or her assistants' and 'All emails sent or received by Anne Freeman of the Defendant within the period [date] to [date] (inclusive) that refer to the meeting held on [date] between Janette Lee and Anne Freeman.'

(b)   It will rarely be appropriate to have a large number of Model C requests because that is likely to make it more difficult for the parties to agree what the Model C requests should be, and increase the complexity, costs and time required to undertake the subsequent review exercise. The larger the number of Model C requests made, the more likely that Model D (equivalent to standard disclosure of specific issues) will be appropriate.

(c)   Using multiple Model C requests can undermine rather than facilitate the use of technology in disclosure. This is another reason for avoiding multiple Model C requests.

10.7.4   Section 2: electronic documents

In cases where search-based Extended Disclosure is sought, the purpose of section 2 is to provide the court with information about the documents held by each party, including:

(a)   where and how those documents are held;

(b)   how the parties propose to process and search those documents; and

(c)   whether there are any points that the parties have not been able to agree through discussions and which they therefore need the court to determine at the CMC.

Section 2 asks various questions about the party's documents, including:

• data sources which the parties propose to search. These can include email servers, cloud-based data storage, back-up systems, social media accounts, mobile phones, tablets and other handheld devices;

• custodians (usually individuals, such as company employees) whose files will be searched;

• date ranges within which searches will be conducted;

- methods of searching that will be used, including the use of keywords and technology-assisted review; and
- estimates of costs for undertaking any required Extended Disclosure.

The explanatory notes make clear that these questions are to be treated as a guide to what the parties can usefully discuss in advance of the CMC.

The parties must confer and seek to agree the contents of section 2 in advance of the CMC. The parties are expected to liaise with each other by 'phone, video conference or in person'. The explanatory notes observe that extensive correspondence in this regard is unlikely to be efficient or helpful.

The claimant is responsible for updating section 2 of the DRD to ensure that it reflects the parties' combined comments and discussions.

The parties must cooperate in finalising the DRD and must seek to resolve any disputes over the scope of any Extended Disclosure sought in advance of the first CMC. A finalised single joint DRD should be filed by the claimant not later than five days before the CMC. The parties must each file a signed Certificate of Compliance once the claimant has filed the DRD.

10.8 COMPLYING WITH AN ORDER FOR EXTENDED DISCLOSURE

10.8.1 Disclosure Certificate and Extended Disclosure List of Documents

An order for Extended Disclosure is complied with by the client undertaking three steps. First, service of a Disclosure Certificate (see PD 57AD, Appendix 4) which also confirms that all known adverse documents (see **10.6.7**) have been disclosed. Second, service of an Extended Disclosure List of Documents (unless dispensed with, by agreement or order). Third, production of non-privileged documents in the client's control (see **10.8.2**).

If you have engaged in search-based Extended Disclosure, the Disclosure Certificate will list the methodology that has been employed during the review of your client's documents and list the broad categories of documents over which you are withholding production, eg on the grounds of legal professional privilege (see further the Legal Practice Guide, **Civil Litigation**). The Certificate contains a long and detailed statement of truth that the client has complied with their disclosure duties and the need to disclose known adverse documents. This statement of truth must be signed by the person within your client's organisation with appropriate authority and knowledge of the disclosure exercise. Can the client's Disclosure Certificate be signed by their legal representative? Yes, but only if they have explained the significance of the Disclosure Certificate to the client and have been given written authority to do so. A copy of the Certificate is at **Appendix 16** to this book.

What if the client cannot produce a particular document because, for example, the document no longer exists or the client no longer has it in their control? In their Extended Disclosure List of Documents, the client should describe each such document with reasonable precision and explain the circumstances in which, and the date when, the document ceased to exist or left their control. If it is not possible to identify individual documents, the class of documents must be described with reasonable precision.

If search-based Extended Disclosure has not been ordered, then the above steps must be completed within 60 days of the first CMC. These steps must still be completed because the duty to disclose known adverse documents applies irrespective of what model of Extended Disclosure is ordered, and therefore there may still be documents to be disclosed at this stage.

10.8.2 Production

Save where otherwise agreed or ordered, the client must produce disclosable electronic documents to the other parties by providing electronic copies in the documents' native format, in a manner which preserves metadata; and normally disclosable hard copy documents by providing scanned versions or photocopied hard copies. Documents are provided at the same time as the Extended Disclosure List of Documents. There is no separate inspection stage as happens under CPR 1998, Part 31.

Electronic documents should generally be provided in the form which allows the party receiving the documents the same ability to access, search, review and display the documents (including metadata) as the party providing them.

Should a client disclose more than one copy of a document? Not unless additional copies contain or bear modifications, obliterations or other markings or features which of themselves cause those additional copies to fall within the client's Initial or Extended Disclosure obligations.

10.9 FAILURE ADEQUATELY TO COMPLY WITH AN ORDER FOR EXTENDED DISCLOSURE

Where there has been or may have been a failure adequately to comply with an order for Extended Disclosure, the court may make such further orders as may be appropriate, including an order requiring a party to (1) serve a further, or revised, Disclosure Certificate; (2) undertake further steps, including further or more extended searches to ensure compliance with an order for Extended Disclosure; (3) provide a further or improved Extended Disclosure List of Documents; (4) produce documents; or (5) make a witness statement explaining any matter relating to disclosure.

Before making an application for any such order, the parties should try to resolve their differences. Consideration should also be given to applying to the court for Disclosure Guidance pursuant to PD 57AD, para 11. Otherwise, an application should be made promptly with a supporting witness statement. The applicant will have to show some basis for going behind the disclosure process which had already been carried out, eg that there is a likelihood, as opposed to a possibility, of further relevant documents existing (*Berkeley Square Holdings Ltd v Lancer Property Assets Management Ltd* [2021] EWHC 849 (Ch)).

10.10 LARGE-SCALE DISCLOSURE

10.10.1 Management and strategy

Disclosure is a large and very important part of the action, in terms of time, cost and strategy. It is therefore essential that it is carefully planned at the outset of the dispute.

Where the court orders the parties to give Extended Disclosure, the parties will need to consider the appropriate methodology for the disclosure exercise, including how best to collect, process, review and produce the documents. The parties must discuss and endeavour to agree the approach to disclosure.

The explanatory notes to the DRD advise that parties should seek to agree the following as early in the process as possible:

(a) how documents are to be identified and collected;

(b) how the documents are to be filtered (ie date ranges, custodians, keyword searches);

(c) whether data exclusion measures should be applied during or post-collection (eg excluding certain document-types or domain names);

(d) how each party intends to use analytics or predictive coding to conduct a proportionate review of the documents;

(e) the approach and format for producing and exchanging documents with the other side, for instance how the documents will be transferred to the other party and how each individual document will be identified in the data-set. This will have an impact on the approach to the review exercise, so parties should endeavour to agree this point at an early stage.

Agreement on these points should ideally be reached before the first CMC, although this may not always be possible.

Do not underestimate just how long it will take to plan how best to review documents and agree that methodology with the other side. The earlier you start, the better.

10.10.2   Computerisation and IT

Many law firms now instruct e-disclosure firms to assist with the disclosure process. These firms will use e-disclosure platforms and software to automate many of the processes that litigators have traditionally carried out.

Clients can sometimes be reluctant about instructing e-disclosure firms, worrying about having to pay another set of fees. Explaining to the client that the e-disclosure firm will, in a couple of hours, reduce the volume of documents that need to be reviewed by up to 20% through de-duplication (a process that it would take a junior litigator many weeks to complete) is an easy way of illustrating the power and value of e-disclosure platforms.

If colleagues are going to be involved in reviewing documents, then they need to have a good working knowledge of the case and the Issues for Disclosure. Circulate copies of your working chronologies, dramatis personae, etc. Take time at the beginning to explain the case and these documents. Diarise regular catch-ups to share ideas and best practice.

Keywords can be a useful way of filtering data-sets. Many e-disclosure platforms will automatically populate a list of all words that appear in a set of documents, which can be a useful starting point in putting together a list of keywords. Other hints and tips on using keywords include:

- Think how best to search against personal names. These are often misspelt, or people will use nicknames or initials.
- In cross-border cases, American spellings should be considered.
- Think of how to reduce the number of documents responsive to keyword searches by combining keywords. Proximity searches can be powerful (eg 'Mary w/p February' will only search for the word Mary in the same paragraph as the word February).
- Alternatively, beware keyword searches that are too prescriptive. Do you need to widen the searches so that it finds variants on a theme (eg litiga* will find 'litigation', 'litigant', 'litigator' etc)?

Keep a note of the methodology that has been agreed and the methodology that you are using. When you receive the other side's Disclosure Certificate, ensure that the methodology listed in it matches the processes that have been agreed.

PART II – OTHER EVIDENCE

10.11   EXPERT EVIDENCE

Although experts' reports are privileged, the rules requiring exchange of expert evidence (see Legal Practice Guide, *Civil Litigation*) mean that the expert evidence which will be used at the trial must eventually be revealed to the other party. If the report is only partly favourable, but the expert will be giving evidence at the trial, the whole report must be revealed and not just the favourable parts. This rule cannot be avoided by the device of sending a favourable report accompanied by a letter setting out the possible weaknesses in the client's case. The letter is part of the report and if the report is revealed the letter must be as well.

Under r 35.10, an expert's report 'must state the substance of all material instructions, whether written or oral, on the basis of which the report was written'. These instructions are not privileged from inspection, although, by r 35.10(4), the court will not usually allow inspection of the instructions by the other party. One problem that may arise from this is that solicitors may be reluctant, when instructing experts, to indicate any possible weaknesses in the claimant's case. As a result, solicitors' instructions to experts may be less helpful than they could be.

A party who instructs an expert therefore has to decide, on receiving the expert's report, whether or not they will call that expert to give evidence at the trial. If so, the full report will have to be disclosed in due course. If the expert is not to be called as a witness, however, because their report is unfavourable, then their report is a privileged document and the other party will not be entitled to production of it.

In the case of *Jackson v Marley Davenport Ltd* [2004] EWCA Civ 1225, the Court of Appeal confirmed that an earlier report made by an expert in preparation of a final report to be exchanged was privileged and therefore not available for inspection. Longmore LJ stated:

> There can be no doubt that, if an expert makes a report for the purpose of a party's legal advisers being able to give legal advice to their client, or for discussion in a conference of a party's legal advisers, such a report is the subject matter of litigation privilege at the time it is made. It has come into existence for the purposes of litigation. It is common for drafts of expert reports to be circulated among a party's advisers before a final report is prepared for exchange with the other side. Such initial reports are privileged.

However, what is the position where a party has obtained an expert's report for use in the proceedings but then decides that they wish to change expert?

In *Hajigeorgiou v Vasiliou* [2005] EWCA Civ 236, the defendants had a valuation carried out by Mr A before the CMC and named him at that hearing as having done so. A consent order was made permitting each party one valuer (unnamed). Subsequently the defendants repented of their reliance on Mr A and instead proposed to rely on Mr B. The claimant contended that the defendants should be refused permission to change expert, or at least that a condition should be imposed requiring the disclosure (and inspection) of Mr A's report. The Court held that because the court order simply allowed each party one valuer, and did not name Mr A, the defendant required no permission from the court to change to Mr B, and so the possibility of adding to any such permission a condition of disclosure of Mr A's report did not arise. The Court then went on to consider whether it would have had the power to impose such a condition. Dyson LJ (as he then was) stated at [29]:

> Expert shopping is undesirable and, wherever possible, the court will use its powers to prevent it. It needs to be emphasised that, if a party needs the permission of the court to rely on expert witness A in place of expert witness B, the court has the power to give permission on condition that A's report is disclosed to the other party or parties, and that such condition will usually be imposed. In imposing such a condition, the court is not abrogating or emasculating legal professional privilege; it is merely saying that, if a party seeks the court's permission to rely on a substitute expert, it will be required to waive privilege in the first expert's report as a condition of being permitted to do so.

Following on from this, in *Edwards-Tubb v JD Wetherspoon Plc* [2011] EWCA Civ 136 the Court of Appeal held that courts had the power to order a party to allow inspection of an expert's report obtained prior to the issue of proceedings (during the course of compliance with the personal injury pre-action protocol) as a condition of granting permission to use a different expert at trial.

The expert's function is not limited to providing a report and giving evidence. When another party's expert report is received, the solicitor will discuss that report with the expert they have instructed. The expert will give advice on the flaws in the other report, its effect, and the questions which need to be asked in cross-examination to show the weaknesses in the report. Such discussions may be interpreted as being part of the instructions to the expert. This might mean that they would have to be disclosed to the court under r 35.10 of CPR 1998. As a result, a solicitor may instruct two teams of experts. The first (expert advisers) will become part of the case management team. They will not be used at the trial, and therefore records of any discussions with them will not have to be revealed to the court. When they have completed their function, a second team of experts (expert witnesses) will be instructed. Their instructions will be disclosed to the court.

It is always worth considering trying to save costs at the trial by arranging a without prejudice discussion of both parties' experts under r 35.12 to narrow the area of disagreement between them.

The Guidance for the Instruction of Experts in Civil Claims (2014) applies to any steps taken for the purpose of civil proceedings by experts or those who instruct them. The introduction to the guidance sets out its objectives:

1.   The purpose of this guidance is to assist litigants, those instructing experts and experts to understand best practice in complying with Part 35 of the Civil Procedure Rules (CPR) and court orders. Experts and those who instruct them should ensure they are familiar with CPR 35 and the Practice Direction (PD35). This guidance replaces the Protocol for the instruction of experts in civil claims (2005, amended 2009).

2.   Those instructing experts, and the experts, must also have regard to the objectives underpinning the Pre-Action Protocols to:–

   a.   encourage the exchange of early and full information about the expert issues involved in the prospective claim;

   b.   enable the parties to avoid or reduce the scope of the litigation by agreeing the whole or part of an expert issue before proceedings are started; and

   c.   support the efficient management of proceedings where litigation cannot be avoided.

3.   Additionally, experts and those instructing them should be aware that some cases will be governed by the specific pre-action protocols and some may be 'specialist proceedings' (CPR 49) where specific rules may apply.

The Guidance runs to 91 paragraphs and is essential reading for experts and those who instruct them.

10.11.1   Expert immunity

Historically, experts who gave evidence in court had immunity from being sued for professional negligence by the party instructing them. The reasoning behind this was to ensure that experts, whose primary duty is to the court, were not reluctant to provide evidence which might be contrary to the interests of their instructing party.

Similar arguments had been used in the past to justify immunity from suit for advocates, but that immunity had been swept away by *Arthur J S Hall v Simons* [2002] 1 AC 615, HL.

In *Jones v Kaney* [2011] UKSC 13 the Supreme Court decided that the time had come to treat experts in the same way and abolish their immunity. Lord Philips stated (at para 56):

> An expert will be well aware of his duty to the court and that if he frankly accepts that he has changed his view it will be apparent that he is performing that duty. I do not see why he should be concerned that this will result in his being sued for breach of duty. It is paradoxical to postulate that in order to persuade an expert to perform the duty that he has undertaken to his client it is necessary to give him immunity from liability for breach of that duty.

10.11.2   Human rights

The case of *Daniels v Walker (Practice Note)* [2000] 1 WLR 1382, provided an interesting insight into how the courts will treat arguments under the Human Rights Act 1998 in relation to the provisions of CPR 1998. The case concerned the use of a single joint expert. The defendant disagreed with the joint expert's report and wanted to instruct another expert. One of the defendant's arguments was that failure to allow the defendant to do this would amount to a breach of Article 6 of the European Convention on Human Rights.

Lord Woolf gave this argument short shrift and said:

Article 6 could not possibly have any application to the issues on the present appeal. The provisions of the CPR made it clear that the obligation on the court was to deal with cases justly.

It would seem, therefore, that attempts to challenge the validity of CPR 1998 on human rights grounds will be met with the riposte that their overriding objective – to deal with cases justly – ensures compliance with the provisions of the European Convention on Human Rights.

10.12   EXCHANGE OF WITNESS STATEMENTS

The requirement that the parties exchange the evidence they intend to call at the trial is another exception to the rules on privilege. As with expert evidence, the parties only have to exchange statements of witnesses who are going to give oral evidence at the trial. If a solicitor has a statement from a witness who does not support the client's case, that statement remains privileged and need not be exchanged.

Again, as with expert evidence, the full statement must be exchanged. A solicitor must not edit out damaging comments in the course of an otherwise favourable statement. They cannot omit something with a view to catching the other party by surprise at the trial. By r 32.10 of CPR 1998, a party will need the permission of the court to call evidence which has not previously been exchanged. The court is unlikely to grant leave if the omission was deliberate. In cases of accidental omission, permission to use the evidence might be granted, but the court would almost certainly grant the other side an adjournment to enable them to consider the new material. It will usually order the party in default to pay the costs wasted by their breach of CPR 1998.

Full details of the rules on exchange of witness statements are set out in the Legal Practice Guide, **Civil Litigation**.

Exchange of witness statements provides the best opportunity to review the case with the client. The parties now know as much about the case as they are going to know (subject to the possible use of requests for further information). It is now possible to make a sensible assessment of the likely outcome of the trial. There will be some cases where it is obvious that the conflict of evidence is so great that the result will depend on the impression that the judge forms of the witnesses. In most cases, however, if the client is litigating as a matter of business rather than as a matter of principle, it will be clear by now whether the case should be settled and, if so, on what terms.

If the matter does come to trial, the exchanged statements will usually stand as the evidence-in-chief of the witness under r 32.5(2) so that the witnesses have to attend only for cross-examination and re-examination.

10.13   FURTHER INFORMATION

In some cases, the exchange of witness statements will still leave the result of the case in doubt. In such cases, one or both of the parties may want to request further information under Part 18 of CPR 1998 in an attempt to clarify their position. Such requests will be granted, however, only if they are likely to help achieve the overriding objective to deal with cases justly (see **Chapter 1**).

10.14   NOTICES TO ADMIT FACTS

Notices to admit facts should be used wherever possible to save time and costs at the trial. Service of a notice to admit facts pressurises the other party to admit facts they know can be proved against them, because if they do not admit those facts, they will have to pay the costs of proving those facts irrespective of the result of the case.

10.15　DETENTION, PRESERVATION AND INSPECTION OF PROPERTY

The court can order that property which is the subject matter of the action shall be detained, preserved, inspected, sampled or experimented on. If a party needs such an order, they will usually seek it at a very early stage of the case, or even before commencing proceedings.

10.16　BANKERS' BOOKS

Sometimes a party needs information about the financial circumstances of their opponent (eg for enforcement or in support of a freezing injunction). The opponent's bank will have that information, but it owes its customer a duty of confidentiality and therefore cannot provide the information unless ordered to do so by a court. Under s 7 of the Bankers' Books Evidence Act 1879 the court can permit a party to inspect and copy bank records for the purposes of the action. The order may be sought without notice to the other party. The bank should be given three days' notice before it has to comply with the order so that it can challenge it if it sees fit.

The application is supported by evidence stating:

(a)　the nature of the proceedings;

(b)　why inspection is required (and that the entries are admissible evidence);

(c)　the period for which inspection is required.

A party cannot use this Act to inspect privileged material.

10.17　SUMMARY

Commercial litigation often involves large amounts of 'documentary' evidence (bearing in mind that material stored on computer is treated in the same way as any paper document). As a result, it is important for clients and lawyers to understand their duties, the rules on disclosure and production, together with the rules on privilege and the different types of documents involved in modern day commercial litigation.

CHAPTER 11

APPEALS

LEARNING OUTCOMES

After reading this chapter you will understand:

- the rules relating to the conduct of appeals in Part 52 of CPR 1998 and the destination of appeals
- the procedure relating to appeals and the time limits for making an appeal.

11.1 INTRODUCTION

The system of appeals in the civil justice system in England and Wales was considered by Lord Woolf in his final *Access to Justice* report (HMSO, July 1996) where he defined the purpose of appeals in these terms:

> Appeals serve two purposes: the private purpose, which is to do justice in particular cases by correcting wrong decisions, and the public purpose, which is to ensure public confidence in the administration of justice by making such corrections and to clarify and develop the law and to set precedents.

A party against whom a judgment or order of the High Court has been made or a determination of a County Court can appeal the result of the hearing rather than the reasons given by the judge for reaching that result (*Anwer v Central Bridging Loans Ltd* [2022] EWCA Civ 201).

So, who can make an appeal? What can be appealed against? Is permission required to make an appeal? On what grounds may an appeal be granted? We will endeavour to answer these questions in this chapter.

11.2 PART 52

Part 52 of the CPR 1998 and the accompanying Practice Directions provide a comprehensive framework for the civil appeals system as it relates to the County Court, High Court and Court of Appeal. It starts with the following important terminology. The 'appeal court' means the court to which an appeal is made. The 'lower court' is the court, tribunal or other person or body from whose decision an appeal is brought. The 'appellant' means a person who brings or seeks to bring an appeal. The 'respondent' is a person other than the appellant who was a party to the proceedings in the lower court and who is affected by the appeal, as well as any person who is permitted by the appeal court to be a party to the appeal.

A crucial aspect of the system is the requirement for permission to appeal – there is generally no automatic right to appeal. By r 52.3, subject only to a few specialist exceptions, an appellant or respondent requires permission to appeal from a decision of a judge in the County Court or the High Court.

A request for permission to appeal can be made orally to the lower court at the hearing at which the decision to be appealed was made or any adjournment of that hearing. If the request is unsuccessful, or no request is made, then the party must apply for permission from the appeal court itself (*FG Financing Ltd & Anor v Lagun* [2023] EWHC 126 (Comm)). A request for permission from the appeal court should be included in the appeal notice (see **11.5**).

The appeal court will usually deal with a request for permission on paper, without a hearing. If the request is refused, the appellant may request an oral hearing. If the request is refused at the oral hearing, that is the end of the matter – there is no further appeal from this final refusal of permission to appeal by the appeal court.

For first appeals, permission to appeal will be given only where the court considers that the appeal would have a real prospect of success or there is some other compelling reason why the appeal should be heard. In *Tanfern Ltd v Cameron-MacDonald* [2000] 1 WLR 1311, Brooke LJ stated that 'real prospect of success' has the same meaning as the test applied in applications for summary judgment. There has to be a realistic, as opposed to a fanciful, prospect of success.

The other ground for granting permission to appeal – there is some other compelling reason why the appeal should be heard – could apply, for example, if there is an important question of law or general policy at stake which requires consideration by the Court of Appeal. This might justify a 'leapfrog appeal' (see **11.3.1**).

What if the appeal is being made against a case management decision such as disclosure, filing of witness statements or experts' reports, directions about the timetable of the claim, adding a party to a claim or security for costs? In addition to the above, the court dealing with the application may take into account whether:

(a)   the issue is of sufficient significance to justify the costs of an appeal;

(b)   the procedural consequences of an appeal (eg loss of trial date) outweigh the significance of the case management decision;

(c)   it would be more convenient to determine the issue at or after trial.

11.3   DESTINATION OF APPEALS

Paragraph 3.5 of PD 52A sets out to which court or judge an appeal is to be made. This may be summarised as follows:

Decision of:	Appeal made to:
District judge of the County Court	Circuit judge
Master or district judge of the High Court	High Court judge
Circuit judge	High Court judge
High Court judge	Court of Appeal

The appeal therefore will normally lie to the 'next court up'. However, this is subject to certain qualifications designed to restrict the possibility of multiple appeals (as to which see **11.3.1**).

11.3.1   'Leapfrog appeals'

Where an appeal is to be heard by a circuit judge or High Court judge, r 52.23 gives the court power to order the appeal to be transferred to the Court of Appeal if it would raise an important point of principle or practice, or there is some other compelling reason for the Court of Appeal to hear it.

In *Clark (Inspector of Taxes) v Perks* [2000] 4 All ER 1, the Court of Appeal suggested that the lower court's power to transfer an appeal to the Court of Appeal should be used sparingly. If the lower court is in doubt as to what to do, it can refer the case to the Master of the Rolls for consideration, as they have an identical power to transfer under s 57 of the Access to Justice Act 1999. However, s 57 does not permit the 'leapfrogging' of an application for permission to appeal, as opposed to an appeal in respect of which permission has been granted; see *In the Matter of Claims Direct Test Cases* [2002] EWCA Civ 428.

11.4 APPEALS FROM THE APPELLATE COURT

Generally, the decision of the appellate court will be the final decision in a case. Second appeals to the Court of Appeal will be very much the exception. By r 52.7, permission is required from the Court of Appeal for any appeal to that court from a decision of the County Court or the High Court which was itself made on appeal.

The Court of Appeal will not give permission unless it considers that (a) the appeal would (i) have a real prospect of success, and (ii) raise an important point of principle or practice; or (b) there is some other compelling reason for the Court of Appeal to hear it.

One reason behind this provision is undoubtedly to deter those litigants who refuse to accept a court's decision and want to appeal as far as they can, or could, go. It should be noted, however, that the prohibition on appeals from the appellate court without permission from the Court of Appeal applies equally to a party who was successful at first instance but then lost the appeal.

11.5 PROCEDURE

If permission to appeal is obtained from the lower court, the appellant must file the appropriate notice in Form N161 (a copy appears at **Appendix 17** to this book) at the appeal court. The time for doing so is normally within the period specified by the lower court or otherwise 21 days after the date of the decision of the lower court which the appellant wishes to appeal.

If an extension of time is needed, the appellant should apply to the appeal court.

Unless the appeal court orders otherwise, the notice must be served on the respondent as soon as practicable, but in any event not later than seven days after it is filed.

If permission to appeal was refused by the lower court, or no application for permission was made, an application for permission from the appellate court must be made in the appropriate section of Form N161.

The grounds of appeal should be set out in Form N161. These should set out clearly why the appellant says:

(a)   that the decision of the lower court is wrong; or
(b)   that the decision of the lower court is unjust because of a serious procedural or other irregularity,

as these are the grounds upon which the appeal court can allow the appeal (r 52.21(3)).

Detailed provisions about the documents to be lodged with the court prior to the hearing of the appeal can be found in PD 52B for appeals in the County Court and High Court, and in PD 52C for appeals to the Court of Appeal.

11.5.1 Respondent's notice (r 52.13)

If the respondent simply wishes the appellate court to uphold the judgment of the lower court, there is no obligation to file a respondent's notice.

However, if the respondent wants to ask the appeal court to uphold the order of the lower court for reasons different from or additional to those originally given by the lower court (as will often be the case), they must file a respondent's notice in Form N162. The respondent must also do so if they wish to seek permission to appeal from the appeal court (a cross-appeal). As to the distinction between an appeal and cross-appeal, see *Braceurself Ltd v NHS England* [2023] EWCA Civ 837 and *Morton and Another v Morton* [2023] EWCA Civ 700.

The time limit for the respondent to file the notice is, in essence, 14 days after it has become clear that the appeal will proceed.

The respondent's notice must be served on the appellant as soon as practicable but in any event within seven days of being filed.

11.5.2 Hearing of the appeal

The general rule is that every appeal will be limited to a review of the decision of the lower court, rather than a complete rehearing (CPR 1998, r 52.21).

Unless it orders otherwise, the appeal court will not hear oral evidence or evidence which was not before the lower court. An example of a situation where the court did decide to allow the appellant to adduce new evidence was *Gillingham v Gillingham* [2001] 1 All ER 52, where a letter containing crucial evidence was allowed to be used although it had not been available at the original hearing.

The appeal court will allow an appeal only if it concludes that the decision of the lower court was wrong or unjust because of a serious procedural or other irregularity in the proceedings in the lower court.

11.6 SUMMARY

There is no automatic right of appeal in civil cases – permission to appeal is invariably required.

Permission can be obtained either from the court which made the decision to be appealed, or from the court which will hear the appeal.

The procedure and time limits for appeals are set out in CPR 1998, Part 52.

SETTLEMENT AND ALTERNATIVES TO LITIGATION

LEARNING OUTCOMES

After reading this chapter you will understand:

- how to use Part 36 of CPR 1998
- the role of ADR in commercial dispute resolution.

12.1 INTRODUCTION

The vast majority of commercial disputes are resolved not by a judge at trial but by the parties reaching a settlement in one form or another. Many disputes are settled without court proceedings being issued; and even where they are issued, most cases will settle before trial. The traditional way of settling disputes has been by direct negotiation between the parties' solicitors. Increasingly, however, disputes are now settled by use of one of the methods of alternative dispute resolution (ADR), most commonly mediation.

In this chapter we shall consider the ways in which parties may settle, together with the use of the Civil Procedure Rules to aid settlement, before going on to consider in the next two chapters two particular alternatives to litigation, namely, arbitration and mediation.

12.2 NEGOTIATED SETTLEMENTS

12.2.1 Disputes settled before the issue of proceedings

Many cases settle in this way. The Civil Procedure Rules themselves, particularly through the Practice Direction on Pre-action Conduct and the Protocols, are designed to encourage settlement of cases without the need for proceedings to be issued. Sanctions, normally in the form of costs, can be inflicted on a party who is deemed by the court to have behaved unreasonably in refusing to settle a case.

Where a dispute is settled without the need for proceedings, it is imperative that the terms of settlement are clearly recorded in writing. Any such agreement should also make it clear whether or not the terms of settlement include the payment of costs and/or interest. If one party does agree to pay the other party's costs then either a figure can be agreed as a term of the settlement, or provided the liability for costs is clearly set out in the agreement, the party entitled to the costs can apply to the court under Part 8 of CPR 1998 for the court to assess those costs. If a party fails to comply with the terms of a settlement (for example by not paying an agreed figure for compensation) then the other party could simply issue proceedings and, if the defaulting party attempts to defend those proceedings, make an application for summary judgment under Part 24 of CPR 1998 on the basis that the defaulting party has no defence with a real prospect of success. This should be fairly straightforward, provided the terms of agreement are clearly expressed.

12.2.2 Settlement after the issue of proceedings

Where a case is settled after the issue of proceedings then the usual way to record that settlement is either by way of a consent order or a *Tomlin* order, whereby the proceedings are stayed on the agreed terms. Again, any agreement reached on the issue of costs and/or interest should be set out as part of the order. See Legal Practice Guide, *Civil Litigation* at **13.3.2**.

12.3 THE USE OF PART 36

A good understanding of Part 36 of CPR 1998 and how to use it effectively in litigation is a key skill for a dispute resolution lawyer. Where proceedings are issued, at some stage in virtually every case it is to be expected that one or other of the parties may make a Part 36 offer. Whilst under r 44.3 of CPR 1998 the court can take into account any admissible offer to settle proceedings in deciding the issue of costs, the advantage of making an offer under Part 36 is that the cost consequences are far more certain.

12.3.1 Costs orders and the impact of Part 36

Traditionally, a solicitor would advise a client at the start of the case that at the end of the case the loser will usually be ordered to pay the winner's reasonable costs – albeit that they would not necessarily be the same as the costs payable by the client to the solicitor under the terms of the retainer. This is embodied in r 44.2(2)(a) of CPR 1998. However, in complex cases where there are several issues to decide, it may be more difficult to ascertain exactly who is the 'winner' in relation to each of the issues before the court.

An example of this came in the case of *Multiplex Constructions (UK) Ltd v Cleveland Bridge UK Ltd* [2008] EWHC 2280 (TCC) (arising out of the construction of Wembley Stadium) and is of general application. The *Multiplex* case was a complex construction dispute involving many issues between the parties. Both parties succeeded and failed on some issues. The end result was that the defendant had to pay the claimant £6.154 million.

The court then had to determine what was the appropriate order for costs. After reviewing the authorities, Mr Justice Jackson derived the following eight principles:

(i) In commercial litigation where each party has claims and asserts that a balance is owing in its own favour, the party which ends up receiving payment should generally be characterised as the overall winner of the entire action.

(ii) In considering how to exercise its discretion the court should take as its starting point the general rule that the successful party is entitled to an order for costs.

(iii) The judge must then consider what departures are required from that starting point, having regard to all the circumstances of the case.

(iv) Where the circumstances of the case require an issue-based costs order, that is what the judge should make. However, the judge should hesitate before doing so, because of the practical difficulties which this causes and because of the steer given by rule 44.2(7).

(v) In many cases the judge can and should reflect the relative success of the parties on different issues by making a proportionate costs order.

(vi) In considering the circumstances of the case the judge will have regard not only to part 36 offers made but also to each party's approach to negotiations (insofar as admissible) and general conduct of the litigation.

(vii) If (a) one party makes an order offer under part 36 or an admissible offer within rule 44.2(4)(c) which is nearly but not quite sufficient, and (b) the other party rejects that offer outright without any attempt to negotiate, then it might be appropriate to penalise the second party in costs.

(viii) In assessing a proportionate costs order the judge should consider what costs are referable to each issue and what costs are common to several issues. It will often be reasonable for the overall winner to recover not only the costs specific to the issues which he has won but also the common costs.

In the *Multiplex* case itself, the application of these principles to the facts of the case resulted in the defendant being ordered to pay 20% of the claimant's costs.

As part of the Jackson reforms introduced in April 2013, CPR 1998, (now) r 36.17(4) was amended to increase the sanctions imposed on a defendant who fails to accept a claimant's Part 36 offer and where judgment thereafter against the defendant is at least as advantageous to the claimant as the proposals contained in that Part 36 offer. In this situation, in addition to the costs and interest sanctions which were already in place, the defendant will normally have to pay an additional amount of 10% of the damages awarded in the case of damages up to £500,000, and 5% of the damages above that figure, up to a maximum additional amount of £75,000. This additional provision is clearly intended to encourage defendants to think carefully before rejecting a reasonable Part 36 offer from the claimant.

In commercial cases, the party receiving a Part 36 offer may not be able to comply with the usual terms for payment within 14 days of acceptance. Indeed, in *Palladian Partners LP v Republic of Argentina* [2023] EWHC 1424 (Comm), the defendant country relied on the state of its economy at the time the offer was made as a reason for not accepting it. However, as Picken J pointed out, it was open to the defendant to have approached the claimants with a counter proposal concerning timing and to have explored with the claimants a regime as regards timing which would have accommodated the difficulties.

12.4 ALTERNATIVES TO LITIGATION

As briefly considered in **Chapter 1**, there is a whole range of ADR options available today, and it is the professional duty of a solicitor to be able to advise a client appropriately on that range of options. Failure to do so may amount to a breach of Principle 7 of the SRA Code of Conduct 2019 – to act in the best interests of your client.

A convenient method of categorising the various ADR options is as determinative methods (ie those which result in a binding decision) and non-determinative methods (ie evaluative processes which result in a voluntary settlement agreement). Determinative ADR processes include the following:

(a) *Arbitration.* This is the most important of the determinative processes and has been in existence for many years. It is considered in detail in **Chapter 13**.

(b) *Expert determination.* In this process the parties agree to appoint an expert who will make a binding decision. Obviously this is an appropriate process only if the parties are prepared to agree to accept the expert's decision. It is perhaps most appropriate in cases where, for example, a valuation is required or a decision is needed on a specific technical point.

(c) *Med-Arb.* This is a two-stage process whereby initially the parties agree to go to mediation, but if that fails to result in a settlement, an arbitration will follow. That of course will produce a binding result.

(d) *Final offer arbitration.* In this form of ADR, the parties agree to appoint a neutral third party to whom they submit their offers of settlement. That third party then chooses one of the settlement offers and the parties are bound by that.

(e) *Statutory adjudication.* This procedure is available under the Housing Grants, Construction and Regeneration Act 1996 to resolve commercial construction disputes and is intended to be quicker and cheaper than arbitration. Parties can have a binding decision within around 35 days. The adjudicator determines disputes that arise in the course of a construction project so that it is not delayed by a lengthy disagreement and/

or litigation or arbitration. The parties may retain the right to litigate the dispute on completion of the project if they so choose. Subject to this, the adjudicator's decision is binding. However, it can be enforced only by issuing proceedings and applying for a summary judgment (*Macob Civil Engineering Limited v Morrison Construction Limited* (1999) 3 EGLR 7, QBD). Such proceedings should be issued in the TCC.

Non-determinative forms of ADR give the parties more control over the outcome. They include:

(a)   *Negotiation between the parties.* We have already considered this at **12.2** above.

(b)   *Mediation.* This is basically an assisted negotiation between the parties facilitated by a neutral third party. Mediation is considered in detail in **Chapter 14**.

(c)   *Conciliation.* This is a more proactive version of mediation, with the third party actively encouraging the parties to settle the dispute by making suggestions regarding the parties' settlement options.

(d)   *Mini-trial.* This normally comprises a tribunal of three people: a neutral chair and a senior representative from each party. Each side makes a presentation to the tribunal which then retires to discuss the dispute. Unless the parties request it, the chair does not make a binding determination.

(e)   *Expert appraisal.* Unlike expert determination, this is a process whereby the expert is asked for their opinion but it is not binding on the parties.

(f)   *Early neutral evaluation.* This is a procedure available in the Commercial Court and the TCC whereby a judge will offer their view of the merits of each party's case. If settlement is not reached then the judge will have no further involvement in the action.

12.5   CHOOSING ADR

A solicitor should discuss with the client the possible uses of ADR whenever a dispute arises in a commercial matter. If the client is willing (or has already agreed) to use ADR, it should be used unless it is obviously inappropriate, for example because an injunction is required or the other party cannot be trusted to comply with an award or to cooperate in the process. In *Dunnett v Railtrack plc* [2002] 2 All ER 850 the Court of Appeal refused to make a costs order against an unsuccessful appellant because the respondent had refused to consider the use of arbitration or mediation to settle the dispute, despite the court, when granting permission to appeal, making a strong suggestion to that effect. There is no point, however, in proceeding with ADR if it looks like failing. In such cases, at the first sign of non-cooperation or lack of trust (eg where the opponent will not help in the selection of the neutral), litigation or arbitration should be used. In *Hurst v Leeming* [2003] 1 Lloyd's Rep 379, the court held that a barrister was justified in refusing to proceed to mediation in a professional negligence case where the attitude and character of the claimant made it very unlikely that mediation would succeed. This does not necessarily mean abandoning ADR. It may be appropriate to continue with ADR in conjunction with litigation, using the latter as a spur to cooperation with the former.

In *Halsey v Milton Keynes General NHS Trust* [2004] EWCA Civ 576 the Court of Appeal laid down guidelines as to the factors which may be relevant to the question of whether a party has unreasonably refused ADR, which may lead the court to depart from the general rule on costs in r 44.3 (that the unsuccessful party will be ordered to pay the costs of the successful party). The Court stated that these factors include, but are not limited to, the following:

(a)   the nature of the dispute;

(b)   the merits of the case;

(c)   the extent to which other settlement methods have been attempted;

(d)   whether the costs of the ADR would be disproportionately high;

(e)   whether any delay in setting up and attending the ADR would have been prejudicial;

(f)   whether the ADR had a reasonable prospect of success.

Lord Justice Dyson, who gave the judgment in *Halsey*, then went on to expand on those guidelines as follows:

17.   **(a) The nature of the dispute.** Even the most ardent supporters of ADR acknowledge that the subject-matter of some disputes renders them intrinsically unsuitable for ADR. The Commercial Court Working Party on ADR stated in 1999:

> 'The Working Party believes that there are many cases within the range of Commercial Court work which do not lend themselves to ADR procedures. The most obvious kind is where the parties wish the court to determine issues of law or construction which may be essential to the future trading relations of the parties, as under an on-going long term contract, or where the issues are generally important for those participating in a particular trade or market. There may also be issues which involve allegations of fraud or other commercially disreputable conduct against an individual or group which most probably could not be successfully mediated.'

Other examples falling within this category are cases where a party wants the court to resolve a point of law which arises from time to time, and it is considered that a binding precedent would be useful; or cases where injunctive or other relief is essential to protect the position of a party. But in our view, most cases are not by their very nature unsuitable for ADR.

18.   **(b) The merits of the case.** The fact that a party reasonably believes that he has a strong case is relevant to the question whether he has acted reasonably in refusing ADR. If the position were otherwise, there would be considerable scope for a claimant to use the threat of costs sanctions to extract a settlement from the defendant even where the claim is without merit. Courts should be particularly astute to this danger. Large organisations, especially public bodies, are vulnerable to pressure from claimants who, having weak cases, invite mediation as a tactical ploy. They calculate that such a defendant may at least make a nuisance-value offer to buy off the cost of a mediation and the risk of being penalised in costs for refusing a mediation even if ultimately successful.

19.   Some cases are clear-cut. A good example is where a party would have succeeded in an application for summary judgment pursuant to CPR 24.2, but for some reason he did not make such an application. Other cases are more border-line. In truly border-line cases, the fact that a party refused to agree to ADR because he thought that he would win should be given little or no weight by the court when considering whether the refusal to agree to ADR was reasonable. Border-line cases are likely to be suitable for ADR unless there are significant countervailing factors which tip the scales the other way. In Hurst, Lightman J said:

> 'The fact that a party believes that he has a watertight case again is no justification for refusing mediation. That is the frame of mind of so many litigants.'

In our judgment, this statement should be qualified. The fact that a party unreasonably believes that his case is watertight is no justification for refusing mediation. But the fact that a party reasonably believes that he has a watertight case may well be sufficient justification for a refusal to mediate.

20.   **(c) Other settlement methods have been attempted.** The fact that settlement offers have already been made, but rejected, is a relevant factor. It may show that one party is making efforts to settle, and that the other party has unrealistic views of the merits of the case. But it is also right to point out that mediation often succeeds where previous attempts to settle have failed. Although the fact that settlement offers have already been made is potentially relevant to the question whether a refusal to mediate is unreasonable, on analysis it is in truth no more than an aspect of factor (f).

21.   **(d) The costs of mediation would be disproportionately high.** This is a factor of particular importance where, on a realistic assessment, the sums at stake in the litigation are comparatively small. A mediation can sometimes be at least as expensive as a day in court. The parties will often have legal representation before the mediator, and the mediator's fees will usually be borne equally by the parties regardless of the outcome (although the costs of a mediation may be the subject of a costs order by the court after a trial). Since the prospects of a successful mediation cannot be predicted with confidence (see further para 27 below), the possibility of the ultimately successful party being required to incur the costs of an abortive

mediation is a relevant factor that may be taken into account in deciding whether the successful party acted unreasonably in refusing to agree to ADR.

22.   **(e) Delay.** If mediation is suggested late in the day, acceptance of it may have the effect of delaying the trial of the action. This is a factor which it may be relevant to take into account in deciding whether a refusal to agree to ADR was unreasonable.

23.   **(f) Whether the mediation had a reasonable prospect of success.** In *Hurst*, Lightman J said that he considered that the 'critical factor' in that case was whether 'objectively viewed' a mediation had any real prospect of success. He continued (p 381):

> 'If mediation can have no real prospect of success, a party may, with impunity, refuse to proceed to mediation on this ground. But refusal is a high risk course to take, for if the Court finds that there was a real prospect, the party refusing to proceed to mediation may, as I have said, be severely penalized. Further, the hurdle in the way of a party refusing to proceed to mediation on this ground is high, for in making this objective assessment of the prospects of mediation, the starting point must surely be the fact that the mediation process itself can and often does bring about a more sensible and more conciliatory attitude on the part of the parties than might otherwise be expected to prevail before the mediation, and may produce a recognition of the strengths and weaknesses by each party of his own case and of that of his opponent, and a willingness to accept the give and take essential to a successful mediation. What appears to be incapable of mediation before the mediation process begins often proves capable of satisfactory resolution later.'

24.   Consistently with the view expressed in this passage, Lightman J said that on the facts of that case he was persuaded that 'quite exceptionally' the successful party was justified in taking the view that mediation was not appropriate because it had no realistic prospects of success.

25.   In our view, the question whether the mediation had a reasonable prospect of success will often be relevant to the reasonableness of A's refusal to accept B's invitation to agree to it. But it is not necessarily determinative of the fundamental question, which is whether the successful party acted unreasonably in refusing to agree to mediation. This can be illustrated by a consideration of two cases. In a situation where B has adopted a position of intransigence, A may reasonably take the view that a mediation has no reasonable prospect of success because B is most unlikely to accept a reasonable compromise. That would be a proper basis for concluding that a mediation would have no reasonable prospect of success, and that for this reason A's refusal to mediate was reasonable.

26.   On the other hand, if A has been unreasonably obdurate, the court might well decide, on that account, that a mediation would have had no reasonable prospect of success. But obviously this would not be a proper reason for concluding that A's refusal to mediate was reasonable. A successful party cannot rely on his own unreasonableness in such circumstances. We do not, therefore, accept that, as suggested by Lightman J, it is appropriate for the court to confine itself to a consideration of whether, viewed objectively, a mediation would have had a reasonable prospect of success. That is an unduly narrow approach: it focuses on the nature of the dispute, and leaves out of account the parties' willingness to compromise and the reasonableness of their attitudes.

27.   Nor should it be overlooked that the potential success of a mediation may not only depend on the willingness of the parties to compromise. Some disputes are inherently more intractable than others. Some mediators are more skilled than others. It may therefore, sometimes be difficult for the court to decide whether the mediation would have had a reasonable prospect of success.

28.   The burden should not be on the refusing party to satisfy the court that mediation had no reasonable prospect of success. As we have already stated, the fundamental question is whether it has been shown by the unsuccessful party that the successful party unreasonably refused to agree to mediation. The question whether there was a reasonable prospect that a mediation would have been successful is but one of a number of potentially relevant factors which may need to be considered in determining the answer to that fundamental question. Since the burden of proving an unreasonable refusal is on the unsuccessful party, we see no reason why the burden of proof should lie on the successful party to show that mediation did not have any reasonable prospect of success. In most cases it would not be possible for the successful party to

prove that a mediation had no reasonable prospect of success. In our judgment, it would not be right to stigmatise as unreasonable a refusal by the successful party to agree to a mediation unless he showed that a mediation had no reasonable prospect of success. That would be to tip the scales too heavily against the right of a successful party to refuse a mediation and insist on an adjudication of the dispute by the court. It seems to us that a fairer balance is struck if the burden is placed on the unsuccessful party to show that there was a reasonable prospect that mediation would have been successful. This is not an unduly onerous burden to discharge: he does not have to prove that a mediation would in fact have succeeded. It is significantly easier for the unsuccessful party to prove that there was a reasonable prospect that a mediation would have succeeded than for the successful party to prove the contrary.

The Court of Appeal reaffirmed these principles in *Burchell v Bullard* [2005] EWCA Civ 358. Ward LJ stated:

> The court [in *Halsey*] has given its stamp of approval to mediation and it is now the legal profession which must become fully aware of and acknowledge its value. The profession can no longer with impunity shrug aside reasonable requests to mediate. The parties cannot ignore a proper request to mediate simply because it was made before the claim was issued.

This final point is reinforced by para 8 of the Practice Direction on Pre-action Conduct which states that whilst ADR is not compulsory, the parties should consider whether some form of ADR procedure might enable them to settle the matter without starting proceedings.

However, in *Daniels v The Commissioner of Police for the Metropolis* [2005] EWCA Civ 1312, the Court of Appeal made it clear that it was entirely reasonable for a defendant, especially a public body such as the police, to refuse to use ADR in circumstances where it wished to contest what it considered to be an unfounded claim. The successful defendants were entitled to their costs.

Whilst 'ordinarily, simple animosity between parties is no basis to refuse mediation', in *Mills & Reeve Trust Corporation Ltd v Martin and others* [2023] EWHC 654 (Ch), Kelly J observed that the case was:

> not an ordinary case of simple animosity ... the fact that the Defendants over a 27 year period have not really agreed about anything to do with the estate bodes ill for the prospects of success of any form of ADR. It is an intractable dispute. Given the strongly held and unwavering views given recently by the First, Second, Third and Sixth Defendants that they will not contemplate mediation or other ADR as there is simply nothing to talk about, ordering a stay and encouraging ADR will just delay matters further before there is a resolution ... Whilst I accept the proposition that some litigants need saving from themselves and using mediation is a good tool to settle disputes, I do not accept that this by itself means an order for a stay for facilitation of mediation or other ADR will assist here. It may well have been that mediation would have assisted at an earlier stage, before the position reached now where the trustees have decided what they wish to do and seek the blessing of the court for their proposed course of action, a decision having been made upon it.

What is the position where one party simply fails to respond to a proposal to use ADR? This point came before the court in *PGF II SA v OMFS Company 1 Ltd* [2013] EWCA Civ 1288. The case concerned a claim for the alleged breach of a tenant's repairing covenants in a commercial lease. The claimant's claim was originally for more than £1.9 million. The defendant denied liability entirely. At or shortly before the commencement of proceedings the claimant made a Part 36 offer of £1.125 million.

Several months later, on 11 April 2011, there was an exchange of e-mail correspondence. The claimant made a second Part 36 offer of £1.25 million plus interest. In a separate letter the claimant invited the defendant to take part in mediation, proposing various dates. The letter concluded by seeking the defendant's agreement to mediate and/or an explanation of any refusal. On the same day the defendant sent the claimant a Part 36 offer of £700,000 inclusive of interest. So the gap between the parties was now £550,000.

Neither Part 36 offer was accepted. The claimant's invitation to mediate received no response from the defendant of any kind. On 19 July the claimant sent a further invitation to the defendant to mediate: 'Please confirm whether your client is willing to attend a mediation and, if so, provide us with dates of availability. If you are not prepared to attend a mediation, please could you let us know why.' A chasing letter was sent on 1 August. There was still no response.

On 20 December the claimant made a further Part 36 offer of £1.05 million plus interest, narrowing the gap to £350,000 plus interest.

The trial was to start on 11 January 2012. In its skeleton argument, exchanged on 10 January, the defendant took up for the first time the point that the air conditioning system in respect of which about £250,000 was claimed for dilapidations, did not form part of the demise. The defendant gave notice of its intention to seek leave to amend its defence to that effect the next day.

The claimant responded the same day by accepting the defendant's Part 36 offer, thereby settling the proceedings save as to costs. The ordinary consequence of the acceptance would have been a costs order whereby the defendant would pay the claimant's costs up to 2 May 2011 and the claimant would pay the defendant's costs from that date until 10 January (CPR 1998, r 36.13(4) and (5)). At the hearing the next day the claimant argued that the usual costs order should not be made for two reasons: (i) the late amendment; and (ii) the unreasonable refusal to mediate (on the basis that the lack of any response equated to a refusal). The late amendment point failed, but the mediation point succeeded to the extent that the judge deprived the defendant of its costs from 2 May, although the judge did not agree with the claimant's request that the defendant pay its costs from that date. So in effect the court ordered each side to pay its own costs from 2 May 2011. The amount involved was about £250,000 for each side.

The defendant appealed and the claimant cross-appealed. Both appeals were dismissed. The defendant's arguments below had been based on three grounds:

(1)   It denied that its silence amounted to a refusal.

(2)   It denied that any deemed refusal was unreasonable.

(3)   It submitted that, since the expenditure of £250,000 odd by each side during the relevant period was attributable to the claimant's failure to accept a reasonable Part 36 offer until the day before trial, no departure from the Part 36 costs consequences should be ordered.

In his judgment in the Court of Appeal, Briggs LJ reviewed the law established in *Halsey* and the interaction of Part 36 and ADR. He referred to the focus in the Jackson Report on proportionality and its relevance to the use of ADR (at [26] and [27]):

> 26.   Secondly, the intense focus in Jackson LJ's report into civil litigation costs upon achieving proportionality between the cost of litigation and the value of that which is at stake led, as I have described, to his clear endorsement of ADR as a process which is still insufficiently understood and still under-used.

> 27.   Thirdly, the constraints which now affect the provision of state resources for the conduct of civil litigation (and which appear likely to do so for the foreseeable future) call for an ever-increasing focus upon means of ensuring that court time, both for trial and for case management, is proportionately directed towards those disputes which really need it, with an ever-increasing responsibility thrown upon the parties to civil litigation to engage in ADR, wherever that offers a reasonable prospect of producing a just settlement at proportionate cost. Just as it risks a waste of the court's resources to have to try a case which could have been justly settled, earlier and at a fraction of the cost by ADR, so it is a waste of its resources to have to manage the parties towards ADR by robust encouragement, where they could and should have engaged with each other in considering its suitability, without the need for the court's active intervention.

Briggs LJ agreed with the trial judge that silence amounted to a refusal and that the refusal was unreasonable. He was not persuaded by the defendant's counsel's argument that 'this was a hard-nosed commercial dispute about money between parties with no continuing relationship, and therefore not susceptible to the ability of a mediator to devise solutions beyond the capacity of the court to order'. He had some sympathy with the defendant's submission that the trial judge had not exercised their discretion properly in departing from the usual costs order under Part 36 in the way they did. He said, however, that whilst he would have exercised his discretion slightly differently (in that he would not have deprived the defendant of all of its costs), the way in which the trial judge had exercised their discretion was within the range of proper responses and therefore he would not interfere with the decision.

At the conclusion of his judgment (at [56]), Briggs LJ made some general remarks about ADR which are of significant importance:

> Finally, as is recognised by the weight placed on the judge's decision in the passage in the ADR Handbook to which I have referred, this case sends out an important message to civil litigants, requiring them to engage with a serious invitation to participate in ADR, even if they have reasons which might justify a refusal, or the undertaking of some other form of ADR, or ADR at some other time in the litigation. To allow the present appeal would, as it seems to me, blunt that message. The court's task in encouraging the more proportionate conduct of civil litigation is so important in current economic circumstances that it is appropriate to emphasise that message by a sanction which, even if a little more vigorous than I would have preferred, nonetheless operates *pour encourager les autres*.

The clear message from this case is that the Jackson reforms have emphasised the crucial role of ADR in our system of litigation and that parties ignore it at their peril.

12.6 THE FUTURE OF ADR

Alternative dispute resolution is becoming increasingly popular. The clear message from cases such as *Halsey* and *Burchell* is that an unreasonable refusal to use mediation, or some other suitable method of ADR, is likely to lead to costs penalties. The use of 'ADR orders' by the courts to encourage this process is likely to increase. However, forcing the parties to the negotiating table may be counterproductive, particularly during the early stages of a dispute when feelings often run high. Also, assessing whether a party has acted with a lack of good faith may be difficult unless the parties or the mediator are required to divulge privileged or confidential information. It is also possible that obliging parties to engage in ADR could be challenged as a contravention of the right to a fair trial under Article 6(1) of the European Convention on Human Rights. This was pointed out by the Court of Appeal in *Halsey v Milton Keynes General NHS Trust* (see **12.5**).

The Civil Justice Council (CJC) ADR Working Group considered the future of ADR during 2016–18 and produced its final report in November 2018. It made a number of recommendations, several of which are intended to increase public awareness of the availability of ADR, including greater encouragement of the use of ADR by government and the courts. One recommendation was that the *Halsey* guidelines for the imposition of costs sanctions should be reviewed and should narrow the circumstances in which a refusal to mediate is regarded as reasonable. It did not, however, recommend that the use of some form of ADR should be compulsory in civil proceedings.

However, following on from this, in July 2021 the CJC published another report on the legality and desirability of compulsory ADR. On legality, it concluded that parties can lawfully be compelled to take part in ADR. On desirability, it identified conditions in which compulsion to participate in ADR could be a desirable and effective development. It concluded its executive summary as follows:

> 8.   In our view, appropriate forms of compulsory ADR, where a return to the normal adjudicative process is always available, are capable of overcoming the objections voiced in the case law and elsewhere and could be introduced.

9. The rules of civil procedure in England and Wales have already developed to involve compulsory participation in ADR at a number of points. These compulsory processes are both successful and accepted.

10. Provided certain factors are borne in mind in designing the scheme, a procedural rule which requires parties to attempt ADR at a certain point or points, and/or empowers the court to make an order to that effect, is, in our opinion, compatible with Article 6 of the European Convention on Human Rights. The factors requiring consideration whenever compulsion is being considered will include:

    • the cost and time burden on the parties;

    • whether the process is particularly suitable in certain specialist areas of civil justice;

    • the importance of confidence in the ADR provider (and the role of regulation where the provider is private);

    • whether the parties engaged in the ADR need access to legal advice and whether they have it;

    • the stage(s) of proceedings at which ADR may be required; and

    • whether the terms of the obligation to participate are sufficiently clear to the parties to encourage compliance and permit enforcement.

11. It is appropriate to permit sanctions for breach of a rule or order requiring participation in ADR. If ADR is no longer 'alternative' or external to civil justice, then parties can surely be compelled to participate in ADR as readily as they can be compelled to disclose documents or explain their cases. The sanction for failure to participate may be to prevent the claim or defence continuing, either by making the commencement of proceedings conditional on entering ADR, or empowering the court to strike out a claim/defence if a party fails to comply with a compulsory ADR order at a later stage in the proceedings. Any strike-out could be set aside if there was a valid reason for non-compliance.

12. This is consistent with the use of initial prompts towards settlement in an online procedure and the active role of a case officer or judge in seeking to facilitate settlement.

13. We do not make detailed proposals for reform in this paper, but make three specific observations on the form compulsory ADR might take:

    • First, where participation in a suitable and effective form of ADR occasions no expense of time or money by the parties, making it compulsory will not usually be controversial.

    • Second, we foresee that greater use of compulsory judge-led ADR processes will prove acceptable, given they are free and appear effective in the contexts in which they are already compulsory.

    • Third, compulsory mediation may be considered, provided it is sufficiently regulated and made available where appropriate in short, affordable formats.

At the moment, there are no definite proposals to amend the rules to bring these proposals into effect for commercial litigation. The idea of compulsory ADR remains controversial within the legal profession.

ARBITRATION

LEARNING OUTCOMES

After reading this chapter you will understand:

- the context of commercial arbitration
- the importance of the arbitration agreement
- how to appoint the arbitrator
- how to commence the arbitration
- the usual procedural matters in an arbitration
- how to prepare for the arbitration hearing
- how to challenge any award made at the arbitration hearing
- how to enforce an arbitration award
- how to stay litigation brought despite there being a valid arbitration agreement.

13.1 INTRODUCTION

In the context of commercial dispute resolution, arbitration is the formal procedure whereby one or more independent parties determine a dispute. Traditionally, arbitration has been prevalent, as a means of dispute resolution, in the shipping and construction industries. Nevertheless, a lawyer may be involved in the arbitration of a wide range of disputes, from landlord and tenant, oil industry, commodities or financial markets disputes to general commercial disputes. Arbitration is considered in this broad commercial context in this chapter.

As discussed in **Chapter 1**, a dispute may be arbitrated because the original contract between the parties provides for the arbitration of any dispute. Otherwise the parties may agree to arbitrate once the dispute has arisen.

Businesspersons frequently refer their disputes to arbitration as it enables them to have those disputes resolved in private, by a person or group of people they have chosen who are experienced in the trade or business in question. Arbitration avoids a public hearing in open court by a judge who may have no special expertise about the matters in dispute, and who will, therefore, have to choose between the conflicting views of each side's expert witnesses.

Another major attraction is the international recognition and support that arbitration has achieved. Treaties such as the United Nations Convention on the Recognition and Enforcement of Foreign Arbitral Awards 1958 ('the New York Convention') ensure widespread acceptance that agreements to refer disputes to arbitration should be upheld by the courts and awards enforced, regardless of the jurisdiction in which they were made. The growth in cross-border commerce has made this increasingly important. The New York Convention has been adopted by over 150 countries. The basic premise of the Convention is to provide for a minimum international standard by which the courts of all its signatory States have to recognise and enforce awards made in another signatory State, without subjecting such an award to procedures that are more onerous than those applied to the enforcement of domestic awards.

As a result, it can be easier in practice to enforce an arbitration award in a different jurisdiction than it is to enforce a court judgment.

Arbitration also enables the parties to decide the procedure the arbitrator will follow and what their powers will be, because this is primarily governed by the terms of their agreement to arbitrate.

Arbitration agreements may be ad hoc agreements tailor-made to a particular dispute or contract. However, many other contracts contain arbitration agreements which incorporate the standard arbitration rules of an established arbitral body. Solicitors involved in arbitration will regularly come across the arbitration rules of bodies such as (among others):

(a)   Chartered Institute of Arbitrators;

(b)   London Maritime Arbitrators' Association;

(c)   Federation of Oils, Seeds and Fats Association (FOSFA);

(d)   Grain and Feed Trade Association (GAFTA);

(e)   International Chamber of Commerce (ICC);

(f)   Royal Institution of Chartered Surveyors;

(g)   Institute of Civil Engineers;

(h)   United Nations' Commission on International Trade Law (UNCITRAL);

(i)   London Court of International Arbitration;

(j)   London Bar Arbitration Scheme;

(k)   Joint Contracts Tribunal (JCT).

Some of these are trade associations or professional bodies. For example, the Royal Institution of Chartered Surveyors and the Institute of Civil Engineers provide arbitration services for construction and engineering disputes. Others are international arbitral organisations specialising in international commercial arbitration, for example ICC, based in Paris, and UNCITRAL. Often, in the case of international transactions, the parties may choose to arbitrate in a country with no connection with the dispute. This is because some countries, such as France and Switzerland, have established solid reputations in conducting arbitrations. In fact, in such countries, arbitration is an industry in itself. The rules of such international arbitral bodies are outside the scope of this book.

This book deals with arbitrations conducted in England and Wales under the Arbitration Act 1996 (AA 1996). The guiding principles behind the statute are set out in s 1:

(a)   the object of arbitration is to obtain the fair resolution of disputes by an impartial tribunal without unnecessary delay or expense;

(b)   the parties should be free to agree how their disputes are resolved, subject only to such safeguards as are necessary in the public interest;

(c)   ... the court should not intervene except as provided by [the Act].

Arbitration in England and Wales has a high reputation throughout the commercial world, both domestically and internationally. As a result, many disputes are dealt with by arbitration in this country even though neither party has any connection with this country and the contract was neither made nor performed in this country (and may not be governed by the laws of this country). Thus arbitration in England and Wales may be selected as the appropriate process for resolution of a £10,000 trade dispute between English tradesmen, as well as of a multi-million pound claim brought by a Saudi Arabian oil dealer against a Malaysian oil refiner. The latter claim may have no connection with England at all, other than the fact that England was chosen as the place of arbitration.

Generally speaking, an arbitrator has the same powers as any court. Nevertheless, in some circumstances the arbitrator will require the court's assistance. For instance, an arbitrator does not have the power to make orders such as injunctions which carry the sanction of imprisonment for non-compliance. In such cases, the parties and/or the arbitrator can seek the aid of the court under ss 42–44 of the AA 1996, so that the court can exercise its wider powers before referring the matter back to the arbitrator.

Another example is that sometimes the parties to a dispute which is being resolved by arbitration will find that the dispute turns on a point of law. Although the arbitrator may decide the point of law for themselves, this may lead to an appeal to the court on that point of law (see **13.8.3**), so it may be preferable to refer the matter to the court under s 45 for a decision on the legal point. Where court involvement is necessary, the matter will normally be dealt with in the Commercial Court. The procedure is set out in CPR 1998, Part 62 and its Practice Direction.

13.2   THE ARBITRATION AGREEMENT

13.2.1   The terms of the agreement

In *Premium Nafta Products Ltd and Others v Fili Shipping Company Ltd and Others* [2007] UKHL 40, the House of Lords reviewed the case law relating to the interpretation of arbitration clauses. The arbitration clause in the case was as follows:

41.   (a)   This charter shall be construed and the relations between the parties determined in accordance with the laws of England.

(b)   Any dispute arising under this charter shall be decided by the English courts to whose jurisdiction the parties hereby agree.

(c)   Notwithstanding the foregoing, but without prejudice to any party's right to arrest or maintain the arrest of any maritime property, either party may, by giving written notice of election to the other party, elect to have any such dispute referred ... to arbitration in London, one arbitrator to be nominated by Owners and the other by Charterers, and in case the arbitrators shall not agree to the decision of an umpire, whose decision shall be final and binding upon both parties. Arbitration shall take place in London in accordance with the London Maritime Association of Arbitrators, in accordance with the provisions of the Arbitration Act 1950, or any statutory modification or re-enactment thereof for the time being in force.

The House of Lords stated that it was time to draw a line under earlier authorities on the distinction between 'disputes arising under' and 'disputes arising out of' an agreement. The House said that its approach to the construction of the arbitration clause was governed by the principle of separability in s 7 of the AA 1996, which states:

> Unless otherwise agreed by the parties, an arbitration agreement which forms or was intended to form part of another agreement (whether or not in writing) shall not be regarded as invalid, non-existent or ineffective because that other agreement is invalid, or did not come into existence or has become ineffective, and it shall for that purpose be treated as a distinct agreement.

The House of Lords held that the construction of an arbitration clause had to start from the assumption that the parties, as rational businesspersons, were likely to have intended any dispute arising out of the relationship into which they had entered, or purported to have entered, to be decided by the same tribunal.

Therefore even if the main contract was invalid or could be rescinded, the arbitration agreement remained valid.

In this particular case, the appellants' argument was that the main agreement had been entered into as a result of bribery. However, that did not show that there was any bribery in relation to the arbitration agreement which remained valid. The arbitration agreement could only be invalidated on a ground which related directly to it.

A clause used by the Chartered Institute of Arbitrators for parties who wish to have future disputes referred to arbitration says:

> Any dispute arising out of or in connection with this contract shall be referred to and finally resolved by arbitration under the Rules of the Chartered Institute of Arbitrators, which Rules are deemed to be incorporated by reference to this clause.

This appears comprehensive enough to cover any dispute which might arise, whether it be about the existence, creation, performance or termination of the contract, or about related pre-contractual matters.

In *Enka Insaat Ve Sanayi AS v OOO Insurance Company Chubb* [2020] UKSC 38, the Supreme Court had to consider how the governing law of an arbitration agreement is to be determined when the law applicable to the contract containing it differs from the 'seat' of the arbitration. The case concerned a power plant in Russia which was severely damaged by fire. The contract contained an arbitration clause under which the seat of the arbitration was London but did not specifically state which law would apply to the arbitration. However, the law applicable to the parties' substantive contractual obligations was Russian law. The court, by a 3:2 majority, held that in this situation the arbitration agreement was governed by the law with which it was most closely connected and that would generally be the law of the seat of the arbitration – so English law in this case.

13.2.2 Incorporating the Arbitration Act 1996

The AA 1996 applies only to arbitration agreements which are in writing (s 5). However, s 5 gives a wide meaning to the term 'agreement in writing'. It covers anything which has been 'recorded by any means' (eg on a mobile phone) and includes:

(a)   exchanges of letters or other communications;

(b)   agreements evidenced in writing (either by the parties or by a third party acting with the authority of the parties); and

(c)   oral agreements to written terms.

By s 5(5), if the parties make written submissions during an arbitration or in court proceedings, and one party alleges that there is a non-written arbitration agreement and the other party does not deny this, those written submissions will create an arbitration agreement to which the AA 1996 can apply.

If there is an arbitration agreement, certain provisions of the AA 1996 are mandatory and will apply irrespective of any attempt by the parties to exclude the Act. These provisions are listed in Sch 1 to the AA 1996. The relevant mandatory provisions of the AA 1996 will be dealt with as and when they are relevant to later parts of this chapter.

A schedule of the main provisions of the AA 1996, showing which are mandatory and which are not, appears at the end of this chapter.

As far as the rest of the AA 1996 is concerned, the parties may, if they wish, make such arrangements as they see fit. The AA 1996 will apply only if the agreement does not cover a particular point which is dealt with in the Act.

13.2.3 Incorporating an arbitration clause

Even if an agreement does not contain an arbitration clause, it is possible to incorporate an arbitration clause from another document into the agreement by referring to the arbitration clause in such a way as to make it part of the agreement (s 6(2)). For example, in a construction contract, a builder and a landowner might agree in writing to refer all disputes to arbitration. The builder may then enter into a sub-contract with a plumber who will do part of the work required under the main contract. That sub-contract may not itself contain an arbitration clause, but a clause which said 'The provisions of the main contract [the contract between the builder and the landowner] shall apply to this contract unless agreed to the contrary' would be sufficient to incorporate the arbitration clause in the main contract into the sub-contract.

By s 7 of the AA 1996, even if the main contract were to be invalid, the arbitration clause would still be effective as far as the sub-contract is concerned.

13.3 APPOINTING THE ARBITRATOR

The arbitration agreement may name the arbitrator. This is rare. It is more usual for the agreement to state how the arbitrator will be appointed.

Section 15(1) provides: 'The parties are free to agree on the number of arbitrators to form the tribunal and whether there is to be a chairperson or umpire.'

13.3.1 Sole arbitrators

By s 15(3), '[i]f there is no agreement as to the number of arbitrators, the tribunal shall consist of a sole arbitrator'.

Section 16(1) makes it clear that the parties can agree their own procedure for appointing a sole arbitrator. If they have not agreed a procedure then, by s 16(3), either party can make a written request to the other to make a joint appointment within 28 days of the request.

If the agreed procedure or the s 16(3) procedure does not work, either party may apply to the court under s 18. The court's powers are listed in s 18(3), but these will not be engaged unless the appointment procedure has been followed and fails (*Global Aerospares Ltd v Airest AS* [2023] EWHC 1430 (Comm)). It will usually appoint an arbitrator, although it may simply give directions to the parties on how to proceed in making the appointment.

> **EXAMPLE**
>
> A and B have an arbitration agreement which provides that the parties shall agree on the identity of a sole arbitrator. When a dispute arises, A writes to B suggesting X as arbitrator. B objects to X as arbitrator. A asks B to suggest an alternative arbitrator. B does not respond. A can apply to the court under s 18. B will have an opportunity to make representations to the court, but if B fails to do so, the court is likely to appoint X as the sole arbitrator.

Very often, the party who initiates the arbitration will submit a list of, for example, three candidates and then the parties will try to agree on one of the candidates.

13.3.2 Three arbitrators

The arbitration agreement may specify three arbitrators. As usual, the parties are free to agree on the procedure for appointing the arbitrators. If they do not do so then, under s 16(5), each party will appoint an arbitrator within 14 days of one party requesting the other to make an appointment. The two arbitrators will then appoint a third arbitrator to act as chairperson of the tribunal.

> **EXAMPLE**
>
> A and B have an arbitration agreement which provides that there should be three arbitrators. When a dispute arises, A writes to B nominating X as an arbitrator and asking B to nominate an arbitrator. B nominates Y. X and Y meet and agree to ask Z to act as their chairperson.

13.3.2.1 One party does not make an appointment

If, in the above example, B had failed to nominate an arbitrator, A would be entitled to rely on the provisions of s 17 of the AA 1996 and give written notice to B that A proposed to appoint X as sole arbitrator. B would then have seven days to appoint B's arbitrator. If B still failed to make an appointment, A would be entitled to confirm X as sole arbitrator. B's only remedy thereafter would be to apply to the court under s 18 and ask the court to revoke X's appointment and to appoint new arbitrators or give directions as to the appointment of arbitrators. On the facts as outlined here, it is unlikely that B's application to the court would be successful.

13.3.2.2 The arbitrators cannot agree on a chairperson

If, in the above example, X and Y had been unable to agree on the identity of the third arbitrator then, unless the arbitration agreement provided otherwise (because the parties are always free to agree on some alternative procedure for dealing with problems in the appointment of an arbitrator, no matter how many arbitrators there may be), either A or B would be entitled to apply to the court under s 18 and ask the court to solve the problem.

13.3.3 Two arbitrators

A tribunal consisting of just two arbitrators creates the obvious risk that the arbitrators will not be able to agree on a solution to the dispute. It is therefore rare to have an arbitration agreement which provides for two arbitrators. The AA 1996 discourages an arrangement for two arbitrators, because s 15(2) says that any agreement which provides for an even number of arbitrators 'shall be understood as requiring the appointment of an additional arbitrator as chairperson of the tribunal'. However, the number of arbitrators is a matter for the parties to the agreement, and if they do want to have an even number of arbitrators, they can do so by expressly stating in their agreement that there shall not be a chairperson. By s 22 of the AA 1996, the parties are free to agree on how the tribunal shall exercise its powers. In the absence of any agreement, s 22 provides that decisions shall be made by a majority vote. If there is no majority and no chairperson (or umpire – see **13.3.4**), the parties will have to apply to the court for directions under s 18.

Where there are to be two arbitrators, the parties can agree on the procedure for appointing the arbitrators. In the absence of any agreement, by s 16(4) each party will appoint its own arbitrator within 14 days of a request from one party to the other to appoint an arbitrator. If one party does not make an appointment, s 17 will apply (see **13.3.2.1**).

13.3.4 Chairperson distinguished from umpire

Where there are three arbitrators, the AA 1996 assumes that one of them will be a chairperson. The parties are free to agree on the chairperson's functions. If they do not deal with this matter in their agreement then, under s 20, all decisions will be made by a majority vote (including the chairperson's vote). If, for example, there are four arbitrators and there is no majority decision, the chairperson has a casting vote.

Although it is more common to have a chairperson, s 15(1) gives the parties freedom to choose an umpire instead. A chairperson is a member of the arbitration tribunal from the outset. An umpire becomes involved later on. Thus the parties might agree to have two arbitrators and that, if the two nominated arbitrators cannot reach agreement on any matter, they shall then appoint an umpire who will resolve the contentious issue for the arbitrators.

It is, of course, for the parties to agree on the procedure for appointing any umpire, but if they have not done so, s 16(6) will apply. Each party will appoint its arbitrator in the usual way (see **13.3.3** for how this is done and how any problems with the appointment are resolved). The two arbitrators will then be free to appoint an umpire at any time. In the absence of any agreement to the contrary, s 16(6) provides that the arbitrators should appoint an umpire as soon as they are unable to agree on any matter. The AA 1996 also requires the two arbitrators to appoint an umpire before the final hearing of the case unless the parties have agreed to the contrary.

Under s 21 of the AA 1996, it is for the parties to agree on the functions of any umpire. In the absence of any agreement, the umpire will attend the proceedings and receive copies of all the papers. They will not, however, take any active part in the arbitration unless and until the arbitrators are unable to agree on a matter. If this happens, the original arbitrators will cease to act and the umpire will take over the case as if they were the sole arbitrator.

13.3.5 Appointing authorities

The parties to an arbitration agreement may agree to ask a third party (eg the President of The Law Society) to appoint an arbitrator for them. This practice has become less common since some appointing authorities started to charge substantial fees for making an appointment.

If the appointing authority fails to make an appointment, the parties can apply to the court under s 18 and ask the court to appoint an arbitrator.

13.3.6 Inability or refusal to act

If a nominated arbitrator is unable or unwilling to take up the post of arbitrator, the parties are free to agree on a procedure for appointing a replacement. If they cannot do so, they may apply to the court under s 18 and ask the court to appoint a replacement or to make directions as to how to resolve the problem.

13.4 COMMENCEMENT OF THE ARBITRATION

13.4.1 How to begin

The arbitration agreement will usually tell the parties how to begin the arbitration. A common procedure is for the applicant to send a written request to arbitrate to the respondent, setting out:

(a) the names and addresses of the parties;

(b) a brief statement of the nature and circumstances of the dispute and the relief being sought; and

(c) who the claimant thinks the arbitrators should be and/or how they should be appointed (if the claimant has to appoint an arbitrator, the request would contain the name and address of the nominated arbitrator).

The request will often be accompanied by a copy of the arbitration agreement.

For the purposes of the Limitation Acts and any time limits in the arbitration agreement itself (see **13.10**), it is necessary to determine when arbitration proceedings have commenced. The parties can reach whatever agreement they see fit on this point. If they have not reached any agreement, s 14 of the AA 1996 will help.

Under s 14, if the arbitration agreement identifies who the arbitrator shall be, the arbitration commences when one party gives written notice to the other requiring them to submit the dispute to arbitration. If, as is more usual, the parties are to appoint the arbitrator or arbitrators when a dispute arises, the arbitration will commence when one party serves the other with written notice requiring it to appoint or agree to the appointment of an arbitrator. Such notice should deal with the following points:

(a)   reference to the arbitration clause in the contract;

(b)   the dispute that has arisen;

(c)   requirement for the party to agree with the appointment of an arbitrator – often the notice will give a list of several proposed arbitrators.

Finally, if the arbitrator is to be appointed by a third party, the arbitration commences as soon as one party asks the appointing authority to make an appointment.

Note: The rest of this chapter assumes that there will be a sole arbitrator. References to the arbitrator include references to a panel of arbitrators.

13.4.2   The arbitrator's duties on being appointed

The arbitrator will be appointed shortly after the commencement of the arbitration. The claimant will send the arbitrator a copy of the arbitration agreement so that the arbitrator can decide not only that they are competent and have the time to do the job, but also that the agreement gives them power to act and that they have been validly appointed. By s 30 of AA 1996, unless otherwise agreed, it is for the arbitrator to decide whether or not there is a valid arbitration agreement, whether the tribunal is properly constituted and what matters have been submitted for arbitration.

At this stage, the arbitrator should disclose any circumstances which might lead any of the parties to doubt the arbitrator's impartiality. The Chartered Institute of Arbitrators has drawn up guidelines of good practice for arbitrators which suggest that the nominated arbitrator should reveal:

(a)   past or present business relationships with any party or important witness;

(b)   substantial social relationships with any party or important witness;

(c)   prior knowledge of the dispute;

(d)   commitments which may affect their availability.

The business or social relationships which the arbitrator should reveal include those of their family, firm and business partners.

13.4.3   Objections to the arbitrator's jurisdiction

Sections 31 and 32 of the AA 1996 deal with challenges to the arbitrator's jurisdiction. Both sections are mandatory (ie the parties cannot exclude them in their arbitration agreement). Section 31 deals with making an objection to the arbitrator; s 32 with making an objection to the court.

Under s 31, a party who wishes to object to the arbitrator's jurisdiction should do so no later than the first step they take in dealing with the merits of the application after the arbitrator has been appointed.

EXAMPLE

A has commenced arbitration proceedings against B. B has reason to believe that the arbitrator appointed by A is not a suitable arbitrator. B can raise an objection immediately or on sending in their defence to A's claim. If, however, B sends in a defence without objecting to the appointment of the arbitrator, B is deemed to have waived their right to object, although under s 31(3) the arbitrator does have a discretion to accept a late objection if they consider that the delay is justified (eg B was not aware of circumstances affecting the arbitrator's suitability when the proceedings began).

Similarly, if any party during the course of the arbitration considers that the arbitrator is exceeding their powers, that party should object immediately or may be taken to have waived the right to do so.

Where an objection is made to the arbitrator's jurisdiction, the arbitrator may deal with the point there and then, or, with the consent of the parties, defer ruling on the jurisdiction point until the arbitrator comes to deal with the merits of the substantive application.

Under s 32, a party to an arbitration may apply to the court to challenge the arbitrator's jurisdiction. A party may do this only with the consent of the other parties or with the consent of the arbitrator. If the application is made with the consent of the arbitrator, the court will consider the application only if:

(a) a decision will save substantial costs;

(b) there has been no delay in making the application; and

(c) there is good reason for the matter to be considered by the court.

Bearing in mind the general principle in s 1 of the AA 1996 that the court should not intervene in an arbitration, successful applications under s 32 are likely to be rare.

By s 73 of the AA 1996, a party who continues to take part in an arbitration after the party knew or should have known that there were grounds for objecting to the jurisdiction cannot subsequently apply to the court under s 32. The parties cannot contract out of s 73. See further **13.8.4**.

13.5 THE PRELIMINARY MEETING

Although there are no rigid procedural rules in arbitration, it is common, once the arbitrator has accepted office, for the arbitrator to arrange a preliminary meeting with the parties. This meeting is the equivalent of the case management conference in a civil case.

13.5.1 Procedure

Under s 34, it is for the arbitrator to decide all procedural and evidential matters, subject to the rights of the parties to agree their own procedure. The arbitrator decides, after consulting the parties, the timetable for resolving the dispute and the procedure to be followed. The issues which may be discussed include those set out in **13.5.1.1** to **13.5.1.7** below. The list is by no means exhaustive. Not all the points will arise in every case. The fact that the parties are able to participate in these matters is one of the great advantages of arbitration.

13.5.1.1 Statements of case

Are written statements of case necessary? If so, when should they be supplied? Can they be amended later? Is a reply needed? Is there a counterclaim? The arbitrator will arrange a timetable for this.

13.5.1.2 Documents

Is disclosure appropriate? If so, what form should it take and what should the timetable be? What documents will be admissible at the hearing of the reference, and how and when should they be presented to the arbitrator? How many copies will be needed at the hearing of the reference?

13.5.1.3 Experts

Is expert evidence needed at all, or will the parties leave the matter to the arbitrator's skill and judgement? If expert evidence is needed, will the arbitrator appoint their own expert, or will the parties call their own experts? If the parties intend to call experts, how many will there be and when (if at all) should there be mutual disclosure of reports? Is oral evidence necessary, or can the matter be disposed of solely on the basis of written reports?

13.5.1.4   Evidence

Should the arbitrator apply strict rules of evidence or not? Will the evidence be oral or documentary? Should it be disclosed in advance? Will the witnesses be sworn? Should there be written requests for further information? Are any orders needed for the preservation of evidence?

13.5.1.5   Points of law

Should points of law be referred to the High Court under s 45 of the AA 1996 (see **13.5.2**), or should the arbitrator be left to take their own legal advice or to reach their own decision in the light of submissions made by the parties' own lawyers?

13.5.1.6   Preservation of property

Under s 38(4), unless agreed to the contrary, the arbitrator can give directions regarding any property involved in the proceedings relating to the inspection, photographing, preservation, custody or detention of that property by the arbitrator, an expert or a party, or to authorise experiments and/or the taking of samples.

13.5.1.7   The hearing

Whose responsibility is it to make the arrangements for the hearing? When and where will it take place? What language should be used at the hearing (one or both of the parties may be from outside the UK) and will translations of documents be required? Will there be oral evidence or submissions, or will the arbitrator just read the documents?

13.5.2   Preliminary points of law

Under s 45 of the AA 1996, a party may apply (on giving notice to the other parties) to the court for a ruling on any question of law arising during the proceedings which substantially affects the rights of one or more of the parties. The application can be made only with the consent of all other parties or with the consent of the arbitrator. If it is made with only the arbitrator's consent, the court will make a ruling only if it is likely to result in a substantial saving in costs and there has been no delay in making the application.

The parties have the right to agree to exclude the court's jurisdiction under s 45. Where one or both of the parties are not based in the UK, they may have agreed to arbitration in England only if there was no risk of being involved in court proceedings in England as well. In such cases, agreements excluding s 45 are likely to be common. Further, it should be noted that, by s 45(1), an agreement that the arbitrator need not give reasons for their decision (see **13.7.3** and **13.8.3**) is deemed to be an agreement to exclude the court's jurisdiction under s 45.

13.5.3   The arbitrator's fee

One additional matter which has to be considered at or before the preliminary meeting (usually when the arbitrator accepts the appointment) is the question of the arbitrator's fee. The arbitrator will indicate how much they will charge for their services (or the basis on which their fees will be calculated) and how much has to be paid in advance (if any). The arbitrator's agreement to act is conditional on reaching satisfactory agreement about their fee.

13.6   PREPARATIONS FOR THE HEARING

13.6.1   The arbitrator's duties

Both in the preparation for the hearing and during the hearing itself the arbitrator must comply with s 33(1) of the AA 1996. This states:

> The tribunal shall—
>
> (a)   act fairly and impartially as between the parties, giving each party a reasonable opportunity of putting his case and dealing with that of his opponent, and

(b)   adopt procedures suitable to the circumstances of the particular case, avoiding unnecessary delay or expense, so as to provide a fair means for the resolution of the matters falling to be determined.

Section 33(2) goes on to provide:

The tribunal shall comply with that general duty in conducting the arbitral proceedings, in its decisions on matters of procedure and evidence and in the exercise of all other powers conferred on it.

At the risk of labouring the obvious, neither the parties nor the arbitrator can contract out of s 33.

13.6.2   The parties' duties

Both in preparing for the hearing and during the hearing itself the parties must comply with s 40 of the AA 1996. This provides:

(1)   The parties shall do all things necessary for the proper and expeditious conduct of the arbitral proceedings.

(2)   This includes—

(a)   complying without delay with any determination of the tribunal as to procedural or evidential matters, or with any order or directions of the tribunal, and

(b)   where appropriate, taking without delay any necessary steps to obtain a decision of the court on a preliminary question of jurisdiction or law ...

(See **13.4.3** and **13.5.2**.)

Again, the parties cannot contract out of s 40, even with the arbitrator's consent.

13.6.3   Correspondence

Although the preliminary meeting deals with the preparations for the hearing, further problems may arise as time passes by. The arbitrator can call further meetings, or they may deal with the problems by correspondence.

Whatever is written to the arbitrator must be copied to the other side. All communications by the arbitrator are sent to both parties.

13.6.4   Want of prosecution

A party who expects to lose the case may try to postpone the inevitable by failing to cooperate with the arbitrator (eg by failing to reply to correspondence or to attend meetings). If the party in default is the claimant then the arbitrator can dismiss the claim for want of prosecution under s 41(3) of the AA 1996, unless the arbitration agreement states to the contrary (as the parties are free to agree on the arbitrator's powers if a party fails to comply with their s 40 duties (see **13.6.2**)). The arbitrator can do this if there has been inordinate and inexcusable delay which creates a substantial risk that it will not be possible to reach a fair decision or which 'has caused or is likely to cause' the respondent serious prejudice. The arbitrator should not exercise their powers under this section where the limitation period has not yet expired, unless there are exceptional circumstances (see *James Lazenby & Co v McNicholas Construction Co Ltd* [1995] 1 WLR 615).

13.6.5   Proceeding without notice

If it is the respondent who is not cooperating, the arbitrator may rely on s 41(4) of the AA 1996, if either the respondent:

(a)   is not present at a hearing of which they had been notified; or

(b)   fails to provide written evidence or submissions after being given proper notice,

and they have not provided a good explanation for their default. This section provides that the arbitrator can deal with the matter on the basis of the arguments and/or evidence provided by the claimant.

13.6.6   Peremptory orders

Under s 41(5) of the AA 1996, if any party fails to comply with the arbitrator's directions, the arbitrator can make a peremptory order giving the party in default a specified period of time to comply with the order. Such an order can perhaps be viewed as the equivalent of an 'unless' order under the CPR 1998 (see Legal Practice Guide, *Civil Litigation* at **9.3.4**). If the party does not comply with the order then, under s 41(7), the arbitrator can either:

(a)   prevent the party in default from relying on any material which was covered by the order; or

(b)   draw any appropriate adverse inference; or

(c)   proceed to make an award on the basis of the existing evidence; or

(d)   impose costs penalties.

EXAMPLE

During the course of an arbitration of a dispute between A and B, the arbitrator orders both parties to exchange the expert reports they propose to rely on at the hearing. A sends B a copy of their expert's report. B fails to provide A with a copy of B's expert evidence. The arbitrator can order B to provide copies of their expert evidence within 14 days. If B still fails to provide copies of their expert evidence, the arbitrator may: (i) direct that B shall not be entitled to use that evidence at the hearing; (ii) infer that the evidence B had was unreliable; (iii) decide the case on the basis of A's expert evidence and any expert evidence the arbitrator may themselves have obtained; and (iv) order B to pay the costs wasted by B's failure to comply with the arbitrator's order.

Alternatively, the arbitrator (or one of the parties acting with the consent of the arbitrator) may apply to the court for an order under s 42 requiring a party to comply with a peremptory order made by the arbitrator. This might be appropriate where, for example, one party has documents which are crucial to the other party's case and they will not hand over the papers to the other party. The advantage of applying to the court is that the court can attach a penal notice to its order so that non-compliance may be punished as a contempt of court.

The power to apply to the court under s 42 can be excluded by the arbitration agreement. It is important to remember that the basic principle is still that the parties are free to agree on what should happen if one party fails to carry out their obligations and that the provisions of ss 41 and 42 apply only in the absence of any agreement to the contrary.

13.6.7   Help from the High Court

In addition to its powers under s 42 of the AA 1996, the court has power under s 44 to make orders relating to:

(a)   taking evidence from witnesses;

(b)   preserving evidence;

(c)   inspecting, photographing, preserving, taking samples or experimenting on any property or goods involved in the proceedings and for the custody or detention of such property. To do this, it can authorise any person to enter the premises of any party;

(d)   selling goods which are involved in the proceedings;

(e)   interim injunctions; and

(f)   appointing a receiver.

The arbitration agreement may exclude all or part of the court's powers under s 44. The court will, in any event, make an order only if the arbitrator has no power to make the order or their order would not be effective.

> **EXAMPLE**
>
> In the course of an arbitration between A and B it becomes apparent that B is about to dispose of B's property in such a way as to make it very difficult to enforce any award which may be made against B at the end of the arbitration. The arbitrator has no power under the arbitration agreement to require B to desist from doing this (or even if they have such power, it is obvious that B will ignore any direction given by the arbitrator). A may apply to the court under s 44 for a freezing injunction (see **Chapter 8**) (with the usual penal notice attached).

The principles applicable to the determination of any application under s 44 are the same as those that apply to making an injunction under s 37(1) of the Senior Courts Act 1981 (see *DP World Djibouti FZCO v Port de Djibouti SA* [2018] EWHC 2340 (Comm) and **6.3**).

Normally, a party can apply to the court under s 44 only if they have the consent of the arbitrator or the other parties. Nevertheless, by s 44(3), in cases of urgency, a party can apply to the court for orders to preserve evidence or assets without first obtaining the arbitrator's consent. The Court of Appeal considered the interpretation of s 44(3) in the case of *Cetelem SA v Roust Holdings Ltd* [2005] EWCA Civ 618, where it upheld the granting of a freezing injunction preventing the defendant from dealing with its shares.

Applications to the court are governed by Part 62 of CPR 1998 and the associated Practice Direction. They will normally be dealt with by the Commercial Court.

13.6.8 Security for costs

Under s 38(3), unless the parties have agreed otherwise, the arbitrator may require an applicant to provide security for the respondent's costs before proceeding any further with the arbitration. However, unless agreed to the contrary, an arbitrator cannot require security for costs solely because the applicant is based outside the UK. One of the objectives of the AA 1996 is to encourage foreign businessmen to use the English arbitration system, and it is important that they should not be deterred by a fear that they might have to put money up front if they were to arbitrate in this country.

The usual ground for ordering security for costs would be because of doubts about the applicant's financial ability to meet any award of costs.

If the applicant fails to provide the required security, the arbitrator can make a peremptory order. If the applicant still fails to comply then, under s 41(6), unless agreed to the contrary, the arbitrator can dismiss the claim.

13.6.9 Provisional awards

By s 39 of the AA 1996, the arbitrator does have power to make a provisional order for the payment of money or disposal of property between the parties or for an interim payment of costs. However, by s 39(4), the arbitrator has this power only if it is expressly conferred by the arbitration agreement.

13.6.10 Without prejudice offers

There will be occasions when the respondent wants to settle and to put pressure on the applicant to do so. The respondent could send the equivalent of a Part 36 offer, ie a letter in which an offer is made 'without prejudice save as to costs'.

13.7 THE HEARING AND THE AWARD

The parties and the arbitrator will settle the arrangements for hearing the reference at the preliminary meeting.

13.7.1   The hearing

By s 46, the arbitrator will decide the dispute under the law the parties have chosen. Section 47 gives the arbitrator power, unless the parties agree otherwise, to make different awards on different issues at different times.

> **EXAMPLE**
>
> During the course of the arbitration, the arbitrator may first hear evidence on whether there has been a breach of contract. If they rule that there has been no breach of contract, that will effectively be the end of the matter. If they decide that there has been a breach of contract, they may then proceed to hear evidence about the amount of harm caused by the breach so that they can decide what compensation to award.

The parties can, of course, agree what powers the arbitrator shall have. In the absence of any agreement to the contrary, the arbitrator may make a declaration, may order payments of money, and has the same powers as a court to order a party to do something or to stop doing it. The arbitrator may also order specific performance of a contract (except one relating to land) and order the rectification, setting aside or cancellation of any document (s 48).

13.7.2   Removal of arbitrator

13.7.2.1   The powers of the parties

The parties may agree what they like regarding their powers to revoke the arbitrator's appointment. In the absence of any agreement to the contrary, s 23 gives the parties power to revoke the arbitrator's appointment if all parties agree in writing.

13.7.2.2   The powers of the court

If the parties cannot agree on the revocation of the arbitrator's powers, either party may apply to the court for an order removing the arbitrator from office on certain grounds. Section 24, which gives this power, cannot be suspended by the agreement of the parties.

The grounds for removing an arbitrator under s 24 are either:

(a)   that there are justifiable doubts about their impartiality;

(b)   that they lack the qualifications required by the arbitration agreement;

(c)   that there are justifiable doubts about their physical or mental ability to conduct the proceedings; or

(d)   that they have failed to conduct the proceedings properly or with reasonable speed, and this will cause substantial injustice.

As far as impartiality is concerned, the test to be applied is that applied to all persons acting in a judicial capacity, ie whether having regard to the relevant circumstances, there was a real danger of bias, in the sense that the arbitrator might unfairly regard or have regarded with favour or disfavour the case of one party. A direct pecuniary interest in the outcome will be assumed to amount to bias and lead to automatic disqualification (R v Gough [1993] AC 646).

If an arbitrator ceases to act for any of the above reasons or because they resign or die, the parties can agree on how the arbitrator should be replaced. If they cannot agree, they should follow the usual procedures for appointing an arbitrator under s 16 or apply to the court under s 18 (see **13.3**).

13.7.3   The award

Although the parties are, of course, free to agree what they like about the form and content of the arbitration award, under s 52, unless agreed to the contrary, the award should be in writing and signed by the arbitrator, and should give reasons for the award. By s 55, unless agreed to the contrary, the arbitrator will serve copies of the award on the parties.

13.7.4 Costs

Under s 61, unless agreed to the contrary, the arbitrator can order one party to pay the costs of the arbitration. Section 61(2) says that, unless agreed to the contrary, the general principle will be that costs should follow the event (ie the loser pays the costs). 'Costs' in this context includes the arbitrator's fees (s 59).

Any provision in an arbitration agreement that one party shall pay the costs of the arbitration in any event is void unless the agreement was made after the dispute arose (s 60).

13.7.5 The arbitrator's fee

Section 56 of the AA 1996 (which cannot be excluded by the parties) gives the arbitrator power to refuse to deliver an award to the parties until the arbitrator's fees and expenses have been paid. Very often, of course, the arbitrator will have required some or all of their fees to be paid before commencing the arbitration. However, in so far as any of their fees and expenses are still outstanding at the time of the award, they will refuse to publish the award until they have been paid. Effectively, this means that the winner will have to pay the fees to the arbitrator in order to get the award and will then seek to recover those fees from the losing party (see **13.9**).

Sections 28 and 56 of the AA 1996 give the court power to resolve any dispute about the amount of the arbitrator's fees.

13.7.6 Interest

Under s 49 of the AA 1996, the parties can agree on the arbitrator's powers to award interest. Unless agreed to the contrary, the arbitrator has power to make such award of interest as they think fit. This includes the power to award compound interest rather than simple interest, which is a power which is not usually available to a court.

13.7.7 Settlement

If the parties do settle their dispute during the arbitration then, by s 51, unless agreed to the contrary, the arbitrator will record the settlement in the form of an agreed award. This will have the same status as an award made after a disputed hearing. All the normal rules relating to the award, costs, and arbitrator's fees and expenses (see **13.7.3–13.7.6**) apply to an agreed award.

13.8 CHALLENGING THE AWARD

Most arbitration agreements stipulate what is to happen if one or more of the parties are dissatisfied with the arbitrator's decision. It is important to remember that what follows in this section of this chapter applies only once the parties have exhausted their remedies under the arbitration agreement.

13.8.1 Issues of jurisdiction

Section 67 of the AA 1996 (which cannot be excluded by agreement) gives a party the right to apply to the court to challenge an award on the grounds of lack of jurisdiction. The courts have so far considered applications on the basis that:

(a)   the arbitration agreement was not binding on the applicant;

(b)   the arbitration clause was void for ambiguity and uncertainty; and

(c)   the arbitrator did not have the jurisdiction to deal with issues covered by their award.

A section 67 challenge involves a rehearing (and not merely a review) of the issue of jurisdiction, so that the court must decide that issue for itself. It is not confined to a review of the arbitrators' reasoning, but effectively starts again; the decision and reasoning of the arbitrators is not entitled to any particular status or weight, although (depending on its cogency) that reasoning will inform and be of interest to the court (*Dallah Real Estate & Tourism Holding Company v Ministry of Religious Affairs of the Government of Pakistan* [2010] UKSC 46).

The parties are permitted to adduce arguments which were not advanced before the arbitrators (*LLC Agronefteprodukt v Ameropa AG* [2021] EWHC 3474 (Comm)).

13.8.2   Issues of fact

Subject to the provisions of the arbitration agreement, the arbitrator's decision is final on questions of fact. There is no right of appeal to the courts on a question of fact.

It is, however, possible to challenge the arbitrator's award on the basis of a serious irregularity affecting the tribunal, the proceedings or the award under s 68(1) of the AA 1996 (which cannot be excluded by the parties). Section 68(2) defines a serious irregularity as an irregularity of one or more of the following kinds which the court considers has caused or will cause substantial injustice to the applicant:

(a)   failure to comply with the general duties imposed on the arbitrator by s 33 (see **13.6.1**);

(b)   exceeding the arbitrator's powers or the powers of anyone else involved in the arbitration (although this would normally fall under s 67 (see **13.8.1**));

(c)   failure to follow agreed procedures;

(d)   failure to deal with all the issues;

(e)   any arbitral or other institution or person vested by the parties with powers in relation to the proceedings or the award exceeding its powers;

(f)   uncertainty or ambiguity as to the effect of the award;

(g)   the award was obtained by fraud or the award (or the way in which it was obtained) is contrary to public policy;

(h)   the award fails to comply with the required formalities;

(i)   an admitted irregularity in the conduct of the proceedings.

The meaning of some of these irregularities is not immediately obvious (eg obtaining an award in a manner which is contrary to public policy) and will have to be clarified by the courts as and when the opportunity arises. It is also unclear why, for example, the court should be asked to interfere with an award simply because of a formal defect (especially as the arbitrator has power under s 57 to correct errors in the award).

The test of serious irregularity has been recognised as imposing a 'high threshold' or 'high hurdle' (*ABB AG v Hochtief Airport GmbH* [2006] EWHC 388 (Comm)). The focus is on due process, not the correctness of the decision reached (*Primera Maritime (Hellas) Ltd v Jiangsu Eastern Heavy Industry Co Ltd* [2013] EWHC 3066 (Comm)). There will be substantial injustice where it is established that, had the irregularity not occurred, the outcome of the arbitration might well have been different (*Vee Networks Ltd v Econet Wireless International Ltd* [2004] EWHC 2909 (Comm)). An applicant need not show that they would have succeeded on the issue with which the tribunal failed to deal or that the tribunal would have reached a conclusion favourable to them; it is necessary only for them to show that their position was reasonably arguable and had the tribunal found in their favour, the tribunal might well have reached a different conclusion in its award. In general, there will, however, be no substantial injustice if it can be shown that the outcome of the arbitration would have been the same regardless of the irregularity (*RAV Bahamas Ltd v Therapy Beach Club Incorporated* [2021] UKPC 8).

If an application under s 68 succeeds, the court will normally refer the matter back to the arbitrator; but if it considers this to be inappropriate, it can set aside all or part of the award.

The Commercial Court may summarily dismiss a challenge to arbitral awards under s 68. The threshold for bringing a successful challenge as set out above is very high, but this does not always deter parties from bringing challenges purely in order to delay enforcement of the award. Paragraph O8.6 of the Commercial Court Guide allows the court to exercise its powers under CPR 1998 to dismiss an application under s 68 of the Act without a hearing, if the court considers that the challenge has no real prospect of success. The respondent to the challenge can also request the court to deal with the application on paper, without an oral hearing. If the court does dismiss the application in this way, the applicant has the right to apply to the court to request a hearing of the application. However, the applicant is at risk of being liable for costs on the indemnity basis if it loses at the hearing.

13.8.3 Issues of law

Under s 69 of the AA 1996, unless otherwise agreed, a party may appeal to the court on any question of law arising out of the award. Where one or both of the parties to the arbitration are based outside the UK, they are likely to prefer finality to the prospect of being involved in litigation in the English courts, so agreements excluding s 69 will be common.

An agreement that the arbitrator need not give reasons for their decision is treated as an agreement to exclude s 69 (s 69(1)).

An appeal can be made only if the court grants permission (or if all parties consent, which is unlikely). The court will grant permission only if a decision will substantially affect the rights of one or more parties and it is 'just and proper' for the court to decide the issue. Even then, the court will intervene only if the arbitrator's decision is obviously wrong or 'the question is one of general public importance and the decision of the tribunal is at least open to serious doubt'.

An application for permission to appeal must identify the question of law to be determined and state the grounds on which it is alleged that permission should be granted. The application will usually be determined without a hearing by the court reading the parties' written submissions.

In many cases, an error of law can be found by studying the way in which the arbitrator has stated the law in their reasons. Has the arbitrator carried out the correct process of not only identifying all material rules of statute and common law, but also identified and interpreted the relevant parts of the contract and identified those facts which must be taken into account when reaching their decision? It is, however, also possible to infer an error of law in those cases where a correct application of the law to the facts found would lead inevitably to one answer whereas the arbitrator has arrived at another: and this can be so even if the arbitrator has stated the law in their reasons in a manner which appears to be correct – for the court is then driven to assume that the arbitrator did not properly understand the principles which they had stated (*The Chrysalis* [1983] 1 Lloyd's Rep 503).

If the court does decide to allow the appeal, it will normally refer the matter back to the arbitrator; but if this is inappropriate, it may vary or set aside the award.

13.8.4 Supplementary provisions

There are certain matters which are common to ss 67, 68 and 69.

By s 70(3), any application or appeal must be made within 28 days of the end of the arbitral process. This might be 28 days from the date of the award, but if the arbitration agreement stipulates that other appeal procedures must be followed before applying to the court, the 28 days will run from the date when the parties were informed of the result of those other procedures.

By s 70(4), the court may require the arbitrator to give reasons or additional reasons for their award.

The court may order the applicant/appellant to provide security for costs and may require the amount of the award to be paid into court pending the court's decision. The applicant/appellant will not be able to proceed until they have complied with these requirements.

By s 71(3), if an award is referred back to the arbitrator, the arbitrator must make a fresh decision within three months (or such other period stipulated by the court).

The provisions of s 73, whereby a party may lose the right to object if they are guilty of unreasonable delay (an example is at **13.4.3**), apply to ss 67 and 68, but not to appeals on a point of law under s 69.

The effect of s 73 is that a party to an arbitration must act promptly if they consider that there are grounds on which they could challenge the effectiveness of the proceedings. If they fail to do so and continue to take part in the proceedings, they will be precluded from making a challenge at a later date. It is unnecessary for an applicant to have had actual knowledge of the grounds of objection in order for them to lose their right to challenge the award. If the respondent can show that the applicant took part or continued to take part in the proceedings without objection after the grounds of objection had arisen, the burden passes to the applicant to show that they did not know, and could not with reasonable diligence have discovered, those grounds at the time.

The relevant question is not when the party has cogent evidence necessary to bring its challenge but when it believed it had grounds for objecting. At that point, it is obliged to raise the objection promptly (*Radisson Hotels APS Denmark v Hayat Otel Isletmeciligi Turizm Yatırım Ve Ticaret Anonim Sirketi* [2023] EWHC 892 (Comm)).

Sections 70, 71 and 73 are all mandatory provisions and cannot be excluded by agreement of the parties.

13.8.5 Further appeals

An appeal from a decision of the court to the Court of Appeal under any of the provisions of the AA 1996 (not just those dealt with in this section of this chapter) can be made only with the permission of the court of first instance (which will usually be the Commercial Court). If the courts continue to follow their previous practices under the earlier legislation, such permission will rarely be granted.

In *Henry Boot Construction (UK) Ltd v Malmaison Hotel (Manchester) Ltd* [2000] 3 WLR 1824, a majority in the Court of Appeal (the matter was obiter) took the view that s 55 of the Access to Justice Act 1999 and r 52.13 of CPR 1998 (see **Chapter 11**) had no effect in relation to an appeal to the Court of Appeal under s 69(8) of the AA 1996. Once a party has obtained permission from the court of first instance to appeal, they are not subsequently required to seek permission from the Court of Appeal.

13.9 ENFORCING THE AWARD

Arbitration is the only alternative to litigation which produces a result which can be enforced without commencing litigation.

The normal way of enforcing the award is under s 66 of the AA 1996 (which cannot be excluded by the parties). This enables the winning party to apply to the High Court for leave to enforce the award as if it were a court judgment.

The procedure is set out in the Commercial Court Guide and is beyond the scope of this book.

If leave is granted, the order must be served on the debtor who has 14 days to apply to have it set aside (eg because the award is tainted by misconduct or is wrong in law). (The order must inform the debtor of this right.) If no such application is made or it fails, the applicant can use all the usual methods of enforcement.

13.10 TIME LIMITS

By s 13 of the AA 1996 (which cannot be excluded by the parties), the Limitation Acts apply to arbitrations in the same way as they apply to other disputes. Most arbitration agreements, however, require the parties to commence the arbitration in a much shorter period than the usual limitation period. Once the time limit in the arbitration agreement has expired, it is normally too late to refer the matter to arbitration, but the arbitration agreement is still effective to prevent either party taking the dispute to the courts, so the aggrieved party will be without a remedy.

Section 12 of the AA 1996 (which cannot be excluded by the agreement of the parties) enables the High Court to grant an extension of time for referring a dispute to arbitration. The parties must first have used any provisions of the arbitration agreement (eg applying to the arbitrator for an extension of time) before applying to the court. The section allows the court only to extend the time for commencing the arbitration.

The grounds for granting an extension are set out in s 12(3). The extension will be granted in only two cases. The first is where 'the circumstances are such as were outside the reasonable contemplation of the parties when they agreed [the time limit]'. The Court of Appeal considered the correct interpretation of this in *Harbour & General Works Ltd v Environment Agency* [2000] 1 WLR 950. The claimant had narrowly missed the time limit because of an administrative oversight. The extension was refused on the basis that this was far from so uncommon as to be treated as beyond the parties' contemplation. The Court of Appeal commented that an extension should only be considered where, had the parties known of the circumstances at the time of the agreement, they would at least have contemplated that the time bar might not apply. The second ground under s 12(3) is that 'the conduct of one party makes it unjust to hold the other party to the strict terms' of the time limit.

EXAMPLE

A and B have an arbitration agreement whereby all disputes must be referred to arbitration within six months of the dispute arising. Such a dispute arises and A wants to refer the matter to arbitration. B persuades A that this is unnecessary because they will be able to negotiate an amicable settlement. The negotiations appear to be proceeding amicably and a settlement is about to be reached. The day after the six-month time limit for referring the dispute to arbitration elapses, B withdraws from the negotiations. The implication is that B was not negotiating in good faith and was simply lulling A into a sense of false security, playing for time until the time limit had expired. This would probably persuade the court to extend the time limit, provided A does not delay in applying to the court.

The provisions were summarised by Foxton J in *National Bank of Fujairah (Dubai Branch) v Times Trading Corp* [2020] EWHC 1983 (Comm) at [29] and [31] as follows:

> So far as s.12(3)(a) and the 'circumstances outside the reasonable contemplation of the parties' test is concerned:
>
> i. The relevant threshold is that 'the circumstances are such as were outside the reasonable contemplation of the parties when they agreed the provision in question, and that it would be just to extend the time'.
>
> ii. This imposes a double requirement. There must be both (i) circumstances outside the parties' reasonable contemplation and (ii) injustice.
>
> iii. To qualify under section 12(3)(a), the relevant circumstances must both have been (a) outside the reasonable contemplation of the parties when the contract was entered into; and (b) such that, if the parties had contemplated them, they would also have contemplated that the time bar might not apply.
>
> iv. Matters are within the 'reasonable contemplation of the parties' if they are 'not unlikely to occur'.
>
> v. Mistakes, oversights and negligence by lawyers or case handlers in relation to the missing of the time bar will not constitute a situation beyond the reasonable contemplation of the parties. However, conduct which goes beyond mere negligence might be. The circumstances must be such that if they had been drawn to the attention of the parties when they agreed the provision, the parties would at the

very least have contemplated that the time bar might not apply – it then being for the court finally to rule as to whether justice required an extension of time to be given.

So far as s.12(3)(b) is concerned, and whether the respondent's conduct makes it unjust not to extend time:

i. A claimant must show some positive conduct on the part of a respondent that renders reliance on the time limit unjust.

ii. The respondent's behaviour does not have to be the sole or even the predominant cause of the failure to meet the deadline, but a causal nexus must exist.

iii. The respondent's conduct does not need to be wrongful or blameworthy. Unintentional conduct on the part of the respondent may suffice.

An arbitration agreement may contain other time limits (eg time limits for serving documents). It is possible (after exhausting all procedures specified in the arbitration agreement) to apply to the court under s 79 for an order extending such time limits. The court will extend the time limit only if 'a substantial injustice would otherwise be done'.

The parties can agree to exclude s 79 in their arbitration agreement. It is likely that such agreements will be common.

13.11   STAYING LITIGATION

Sometimes one of the parties to an arbitration agreement issues court proceedings instead of referring the dispute to arbitration. The defendant must, of course, acknowledge service of the claim form or the claimant will enter a default judgment against them. Having done so, the defendant can then apply to the court under s 9 of the AA 1996 for an order staying the court proceedings and referring the matter to arbitration. By s 9(1):

> A party to an arbitration agreement against whom legal proceedings are brought (whether by way of claim or counterclaim) in respect of a matter which under the agreement is to be referred to arbitration may (upon notice to the other parties to the proceedings) apply to the court in which the proceedings have been brought to stay the proceedings so far as they concern that matter.

Can an application be made notwithstanding that the matter is to be referred to arbitration only after the exhaustion of other dispute resolution procedures? Yes, this is provided for in s 9(2). This means s 9 applies notwithstanding that the designated seat of an arbitration is outside England and Wales (*Lifestyle Equities CV v Hornby Street (MCR) Ltd* [2022] EWCA Civ 51).

By s 9(3):

> An application may not be made by a person before taking the appropriate procedural step (if any) to acknowledge the legal proceedings against him or after he has taken any step in those proceedings to answer the substantive claim.

A 'step in [the] proceedings to answer the substantive claim' would usually be the service of a defence. In *Bilta v Nazir and Others* [2010] EWHC 1086 (Ch), the court held that seeking an extension of time to serve the defence and obtaining a consent order confirming the agreement to extend time did not amount to such a step. The court held that the defendant was entitled to have more time to consider the case to be put against it and to decide what position to adopt as regards court proceedings or arbitration.

The court also held that Part 11 of the CPR 1998 did not apply to such applications, which were governed by r 62.8. Unlike Part 11, this does not impose a time limit of 14 days (28 days in the Commercial Court and Circuit Commercial Courts) from filing the acknowledgement of service within which the application must be made.

When applying for a stay under s 9, the defendant must prove that the parties to the action are parties to the arbitration agreement and the dispute in the litigation is a matter which falls within the scope of the arbitration agreement. As Lord Hodge observed in *Republic of*

Mozambique (acting through its Attorney General) v Credit Suisse International [2023] UKSC 32 at [73]–[78]:

> In carrying out this exercise the court must ascertain the substance of the dispute or disputes between the parties. This involves looking at the claimant's pleadings but not being overly respectful to the formulations in those pleadings which may be aimed at avoiding a reference to arbitration by artificial means. The exercise involves also a consideration of the defences, if any, which may be skeletal as the defendant seeks a reference to arbitration, and the court should also take into account all reasonably foreseeable defences to the claim or part of the claim.
>
> Secondly, while article II(3) of the New York Convention, which requires that the court refer a matter to arbitration, is silent as to the stay of the court proceedings, legislation implementing this provision of the New York Convention has generally made express provision for a stay pro tanto. Section 9 of the 1996 Act has done so expressly. The 'matter' therefore need not encompass the whole of the dispute between the parties.
>
> Thirdly, a 'matter' is a substantial issue that is legally relevant to a claim or a defence, or foreseeable defence, in the legal proceedings, and is susceptible to be determined by an arbitrator as a discrete dispute. If the 'matter' is not an essential element of the claim or of a relevant defence to that claim, it is not a matter in respect of which the legal proceedings are brought. I agree with the statement of Sundaresh Menon CJ in para 113 of *Tomolugen* that a 'matter' requiring a stay does not extend to an issue that is peripheral or tangential to the subject matter of the legal proceedings. I agree with Foster J's third proposition in *WDR Delaware* that a 'matter' is something more than a mere issue or question that might fall for decision in the court proceedings or in the arbitral proceedings.
>
> A focus on the substantial nature and relevance of a referred matter to the legal proceedings is consistent with international jurisprudence, including *Lombard North Central*, *Quiksilver*, *Tomolugen* and *Ting Chuan*. It is also consistent with the Australian jurisprudence in *Tanning* and *WDR Delaware*.
>
> Fourthly, the exercise involving a judicial evaluation of the substance and relevance of the 'matter' entails a question of judgment and the application of common sense rather than a mechanistic exercise. It is not sufficient merely to identify that an issue is capable of constituting a dispute or difference within the scope of an arbitration agreement without carrying out an evaluation of whether the issue is reasonably substantial and whether it is relevant to the outcome of the legal proceedings of which a party seeks a stay whether in whole or in part. In so far as the summary of the law in *Sodzawiczny*, if read by itself, may suggest otherwise, it is in error.
>
> The existing jurisprudence also supports a fifth point. There may not yet be a consensus on this matter, but common sense lends further support. When turning to the second stage of the analysis, namely whether the matter falls within the scope of the arbitration agreement on its true construction, the court must have regard not only to the true nature of the matter but also to the context in which the matter arises in the legal proceedings.

By s 9(4), the court will grant a stay unless it is satisfied that 'the arbitration agreement is null and void, inoperative, or incapable of being performed'. It will be very rare for these conditions to be satisfied, so the normal course of action will be for the court to grant a stay. In doing so, the fact that the court has powers which the arbitrator does not have (eg to grant summary judgment) is irrelevant. It is also irrelevant that the dispute is about a point of law or, even, that the claimant does not think that there is a dispute and is alleging that the attempt to refer the matter to arbitration by the defendant is simply a ploy to delay payment of compensation. There was a dispute where a claim was made, which the other party refused to admit or did not pay, whether or not there was any answer to the claim in fact or in law (see *Halki Shipping Corporation v Sopex Oils Ltd, The Halki* [1998] 1 WLR 726).

The fact that the defendant wishes to refer the matter to arbitration only so that they can defeat the claimant's action, by relying on a clause in the arbitration agreement which says that it is too late for the matter to be referred to arbitration, is not a ground for refusing to stay the litigation. Such matters should be dealt with by an application to the court under s 12 (see **13.10**).

13.12   SERVICE OF DOCUMENTS

The parties can reach their own agreement on how documents should be served during the course of the arbitration. Otherwise, s 76 states that a properly addressed, pre-paid envelope delivered by post to the addressee's last known place of residence or business address, or to the registered or principal office of a corporation, is effective service. If this is not reasonably practical (eg the other party's address is not known), the court can make directions as to service (eg the document shall be sent to the address of the other party's accountant) or may dispense with service.

13.13   JUDGE-ARBITRATORS

Under s 93 of the AA 1996, a judge can accept appointment as a sole arbitrator or as an umpire if the Lord Chief Justice is satisfied that they can be freed from their other duties. Schedule 2 to the AA 1996 makes certain modifications to the normal rules where the arbitration is being conducted by a judge.

Applications to the court where the arbitrator is a judge will be made to the Court of Appeal.

Where the arbitrator is a judge, they can grant permission to enforce the award under s 66 (see **13.9**) without the need for a separate application for permission.

The other provisions of Sch 2 are technical in nature and beyond the scope of this book.

13.14   EXPERT DETERMINATION

Expert determination is closely related to but different from arbitration. Again, the parties to a dispute seek to have it resolved by a person they have chosen rather than by the court. There are, however, significant differences between arbitration and expert determination.

An arbitrator's award is enforceable in the courts. An expert's award is not, save that the successful party can bring a breach of contract action against a party who does not comply with the expert's decision. They will also apply under Part 24 for summary judgment if there is a contract whereby the parties have agreed to accept the expert's decision. As a result, the court has much less formal control over the actions of an expert than over an arbitrator. (However, if the court considers that the expert has been guilty of misconduct, it is unlikely to grant judgment to the party seeking to enforce the expert's award.)

As an expert is not performing a judicial function, they can be sued in negligence if they make a mistake, although, since they will not usually be obliged to give reasons for their decision, they may be difficult to challenge. An arbitrator has immunity under s 29 of the AA 1996 for anything done as arbitrator unless it was done in bad faith.

If the parties use expert determination, they will not be able to make use of the AA 1996. The agreement appointing the expert may have to be carefully drafted. There should be provision for the expert to be appointed by an appointing authority if the parties cannot agree on whom to appoint. The court has no power to appoint the expert.

13.15   SUMMARY

Many commercial contracts contain arbitration clauses under which disputes between the parties will be resolved by way of arbitration rather than court proceedings.

Arbitration is a formal dispute resolution process under the control of an independent arbitrator or panel of arbitrators rather than a judge.

The parties involved are often free to decide the procedure they wish to follow, although many professional and commercial bodies have standard arbitration rules.

Arbitrations in England and Wales are regulated by the Arbitration Act 1996.

Decisions of arbitrators are enforceable through the courts.

13.16   THE ARBITRATION ACT 1996 AT A GLANCE

SECTION NUMBER	SUBJECT	IS IT MANDATORY?
s 1	Guiding principles	N/A
s 5	Agreements to be in writing – widely defined	N/A
s 9	Staying legal proceedings	Yes
s 12	Power of court to grant extensions of time for the commencement of arbitration proceedings	Yes
s 13	Limitation Act applies to arbitration proceedings	Yes
s 14	Commencement of arbitration proceedings – written notice	No
ss 15 and 16	Appointment of arbitrators	No
s 24	Power of court to remove arbitrator	Yes
s 33	Arbitrators' duties	Yes
s 34	Power of arbitrators over procedural and evidential matters	No
s 38	General powers of arbitrators including power to award security for costs	No
s 40	General duty of parties	Yes
s 41	Powers of arbitrators where party in default – power to make peremptory orders	No
s 42	Enforcement of peremptory orders through the courts	No
s 45	Power of arbitrators to make different awards on different issues at different times	No
s 47	Ability of arbitrators to make different awards on different issues at different times	No
s 56	Ability of arbitrators to withhold award in the event of non-payment	Yes
s 60	Prohibition on agreement to pay costs in any event	Yes
s 61	Arbitrators' ability to award costs	No
s 66	Enforcement of the award	Yes
ss 67 and 68	Right to challenge the award – substantive jurisdiction and serious irregularity	Yes
s 69	Appeal on question of law	No
s 79	Power of court to extend time limits relating to arbitration proceedings	No
Sch 1	Mandatory provisions of Part 1	N/A

MEDIATION

> **LEARNING OUTCOMES**
>
> After reading this chapter you will understand:
>
> - how to prepare for a mediation
> - how the mediation is conducted.

As we have already seen at **12.4**, mediation is a form of non-determinative ADR, and is without doubt the most popular. One of its attractions for parties involved in a dispute is the fact that any agreement reached at the mediation must be consensual – it cannot be imposed by the mediator. The Centre for Effective Dispute Resolution (CEDR) defines mediation as

> a flexible process conducted confidentially in which a neutral person (the mediator) actively assists parties in working towards a negotiated agreement of a dispute or difference, with the parties in ultimate control of the decision to settle and the terms of resolution.

14.1 WHEN TO MEDIATE?

Mediation is a key tool in dispute resolution, and in many cases its use should be part of your overall strategy to resolve the dispute on the best possible terms for the client. As we have already seen, there are professional obligations to discuss some form of ADR with the client and also a case management power of the court under CPR 1998 (r 1.4(2)(e)). Mediation can take place at any time during the course of the dispute resolution process – before any court proceedings are issued or during those court proceedings. It can even take place after judgment, for example when an appeal is pending. It should not be considered as an 'either or' option – litigate or mediate – but as an important method of trying to achieve your client's objectives. Whether, when and how you should use mediation to do this will often be a key part of your dispute resolution strategy.

14.2 SETTING UP THE MEDIATION PROCESS

Once the parties have agreed to mediate, what needs to be done to begin that process? In a contractual dispute, there may well be a term in the contract (similar to an arbitration clause) which deals with the mediation process to be followed. If not, the parties will have to reach agreement as to how the mediation is to be conducted and, of course, who is going to act as the mediator.

The parties can either select a mediator themselves or request an ADR organisation, such as CEDR or the ADR Group, to appoint a mediator on their behalf. The parties will also have to make arrangements relating to the venue for the mediation.

Although one of the main advantages of mediation is that it is generally far less expensive than proceeding to trial, there will of course be costs involved in the mediation process. The parties will have to agree who is to be responsible for the mediator's costs and the costs of the venue where the mediation is to take place. Usually, these will be shared between the parties, and the parties will also usually agree to pay their own legal costs of the mediation in the event of a successful outcome. If the mediation fails, however, it is quite likely that the costs incurred by a party in relation to the mediation will form part of the overall costs of the case, which will usually be paid by the unsuccessful party subject to assessment by the court.

14.3   PREPARING FOR THE MEDIATION

As with advocacy at any court hearing, thorough preparation is the key to ensuring that you are able to achieve the best outcome for your client at the mediation. You will need to have a clear understanding of the strengths and weaknesses of your client's case, and the risks associated with proceeding to trial should the mediation prove unsuccessful. You will need to decide who is going to attend the mediation on behalf of the client (ensuring that whoever does attend has authority to settle the case) and also decide which members of the legal team should be there. For example, if you have already instructed counsel in the case, should counsel be present at the mediation or should it simply be conducted by the solicitors involved? If experts have been instructed, will it help if those experts are also present?

Prior to the mediation taking place, the parties should always try to agree a bundle of relevant documents which will be used during the mediation. Further, it will usually be the case that each party, or the parties jointly, prepares a case summary setting out the case as they see it for submission to the mediator in advance of the mediation. Before attending the mediation itself, you should clearly explain to the client the way in which the mediation is going to be conducted and also the consequences of failing to reach agreement at the mediation.

14.4   THE MEDIATION

The way in which the mediation is conducted may well have been set out in the mediation agreement, but it is essential that the procedure is flexible and suits the needs of the parties. Whilst there is no fixed format for the conduct of a mediation, it is common for the mediator to invite each party to make an opening statement. Following the opening statements, it is usual for each party to retire to separate rooms and for the mediator then to engage in private sessions with each party to discuss their positions, concerns, needs and wants. The mediator is not simply a messenger, however; as an active participant in the mediation they will encourage each party to consider various options based on the information the mediator has gleaned from them during the private sessions.

If the parties are able to reach a settlement then it is essential – and indeed this is usually a term of the mediation agreement – that such settlement be recorded in writing and signed by all parties at the mediation. The agreement must be drafted carefully, which may take some time, but that is a small price to pay for certainty. If the agreement is not completed at the mediation then there is always a risk that the parties may change their minds overnight. If proceedings have already been started, the parties will subsequently have to lodge a consent order with the court setting out the basis on which the action has been settled.

If no agreement is reached at the mediation then this does not necessarily mean that the mediation has been fruitless; the parties may now have a better understanding of where the other stands on the issues in the case, and many cases do settle after what, on the face of it, appears to be an unsuccessful mediation.

As mediations are conducted on a 'without prejudice' basis, the general rule is that nothing discussed or revealed at the mediation may be revealed to the court should the proceedings continue.

ENFORCEMENT AND INSOLVENCY

> **LEARNING OUTCOMES**
>
> After reading this chapter you will understand:
>
> - how to enforce a judgment
> - the use of insolvency proceedings as an alternative to litigation
> - the advantages and disadvantages of using insolvency proceedings.

15.1 INTRODUCTION

As we saw in **Chapter 1**, financial considerations are a central issue in CDR. There is absolutely no point in taking proceedings against a party if at the end of the day you will not be able successfully to enforce any agreement reached or judgment obtained. The ability to enforce any judgment or agreement, and the prospects of success in doing so, must be a consideration throughout.

15.2 ENFORCEMENT – A REMINDER OF THE BASICS

Enforcement against a judgment debtor is dealt with in detail in the Legal Practice Guide, **Civil Litigation**. This chapter reconsiders briefly these main points and then looks at some methods of enforcement which are usually more relevant to commercial litigation than to other types of litigation.

Note that as the Commercial Court is not an enforcement court, proceedings for the enforcement of a judgment or order for the payment of money given in the Commercial Court will automatically be referred to a master or district judge of the King's Bench Division of the High Court.

15.2.1 Locating the assets

A solicitor must consider enforcement at the beginning of the case, not at the end. There is no point in suing a person who cannot meet any judgment which may be obtained against them. Before issuing proceedings, a solicitor must be satisfied that the defendant has assets which will meet any judgment obtained against them, and that those assets can be traced. Many apparently affluent debtors turn out to have no significant assets when their creditors finally catch up with them.

Sometimes the client already has the necessary information about the proposed defendant (eg because enquiries were made about their finances before entering into the original contract), but it will often be necessary to use enquiry agents to make further enquiries about their financial status. An oral examination under CPR 1998, Part 71 can be used as a means of establishing a judgment debtor's finances, but only at the end of the case once judgment has been obtained. It is too late then to find out whether the judgment debtor was worth suing.

In appropriate cases, a claimant can use a freezing injunction to preserve the defendant's assets pending judgment. If the claimant obtains such an injunction, they can also obtain an order for disclosure of the defendant's assets, whereby at a very early stage of the proceedings, the defendant has to produce evidence about their assets (usually limited to those within the jurisdiction). In appropriate cases, the defendant can be cross-examined about that evidence (see **8.6.2**).

15.2.2   The standard methods of enforcement

15.2.2.1   Taking control of goods (CPR 1998, Part 83)

This is seizure and sale of the debtor's goods. In the High Court, this is carried out by a High Court Enforcement Officer, and in the County Court by a bailiff (enforcement officer). This can be a quick and effective method of enforcement as often the mere threat of a seizure of goods is enough to produce payment from the debtor. Further details concerning the procedure can be found in the Legal Practice Guide, *Civil Litigation*.

15.2.2.2   Third party debt orders (CPR 1998, Part 72)

Third party debt orders allow the judgment creditor to intercept money owed to the judgment debtor by a third party and have the money paid to the judgment creditor in total or partial satisfaction of the judgment debt. These proceedings are often used where the judgment debtor has a bank or building society account, so that the money in that account can be paid to the judgment creditor.

The judgment creditor applies without notice, with supporting evidence, for an order to show cause. This order, called an interim third party debt order, freezes the money owed to the judgment debtor, pending an on notice hearing. The judgment creditor then serves the order on the third party. If the third party is a deposit-taking institution (eg a bank, building society or finance house) the judgment creditor should serve the third party at its head office. It is also good practice to serve a copy on the branch where the judgment debtor has their account. The judgment creditor will then serve the order on the judgment debtor.

There will then be an on notice hearing at which the court will decide whether to order the third party to pay the money to the judgment creditor. At that hearing, the court will also consider whether the order would prejudice other creditors of the judgment debtor. If the third party does not appear or does not dispute the debt, the court will usually make the interim order final, ie a final order which will be enforced against the third party. If the third party denies the debt, the court will have to investigate their claim before deciding whether to order them to pay the judgment creditor or to refuse to make the order final.

15.2.2.3   Charging orders on land (CPR 1998, Part 73)

A charging order gives the judgment creditor a charge over the judgment debtor's land. If the land is jointly owned then (if the co-owner is not a party to the debt) only the judgment debtor's beneficial interest in the land can be charged.

The judgment creditor applies without notice for an interim charging order, giving full details of any other creditors known to them. The interim charging order temporarily charges the judgment debtor's land and fixes a hearing date when the judgment creditor will apply for the order to be made final. The judgment creditor then serves the order on the judgment debtor. The court may also direct them to serve the order on one or more of the judgment debtor's other creditors and any other interested person (eg the judgment debtor's spouse, civil partner or any other person living in the property). These people will be able to argue at the hearing that the order should not be made final.

In the meantime, the judgment creditor will register the interim order at HM Land Registry or the Land Charges Registry, as appropriate, to prevent any dealings with the land pending the hearing. Where the land is registered land, the order is protected by a notice at HM Land Registry. In the case of unregistered land, the order is registered at the Land Charges Registry as an order affecting land. If the land is jointly-owned land and one of the owners is not a debtor, then a caution may be lodged if it is registered land. However, where the land is unregistered land, it may not be protected by registering a Land Charge (see Sch 3, para 12 to the Trusts of Land and Appointment of Trustees Act 1996, which inserts s 6(1A) into the Land Charges Act 1972). There may be little point in practice, therefore, in obtaining a charging order over a debtor's beneficial interest in jointly-owned unregistered land, when it cannot be protected by registration.

The judgment creditor should also give notice of the order to anyone else who has a charge over the land.

The court has a discretion whether to make the charging order final, although the burden of proof is on the judgment debtor and the others opposing the order. It will not make the order final if there is a reasonable chance that the debt will be paid in the near future or if the debt is relatively small compared to the value of the property to be charged. Nor will it make the order if it would give the applicant an unfair advantage over the other creditors. If the judgment debtor has been made bankrupt or wound up, the order will normally be refused (*Roberts Petroleum Ltd v Bernard Kenny Ltd* [1983] 2 AC 192). If the court does not make the order final, it will discharge the order.

Sometimes the judgment debtor will be involved in divorce proceedings when the judgment creditor applies for the charging order. If the judgment debtor's spouse is seeking a transfer of property order under s 24 of the Matrimonial Causes Act 1973, the application for a charging order should be transferred to the Family Division, so that that court can deal with both matters at the same time. Even so, that court is unlikely to transfer the property to the judgment debtor's spouse if this would defeat the claims of the creditors. The most the court is likely to do is to protect the spouse's right to occupy the house by placing restrictions on the circumstances in which it can be sold (*First National Securities Ltd v Hegerty* [1984] 3 WLR 769; *Harman v Glencross* [1986] 2 WLR 637).

If the court makes the order final, the judgment creditor will register it in the same way as the interim order. This ensures that when the judgment debtor sells the land, the judgment creditor is paid from the proceeds of sale. In the meantime the charge merely provides the judgment creditor with security. However, it may be some time before the judgment debtor decides to sell the land and the judgment creditor is paid from the proceeds of sale. If, therefore, the judgment creditor wishes to force the judgment debtor to sell the land, to realise the monies, they may apply for an order for sale. This is done by commencing new proceedings using the Part 8 procedure. It is in the court's discretion whether it makes an order for sale, and it is unlikely to do so if the amount of the debt secured by the charge is small.

15.3 INSOLVENCY PROCEEDINGS

Insolvency proceedings can be used as a means of enforcement because, once a judgment creditor has attempted to enforce a judgment and that judgment remains unsatisfied, that is evidence that the judgment debtor is unable to pay their debts (Insolvency Act 1986, ss 123(1) and 268(1)).

However, a judgment creditor who finds that they have to use insolvency proceedings after they have used litigation unsuccessfully, is probably a judgment creditor who made inadequate enquiries before commencing the litigation. The judgment creditor now finds themselves in the position of having sued a person who was not worth suing, and the litigation was probably a waste of time and money. The time to decide on whether or not to commence insolvency proceedings is before litigation, not afterwards.

In the case of an undisputed debt of £750 or more owed by a company, a creditor can serve a statutory demand on a debtor. For individual debtors the figure is £5,000. If the debtor does not pay the debt within three weeks, this is also evidence of inability to pay debts and entitles the creditor to issue insolvency proceedings.

In the case of undisputed debts of £750/£5,000 or more, therefore, a creditor has a choice. They can serve a statutory demand and follow it up by insolvency proceedings. Alternatively, they can send a letter before action and follow it up with court proceedings, an application for summary judgment if the debtor attempts to defend the proceedings, and then take the usual steps to enforce that judgment if payment is still not forthcoming.

15.3.1   The advantages of the insolvency route

Many debtors are not particularly worried about the prospect of being sued. Court proceedings take time and cost the creditor money. Although the creditor may get an order for costs, this will not cover all their legal costs, so they will never recover the full amount of the debt because they will have to use part of it to pay their unrecovered costs. The debtor will also have to pay interest on the debt from the time proceedings were issued, but they may regard this as an acceptable price to pay for being able to avoid paying the debt for a few more months. There may also be scope for negotiating a reduction in the debt during the proceedings.

Importantly, most litigation is not very public. It is unlikely to become public knowledge that the debtor is being sued, and anyone who does learn of this may not be unduly worried by the knowledge, given that most businesses are involved in litigation at some time or other.

On the other hand, insolvency proceedings are public knowledge. Winding-up petitions are advertised, and credit reference agencies take note of such advertisements and pass the information on to their customers. This will affect the debtor's ability to obtain credit in future and this will damage their business, possibly irreparably.

For many debtors, therefore, the threat of insolvency proceedings is far more potent than the threat of litigation and is far more likely to result in immediate payment. It is, perhaps, also fair to say that some creditors take a certain pride in threatening insolvency proceedings.

15.3.2   The disadvantages of insolvency proceedings

A statutory demand is fine if it produces payment. The problem arises if the debtor still does not pay. The creditor then has to decide whether to take the matter further by issuing insolvency proceedings. It will appear odd if they do not carry through the threat, but if they do issue a winding-up petition, they will have to advertise it. This will result in all the other creditors joining in to pursue their claims, and it may then become impossible for the creditor who initiated the proceedings to recover all of their debt. Indeed, if they are an unsecured creditor and not a preferential creditor, they may end up with little or nothing.

15.3.3   The statutory demand procedure – corporate debtors

The procedures for serving a statutory demand against a corporate debtor and an individual debtor (see **15.3.4**) are very similar, but it is important to take care to apply the appropriate Rules in each case and not to assume that they are the same. The procedures for challenging the statutory demand are very different.

An example of a statutory demand against a corporate debtor can be found in **Appendix 18** to this book.

15.3.3.1   Use and abuse

The statutory demand is intended to give a clear warning to a debtor company that unless it pays the debt in the next three weeks, it is at risk of being compulsorily wound up. The procedure is only available for undisputed debts of at least £750. It is an abuse of process to serve a statutory demand when the creditor knows that the debt is disputed. It is, however, legitimate to use a statutory demand where there is an undisputed debt of at least £750, even though the exact amount of the debt is in dispute.

15.3.3.2 Prescribed form

The Insolvency Rules 2016 set out the form that a statutory demand must take. It must name the parties and specify the amount of the debt. It must also give full details of when the debt was incurred and the consideration for the debt.

15.3.3.3 Service

Section 123(1)(a) simply says that the statutory demand should be served by leaving it at the debtor company's registered office. It does not say who should leave it there.

Many solicitors regard the safest course of action as being to serve the demand personally, although *Re a Company (No 008790 of 1990)* [1992] BCC 11 decided that the demand had been properly served if the demand was left at the registered office by any person, including a postal worker. The crucial point is, perhaps, that it is all too easy for the company to deny ever receiving a statutory demand sent by ordinary post. At the very least, the demand should be served by recorded delivery so that someone has to sign to acknowledge receipt.

15.3.3.4 Time period

The statutory demand allows the debtor three weeks to pay the debt. This excludes the day of service. If a statutory demand is served on 1 March, time does not start to run until 2 March. The three-week period then elapses on 22 March, but the creditor cannot issue a petition until the day after time has expired (ie 23 March). Obviously, if payment was received on 23 March the creditor would not actually issue a petition, but it would be a brave debtor who deliberately delayed payment until then. If the creditor legitimately issues a petition before payment is received, the debtor will usually have to reimburse the creditor for the costs of doing so.

15.3.3.5 Disputed statutory demand

In personal insolvency cases, the debtor can apply to set aside the statutory demand (see **15.3.4**). There is no formal procedure for setting aside a statutory demand served on a company. However, given the devastating effect which a winding-up petition can have on a company's business reputation, and the right of a company to protect its legitimate business interests, the courts will grant an injunction to restrain the presentation of an unjustified winding-up petition.

The grounds for seeking an injunction to restrain a winding-up petition will usually be that the debt is disputed and that the statutory demand was therefore an abuse of process. Injunctions have also been granted, however, on the basis that the statutory demand was not properly served, or that it contained errors which made it misleading. Procedural or drafting errors will result in an injunction only if the debtor can show that it has been prejudiced by the errors.

If an injunction restraining the petition is granted, the creditor will almost certainly be ordered to pay the debtor's costs.

15.3.4 The statutory demand procedure – individual insolvency

The rules on the use and abuse of statutory demands are the same for both individual and corporate insolvency (see **15.3.3**).

15.3.4.1 Prescribed forms

There are three types of statutory demand forms prescribed in r 10 of the Insolvency Rules 2016. There is one form for judgment debts, one for immediate debts and one for future debts. However, provided the debtor has not been misled and they can identify the issues in the claim, the fact that the creditor has used the wrong form will not invalidate the statutory demand (see *Re a Debtor (No 1 of 1987)* [1989] 1 WLR 271).

15.3.4.2   Service

Although r 10.3 of the Insolvency Rules 2016 treats personal service as being the usual method of serving a statutory demand (because this is the easiest way to rebut claims that the debtor never received the demand), it recognises that it is much easier for an individual debtor to evade service of a statutory demand. It therefore simply requires the creditor to do all that is reasonable to bring the statutory demand to the debtor's attention. This might include postal service (preferably by recorded delivery), or even substituted service on someone who, or by some means which, is likely to bring the statutory demand to the debtor's attention. Evidence of service other than personal service will be relevant in any application to set aside the statutory demand or any other challenge to later bankruptcy proceedings.

Rule 10.3 allows the creditor to rely upon any acknowledgement by the debtor that they have received the demand. Any method of service will be effective if it provokes a response (no matter how crude) from the debtor which shows that they have, in fact, received the demand.

15.3.4.3   Time period

The period for compliance with the demand is exactly the same (and is calculated in the same way) as for corporate insolvency. However, s 270 of the Insolvency Act 1986 allows the creditor to present a petition in less than three weeks if they can prove that there is a serious risk that the value of the debtor's assets is about to diminish significantly (eg they are trying to move their property out of the country).

15.3.4.4   Setting aside the statutory demand

On service of the statutory demand, the debtor has 18 days in which to apply to set aside the statutory demand. The debtor will apply to the court which would have jurisdiction to hear the bankruptcy petition. There is a prescribed form of application and supporting affidavit. The debtor must use these. A letter to the court will not suffice (see *Ariyo v Sovereign Leasing plc* (1997) *The Times*, 4 August).

If the application to set aside the statutory demand is clearly doomed to fail, the court can dismiss it summarily without a full hearing. If there is to be a full hearing, all parties must be given at least seven days' notice of that hearing. The application will succeed if the court is satisfied that there are substantial grounds for disputing the debt, or if the debtor has a good right to a counterclaim or set-off, or if the creditor has adequate security for their debt or if the demand ought to be set aside on other grounds.

Matters of form are rarely good grounds for setting aside a statutory demand. Normally, the debtor will have to satisfy the court that it is unjust for the creditor to rely on the demand as proof of the debtor's inability to pay their debts by, for example, showing that they have paid the undisputed part of the debt, or that the undisputed part of the debt is less than £5,000.

15.3.5   The subsequent procedure

15.3.5.1   Corporate debtors

If the statutory demand is not challenged successfully, the next stage is to issue a winding-up petition against the company. The facts in the petition must be verified by a statement of truth. A hearing date will be fixed by the court. This will probably be in some six to eight weeks' time.

The petition must then be served on the company. Following service, the petition must be advertised in the *London Gazette* at least seven days after service has taken place and at least seven days before the hearing of the petition. Advertisement of the petition is a key stage in the process. This is because it alerts other creditors to the situation and can result, for example, in the company's bank freezing the company's account. There may also be difficulties in relation to any settlement which is subsequently reached between the creditor and debtor company.

At least five days before the date of the hearing, the petitioning creditor must file a Certificate of Compliance on all statutory matters (for example service and advertisement). At the hearing itself, although the court has the discretion to dismiss or adjourn the petition, provided the debt is still outstanding and the procedural requirements have been complied with, the petitioning creditor is usually entitled as of right to a winding-up order. Once this happens the Official Receiver will be notified.

15.3.5.2 Individual debtors

Again, assuming that the statutory demand is not challenged successfully, the next stage is to issue a bankruptcy petition against the individual. Again the court will fix a hearing date, but one significant difference between bankruptcy and the winding-up procedure is that there is no requirement for the bankruptcy petition to be advertised. If a bankruptcy order is made at the hearing then the Official Receiver will become the trustee in bankruptcy of the debtor.

15.3.6 Effect of insolvency proceedings on other proceedings

Once a winding-up or bankruptcy petition has been presented, the court has power to stay any other proceedings against the debtor pending the outcome of the insolvency proceedings (Insolvency Act 1986, ss 126 and 285). The court will be likely to grant a stay since any such proceedings will be a waste of time and money if the petition is successful.

The reason for this is that, if a winding-up or bankruptcy order is made, any enforcement proceedings commenced after the presentation of the petition are void, unless the court orders otherwise, and any enforcement proceedings which are incomplete will be set aside (Insolvency Act 1986, ss 128, 183, 184 and 346).

15.3.7 Settlement of insolvency proceedings

If a creditor and debtor reach a settlement of their claim after service of a statutory demand and before the presentation of a petition, the settlement should be entirely safe for both parties. It simply means that the statutory demand has achieved its intended result, and there is no real risk of the settlement being set aside as a preference, since a payment made by the debtor to ward off insolvency proceedings is a payment made for good consideration.

Settlements made after the presentation of the petition are rather more unreliable. The settlement may still be valid as between creditor and debtor if it is made for good consideration (eg, payment is made in return for withdrawal of the petition); but the presentation of an insolvency petition is a public act (especially once a winding-up petition has been advertised), and the debtor may find that even though they have settled the claim by the petitioning creditor, some other creditor may apply to be substituted as a new petitioning creditor so that the debtor is still faced with the imminent threat of insolvency.

15.3.8 Maximising the assets

If the case does go all the way and the debtor company is wound up, creditors should remember the rules on wrongful and fraudulent trading which can result in directors of a company being required to make personal contributions to the company's assets to help meet its debts. Those directors may also face disqualification proceedings, and the threat of such proceedings may persuade directors to make voluntary contributions without any need for wrongful or fraudulent trading proceedings.

Creditors should also remember the rules on preferences which relate to both corporate and individual insolvency proceedings, and which can result in the setting aside of transactions, especially with 'connected persons', leading to the recovery of assets previously disposed of by the debtor.

These topics are covered in more detail in the Legal Practice Guide, **Business Law and Practice**.

15.3.9 Voluntary procedures

This chapter has dealt with compulsory insolvency. Readers should remember that there is a wide range of voluntary procedures whereby a debtor can enter into a composition with their or its creditors. These are dealt with in the Legal Practice Guide, **Business Law and Practice**.

15.4 SUMMARY

Enforcement should be considered before commencing proceedings, and if the proposed defendant is not worth suing, the client should write off the debt or consider whether insolvency proceedings would be appropriate. Insolvency proceedings are not appropriate if the debt is disputed.

If judgment is obtained against the defendant, it can potentially be enforced against their goods by execution, against their bank account (or other debts owed to the judgment debtor) by third party debt proceedings and against their beneficial interest in land by a charging order. Charging orders can also be made against other properties listed in the Charging Orders Act 1979.

Insolvency proceedings are an alternative to litigation followed by enforcement of a judgment. Ironically, insolvency proceedings (or the threat of them) are likely to be more effective against a solvent debtor than an insolvent debtor.

FOREIGN ELEMENT

FOREIGN ELEMENT: COMMENCING PROCEEDINGS

LEARNING OUTCOMES

After reading this chapter you will understand:

- when permission of the court is not required to serve proceedings out of the jurisdiction
- how to obtain the court's permission to serve proceedings out of the jurisdiction
- the circumstances in which proceedings commenced in England and Wales may be stayed
- the advantages and disadvantages of litigation abroad.

16.1 INTRODUCTION

When first instructed in relation to a potential piece of litigation, the solicitor will have to consider, as one of the preliminary steps, where the action should be conducted or, if an action has already commenced, whether proceedings have been issued in the correct country. These preliminary considerations are essential, particularly where one of the parties, or the subject matter of the action, is foreign or located abroad.

There are limited circumstances when a foreign individual or company may be served in the jurisdiction. Otherwise, we are concerned with when service may be effected out of the jurisdiction either with the court's permission (CPR 1998, r 6.36 and PD 6B) or without the court's permission (rr 6.32 and 6.33). In this chapter, we will start by looking at the circumstances where permission of the court is not required to serve a claim form out of the jurisdiction.

16.2   SERVICE OF THE CLAIM FORM WHERE THE PERMISSION OF THE COURT IS NOT REQUIRED – SCOTLAND AND NORTHERN IRELAND

16.2.1   Jurisdiction and the United Kingdom

By CPR 1998, r 2.3(1), 'jurisdiction' means, unless the context requires otherwise, England and Wales and any part of the territorial waters of the United Kingdom (UK) adjoining England and Wales. Scotland and Northern Ireland are part of the UK but are separate legal jurisdictions. So, in what circumstances can proceedings issued in the High Court or County Court in England and Wales be served on a defendant in Scotland or Northern Ireland without the permission of the English and Welsh courts?

16.2.2   CPR 1998, r 6.32

The starting point is that the English court must have power to determine each claim made in the claim form under any of rules 3 to 13 of Schedule 4 to the Civil Jurisdiction and Judgments Act 1982. For example, a person domiciled in a part of the UK may, in another part of the UK, be sued in matters relating to a contract, in the courts for the place of performance of the obligation in question and, in matters relating to tort, in the courts for the place where the harmful event occurred or may occur.

In addition, no proceedings between the parties concerning the same claim must be pending in the courts of any other part of the UK.

Finally, the defendant must either be domiciled in the UK, or a party to an agreement conferring jurisdiction, or exclusive jurisdiction is allocated by para 11 of Schedule 4 to the 1982 Act.

EXAMPLE 1

An English businessperson contracts with a Scottish company to build a factory for them in England and there is a dispute about the construction of the building. The English businessperson can sue in England because that is the place where the factory was to be built.

EXAMPLE 2

A Northern Ireland company supplies an English company with machinery. The English company alleges that it was not fit for its particular purpose. The English courts where the goods were delivered will have jurisdiction: the disputed term is the obligation to supply goods fit for their purpose and this obligation is performed at the time of delivery.

What if the English company had not paid for the machinery? Assuming that payment was to be made to a bank in Northern Ireland, the Northern Ireland company could take proceedings for non-payment of any balance due in Northern Ireland.

16.3   SERVICE OF THE CLAIM FORM WHERE THE PERMISSION OF THE COURT IS NOT REQUIRED – OUT OF THE UNITED KINGDOM

16.3.1   2005 Hague Convention

In some cases, a party may be able to rely on the 2005 Hague Choice of Court Convention which applies to exclusive choice of court agreements entered into after 1 October 2015. CPR 1998, r 6.33(2B)(a) enables a party to issue proceedings in this country against a defendant domiciled in another contracting country (which includes all EU states, Mexico, Montenegro and Singapore) and serve them abroad without requiring permission to do so.

Article 3 of the Convention defines exclusive choice of court agreements as follows:

For the purposes of this Convention—

(a)   'exclusive choice of court agreement' means an agreement concluded by two or more parties that meets the requirements of paragraph c) and designates, for the purpose of deciding disputes which have arisen or may arise in connection with a particular legal relationship, the courts of one Contracting State or one or more specific courts of one Contracting State to the exclusion of the jurisdiction of any other courts;

(b)   a choice of court agreement which designates the courts of one Contracting State or one or more specific courts of one Contracting State shall be deemed to be exclusive unless the parties have expressly provided otherwise;

(c)   an exclusive choice of court agreement must be concluded or documented—

    (i)   in writing; or

    (ii)   by any other means of communication which renders information accessible so as to be usable for subsequent reference;

(d)   an exclusive choice of court agreement that forms part of a contract shall be treated as an agreement independent of the other terms of the contract. The validity of the exclusive choice of court agreement cannot be contested solely on the ground that the contract is not valid.

16.3.2 Jurisdiction clause in contracts

In cases where the Hague Convention does not apply, CPR 1998, r 6.33(2B)(b) permits service out of the jurisdiction without permission where 'a contract contains a term to the effect that the court shall have jurisdiction to determine the claim'. This provision will be relevant where the defendant resides in a non-Hague Convention country or where the jurisdiction clause is not exclusive, which is a requirement of the Hague Convention. If a party wants any dispute arising out of a contract to be determined in the English and Welsh courts, it is therefore crucial to include such a jurisdiction clause.

If the defendant contests the claimant's right to rely on r 6.33(2B)(b), the relevant question for the court to determine is whether there is a good arguable case based on plausible evidence that (a) the contract in respect of which the claim is made exists and is legally binding, (b) the contract contains a valid and effective jurisdiction agreement in favour of the English courts that is binding on the defendant, and (c) the dispute falls within the scope of that jurisdiction agreement (*Pantheon International Advisors Ltd v Co-Diagnostics Inc* [2023] EWHC 1984 (KB)). The burden of proof falls on the claimant to establish the English court's jurisdiction. However, it is not a burden on the balance of probabilities as the court cannot weigh the evidence in its totality as at trial. In *Kaefer Aislamientos v AMS Drilling Mexico* [2019] EWCA Civ 10 at [80], Green LJ referred to 'the burden of persuasion'.

16.4 THE COMMON LAW RULES

16.4.1 Suing in England

16.4.1.1 Individual defendants

The English and Welsh courts can hear any proceedings if the claim form was served on the defendant while they were present in England and Wales – no matter how briefly. It is the act of uncontested service which establishes jurisdiction (*Pantheon International Advisors Ltd v Co-Diagnostics Inc* [2023] EWHC 1984 (KB)) at [16]).

16.4.1.2 Corporate defendants

If a foreign company has an established place of business within the jurisdiction, proceedings can be served on it there under s 1139 of the Companies Act 2006 in order to give the English and Welsh courts jurisdiction. The claim form must be addressed to the person whose name has been delivered to the Registrar of Companies as a person resident in Britain who is authorised to accept service on the company's behalf.

16.4.1.3   Permission to serve out of the jurisdiction

If it is not possible to effect service within the jurisdiction, the claimant needs permission under r 6.36 of CPR 1998 to serve the claim form out of the jurisdiction. The claimant must show that the matter falls within para 3.1 of PD 6B. There are over 20 jurisdictional categories or 'gateways' set out there. The objective is to enable the court to exercise jurisdiction over defendants where the subject matter of the dispute has a sufficiently close connection with England or Wales. The more important gateways include the following:

(a)   The claim is in respect of a contract made within the jurisdiction, concluded by the acceptance of an offer that was received within the jurisdiction; made by or through an agent trading or residing within the jurisdiction; or which is governed by the law of England and Wales.

(b)   The claim is made in respect of a breach of contract committed within the jurisdiction.

(c)   The claim is made in tort where the damage was sustained within the jurisdiction or the damage sustained resulted from an act committed within the jurisdiction.

   In FS Cairo v Brownlie [2021] UKSC 45, the Supreme Court, in upholding the earlier decision of the Court of Appeal, confirmed that this ground included cases where, although the original incident was a car accident in Egypt, the claimant had sustained damage within the jurisdiction (England and Wales) as she continued to suffer after returning home.

(d)   The claim is made against a person (the 'defendant') on whom the claim form has been or will be served, and there is between the claimant and defendant a real issue to be tried and the claimant wishes to serve the claim form on another person who is a necessary or proper party to that claim.

Unless conceded by the defendant, the claimant must satisfy the court that there is a good arguable case that the claim falls within the para 3.1 gateway(s) relied on. In this context, 'good arguable case' connotes that one side has a much better argument than the other (Canada Trust Co v Stolzenberg (No 2) [1998] 1 WLR 547 at 555–7 per Waller LJ, affirmed [2002] 1 AC 1; Bols Distilleries BV v Superior Yacht Services [2006] UKPC 45 at [26]–[28]).

By r 6.37(1), an application for permission under r 6.36 must set out which gateway in para 3.1 of Practice Direction 6B is relied on; that the claimant believes that the claim has a reasonable prospect of success; and the defendant's address or, if not known, in what place the defendant is, or is likely, to be found.

By r 6.37(3), the court will not give permission unless satisfied that England and Wales is the proper place in which to bring the claim.

So, even if para 3.1 applies, the claimant will not be given permission unless they also establish that the claim has a reasonable prospect of success and that England is the most convenient place for the case to be tried (see Seaconsar (Far East) Ltd v Bank Markazi Jomhouri Islami Iran [1993] 4 All ER 456 and Spiliada Maritime Corp v Cansulex Ltd, The Spiliada [1987] AC 460 respectively).

How does the court determine the reasonable prospects of success test? The claimant must satisfy the court that in relation to the foreign defendant there is a serious issue to be tried on the merits, ie a substantial question of fact or law, or both. The same test is used as for summary judgment, namely whether there is a real (as opposed to a fanciful) prospect of success (Altimo Holdings and Investment Ltd v Kyrgyz Mobile Tel Ltd [2011] UKPC 7).

When determining if England and Wales is the proper place in which to bring the claim, the court must identify the forum in which the case can be suitably tried for the interests of all the parties and for the ends of justice. The burden of proof rests on the claimant not only to persuade the court that England is the appropriate forum for the trial of the action but that it is clearly or distinctly so, and that in all the circumstances the court ought to exercise its discretion to permit service of the proceedings out of the jurisdiction.

What factors may affect whether or not England and Wales is the appropriate forum? These may include:

- what are, or what are likely to be, the issues between the parties which will ultimately be required to be determined at any trial;
- where the issues will require the assessment of many documents in a foreign language, this may point away from England being the most appropriate forum;
- the law governing the relevant transaction;
- the places where the parties reside and carry on business;
- the location of witnesses and documentary evidence; and
- delays, costs rules, convenience and expense.

The claimant applies for permission without notice with supporting evidence. This is usually a witness statement from the claimant's solicitor conducting the case. The evidence should deal with the matters referred to above. As the application is made without notice, it must also give details of anything that casts doubt on the application (the duty of full and frank disclosure – see **6.8**). In the Commercial Court, the Guide in Appendix 9 gives the following advice.

> The claimant should also present evidence of the considerations relied upon as showing that the case is a proper one in which to subject a party outside the jurisdiction to proceedings within it (stating the grounds of belief and sources of information); exhibit copies of the documents referred to and any other significant documents; draw attention to any features which might reasonably be thought to weigh against the making of the order sought; and otherwise comply with the duty of full and frank disclosure to the Court.

In *Gulfvin Investment Ltd v Tahrir Petrochemicals* [2022] EWHC 1040 (Comm), Baker J found as follows:

> 18. Whilst ultimately not determinative, Gulfvin's very experienced litigation solicitor, in his witness statement in support of the without notice application for permission to serve out, felt unable to put the matter higher than this, namely that '*Gulfvin does not believe that a more appropriate and convenient alternative forum than England exists in which to try this dispute*'. That would be sufficient, if the court concurred with Gulfvin's view, to see off a *forum non conveniens* application. It is not good enough for permission to serve out where the claimant must demonstrate that England and Wales is either the only sensibly available forum or is clearly and distinctly more appropriate than any other such forum.

16.4.1.4 Service of documents subsequent to the claim form

By r 6.38, any application notice issued or order made in any proceedings, or other document which is required to be served in the proceedings, may be served on a defendant out of the jurisdiction without permission where (a) the claim form has been served on the defendant out of the jurisdiction with permission; or (b) permission is or was not required to serve the claim form (whether within or out of the jurisdiction).

16.5 SERVICE

16.5.1 Documents additional to the claim form

As we have seen at **16.2** and **16.3**, if the claim falls within the provisions of CPR 1998, r 6.33(2B)(a) (Hague Convention cases) or r 6.33(2B)(b) (contract contains a jurisdiction clause in favour of England and Wales), the claimant does not need permission to serve out of the jurisdiction. However, the claim form must be accompanied by practice form N510, setting out the grounds under r 6.33 on which the claimant relies.

16.5.1.1   Deadline for service

The claim form must be served within six months after the date of issue (as compared with four months where it is served within the jurisdiction). The fact that the law of the State where the claim form is served allows a longer period is irrelevant (*Abdullah Ali Almunajem Sons Co v Recourse Shipping Co Ltd* [1994] 1 Lloyd's Rep 584).

16.6   STAYING ENGLISH PROCEEDINGS

If a claimant sues a foreign defendant in England, the defendant may seek a stay of proceedings so that the matter can be litigated in another country.

16.6.1   Foreign defendant served in UK

We saw at **16.4.1.1** that service may have been effected on a foreign defendant when they were temporarily present in England and Wales. Obviously, the defendant may submit to the jurisdiction by filing a defence but otherwise they may apply for the proceedings to be stayed, or jurisdiction declined, usually on the ground that there is another more appropriate forum (see **16.6.3**).

16.6.1.1   The parties are based in different parts of the UK

A defendant may object to the jurisdiction of the English courts on the ground, for example, that it would be more convenient for the action to be tried by the courts of Northern Ireland (*Cumming v Scottish Daily Record and Sunday Mail* [1995] EMLR 538).

The defendant can also object to proceedings in one part of the UK on the grounds that proceedings have already been commenced in another part of the UK.

16.6.2   One of the parties is based outside the UK

Where the court gave permission for a party to be served outside the UK, that party can object to the jurisdiction of the English courts on the ground that the English courts are not the most appropriate for resolving the dispute. They will have to prove that it is possible for the claimant to issue proceedings in another State. The defendant may also try to argue that the gateway relied upon by the claimant under para 3.1 of PD 6B is not established or that the claimant does not have a claim with a reasonable prospect of success. The claimant then has to prove that the English courts are the most convenient place to deal with the litigation bearing in mind the convenience of the parties and the witnesses and the interests of justice (*Spiliada Maritime Corp v Cansulex Ltd, The Spiliada* [1987] AC 460 and see further **16.4.1.3**).

In *Connelly v RTZ Corporation* [1997] 3 WLR 373, the claimant commenced proceedings in England against defendants based in Namibia. The defendants objected to the jurisdiction on the grounds that the incident occurred in Namibia and all the witnesses lived in Namibia. The claimant argued that they could not afford to bring proceedings in Namibia because they would not qualify for legal aid there, and that the only way in which they could afford to bring proceedings anywhere in the world was to bring them in England where they could get legal aid. The House of Lords decided that the English courts were the most convenient place to deal with the case (on the basis that it was more convenient to have an inconvenient trial than no trial at all).

16.7   WHERE TO SUE (OR BE SUED)

An English client will usually prefer to resolve their disputes in England, and their solicitor must study the jurisdiction rules carefully to achieve this result wherever appropriate. There are, however, two significant potential drawbacks to English proceedings against a foreign defendant:

(a)   If the contract is governed by foreign law, the parties will have to call expert evidence regarding the law in question. This can be very expensive.

(b) If the defendant's property is outside the jurisdiction, there can be a delay in enforcing judgment (see **Chapter 17**).

16.8 THE PERILS OF FOREIGN LITIGATION

There will be cases where it is not possible to avoid litigation in a foreign country, or where it is desirable to take proceedings abroad. A solicitor will instruct foreign lawyers as agents, but they will still have to bear certain dangers in mind.

16.8.1 Limitation periods

Foreign limitation periods may be much shorter than the English equivalents.

16.8.2 Causes of action

Some countries may not recognise a cause of action which is part of English law. Others may allow claims which would not be actionable here.

16.8.3 Remedies

Remedies may differ, especially at the interim stage. For example, not all countries have an equivalent to search orders, while other countries exercise much tighter control over the defendant's property pending trial under a freezing injunction and give creditors greater rights to an early judgment.

16.8.4 Time

The time it takes for an action to come to trial can vary widely from State to State. There is a significant difference between, for example, the pace of German and Italian litigation.

16.8.5 Costs

In most countries costs follow the event, but this is not always the case, and even where costs are awarded to the winner, they may be based on the value of the claim rather than the amount of work involved. Contingency fee systems are common.

16.8.6 Judicial expertise

In some countries, the judges will have considerable commercial expertise, being local businesspersons themselves. Alternatively, the judges may be aided by lay assessors.

16.8.7 Miscellaneous

There may also be different rules on, for example, whether a claim carries interest or on the enforcement of judgments.

16.9 COMMON LAW VERSUS CIVIL LAW

Common law systems, like those used in the USA and most Commonwealth countries, will have many features with which an English lawyer will be familiar, although there may well be differences in, for example, contingency fees, the level of costs and the amount of pre-trial disclosure.

Civil law systems are very different. For a start, there will be no (or very limited) disclosure of documents. The main difference, however, lies in the role of the judge. We are used to the case building to a formal ending (the trial) at which the parties have a major say in what evidence the judge is to hear. That is not what happens in most of the rest of Europe.

Under the civil code systems, if the parties choose to litigate then, generally, they place themselves in the hands of a judge who has to decide where the truth lies. The judge investigates the case. They interview the parties. They then decide what witnesses they would like to hear and question those witnesses. In some countries, the parties' lawyers are then entitled to ask their own questions of the witness. In other countries, the lawyers are not allowed to speak to the witnesses at all.

The judge also decides whether expert evidence is needed, and if it is, they usually choose who that expert will be. It can be extremely difficult to challenge the views of such an expert.

As a result, litigation elsewhere in Europe places much greater emphasis on detailed statements of case and written evidence than an English lawyer is accustomed to. On the other hand, the rules on admissibility of evidence tend to be less complex and cross-examination of witnesses is relatively rare.

The CPR 1998 have reduced, to some extent, the differences between English and European litigation, as English judges take more and more responsibility for managing the case, appointing experts and deciding what evidence they wish to hear.

16.10   ROME I – REGULATION 593/2008

Rome I, which applies to the Member States of the EU, deals with the choice of laws in the context of contractual obligations. Following Brexit, Rome I has been converted into UK law as retained EU law so the provisions set out below continue to operate in UK domestic law. The same applies to Rome II – see **16.11**.

Neither Rome I or II deal directly with jurisdiction.

16.10.1   The basic position under Rome I

Article 1(2) specifies the matters to which the Regulation does not apply, for example wills and probate, and matters governed by company law.

Article 3(1) allows the parties to choose the law of the contract, either expressly or impliedly. If they have done so, then that is the applicable law that governs the contract.

If no such choice has been made then the rules in Article 4 apply. Typically, in a sale of goods contract, this means that the law of the country where the seller has their habitual residence will apply, unless the buyer is a consumer, who cannot be denied the use of laws which cannot be derogated from in their own jurisdiction.

16.10.2   Other exceptions to the seller's law applying

Article 4(1)(c) deals with a right in 'immovable property'. The presumption here is that the contract is governed by the law of the country where the immovable property is situated. This does not apply to contracts for repair or construction of immovable property.

Article 5(1) provides that, in a contract for the carriage of goods (not *sale* of goods), it is the country where the carrier has its place of business if that is also the country of loading or discharging the goods, or if it is also the country where the consignor has its principal place of business.

Article 4(4) provides that the court may decide that the contract is more closely connected with another country and apply that country's laws.

16.10.3   Local 'mandatory rules'

There are limitations on the use of the applicable law. If any provisions of the applicable law conflict with local laws of the jurisdiction where the dispute is heard, relating to the contract, those conflicting provisions of the applicable law cannot validly be used. These local law provisions are the 'mandatory rules' which are referred to in Article 9 of the Regulation. These are 'rules' which cannot be derogated from (eg, in the case of the UK, the Financial Services and Markets Act 2000). Article 9 provides that the choice of foreign law by the parties will not prejudice the application of the mandatory rules of the home country to the contract. So, even if the applicable law was held to be, say, Austrian law, the Financial Services and Markets Act

2000 could also apply to a relevant dispute heard by a court in England and Wales, and would override any inconsistent provisions in Austrian law.

16.10.4 Exceptions for consumer and employment contracts

Articles 6 and 8 are intended to give protection to the weaker party to a contract.

Article 6 deals with certain types of consumer contract. Where no choice has been made, such contracts are governed by the law of the consumer's habitual residence. Where a choice has been made, the chosen law operates subject to any rules for the protection of the consumer applicable in the consumer's country of habitual residence.

Article 8 deals with individual contracts of employment. Where there is no choice of law in the contract then the presumption is that contained in Article 8(2). This is basically that the law is that of the country where the work takes place, or where the business is situated if the work takes place in a different country. However, a contractual choice of law cannot operate so as to deprive the employee of the protection of the mandatory rules which would apply under Article 8(2).

16.11 ROME II – REGULATION 864/2007

Non-contractual obligations are dealt with under what is generally referred to as 'Rome II'. In brief this states that the applicable law for the resolution of non-contractual disputes (ie torts) is determined on the basis of where the damage occurs or is likely to occur, regardless of the country or countries in which the act giving rise to the damage occurs.

16.12 SUMMARY

The law relating to jurisdiction is quite complicated. The key issue is to appreciate when proceedings can be served out of the jurisdiction without permission of the court (CPR 1998, r 6.33) and when that permission is required (r 6.36).

The current position therefore is that permission will not be required if the case is covered by the Hague Convention (exclusive choice of court agreement conferring jurisdiction on UK courts) or, if not, the contract contains a jurisdiction clause conferring jurisdiction on UK courts (r 6.33(2B)). These cases will all relate to commercial contractual disputes.

In other types of dispute, permission of the court will be required to serve the defendant out of the jurisdiction – but remember that if it is possible to serve the defendant within the jurisdiction (even if the defendant is domiciled abroad) no such permission is required. It is open to a defendant to challenge the jurisdiction of UK courts on the basis that a court in a different country would be a more convenient court to hear the case.

FOREIGN ELEMENT: ENFORCEMENT PROCEEDINGS

LEARNING OUTCOMES

After reading this chapter you will understand:

- the methods of enforcing a judgment obtained in England and Wales outside the jurisdiction
- the methods of enforcing a judgment obtained outside the jurisdiction within England and Wales.

17.1 INTRODUCTION

The methods of enforcing English judgments abroad and foreign judgments in England depend on the arrangements (if any) which have been made with the foreign country in question either by Treaty or Convention. There are four different systems:

(a) The Hague Convention addresses enforcement of judgments obtained in cases covered by that Convention – ie contractual disputes where there was an exclusive jurisdiction clause in the contract.

(b) Registration systems have been established under the Administration of Justice Act 1920 (AJA 1920) and the Foreign Judgments (Reciprocal Enforcement) Act 1933 (FJ(RE)A 1933). They cover most Commonwealth and former Commonwealth States, and some European States like Malta.

Countries covered by the AJA 1920 include Barbados, the Falkland Islands, Hong Kong, Jamaica, Malaysia, most of the Australian states, New Zealand, Singapore and Zimbabwe. Examples of other countries to which the provisions of FJ(RE)A 1933 apply include Israel, one Australian state (namely the Australian Capital Territory), Canada, the Isle of Man, Guernsey, Jersey, India and Pakistan.

(c) There are many countries not covered by the above systems. The USA is probably the most important example. Enforcement of judgments of the courts of these countries is covered by the common law.

(d) It is important to realise that many foreign courts are very reluctant to enforce default judgments. If most of the defendant's assets are located abroad, it would be wise to ascertain if the courts of the country where the assets are located will recognise and enforce default judgments. If there is likely to be a problem about this then, even though the claimant may be entitled to a default judgment, the claimant should set the matter down for trial after the defendant has failed to acknowledge service of the claim form or to serve a defence (giving the defendant notice of this), and prove the case by calling evidence at the trial (*Berliner Bank v Karageorgis* [1996] 1 Lloyd's Rep 426).

17.2 THE HAGUE CONVENTION

17.2.1 Recognition

Article 8 of the Convention provides that a judgment given by a court in a contracting state designated in an exclusive choice of court agreement shall be recognised and enforced in other contracting states. Only judgments in civil and commercial matters are covered, but this is subject to a long list of matters excluded by Article 2 that includes wills and succession, insolvency, consumer, employment and insurance and arbitration. A judgment includes not only any decision on the merits of a claim given by a court, but also a default judgment.

17.2.2 Registering the judgment

The party seeking recognition or enforcement must produce the following documents:

- a complete and certified copy of the judgment;
- the exclusive choice of court agreement;
- documents necessary to establish that the judgment has effect or is enforceable in the state where it was obtained;
- any other documents the enforcing court may require in order to verify that the conditions for enforcement have been met;
- certified translations of these documents if they are not in an official language of the enforcing state.

17.3 THE UNITED KINGDOM

17.3.1 Recognition

Broadly, judgments obtained in Scotland and Northern Ireland are recognised in England and Wales.

17.3.2 Registration in England

The applicant obtains a certificate relating to the judgment and a certified copy. The applicant must lodge this in the Royal Courts of Justice within six months. If the judgment is a money judgment, it is then enforceable here as if it were an English judgment.

If the judgment is a non-money judgment, the creditor must apply for leave to enforce it in England (CPR 1998, r 74.16). The creditor applies without notice, but the court can require them to issue a Part 8 claim form. The application is supported by a certified copy of the judgment. If the courts grant an order for registration of the judgment, notice of registration must be served on the respondent and the respondent can apply to have the registration set aside.

17.3.3 Enforcing an English judgment in Scotland and Northern Ireland

17.3.3.1 Money judgments

Where a money judgment has been obtained, the creditor applies for a certificate regarding the judgment, and files written evidence which states:

(a)   the amount due under the judgment plus details of any interest;

(b)   that the time for appealing has expired and no stay of execution has been granted;

(c)   the addresses of the parties.

If a certificate is granted, it must be registered in the appropriate court within six months so that it can be enforced as if it were a judgment of that court.

17.3.3.2 Other judgments

Where the judgment is other than for money, the applicant applies without notice for a certified copy of the judgment with the certificate and supporting evidence described above.

17.4 REGISTRATION UNDER THE FOREIGN JUDGMENTS (RECIPROCAL ENFORCEMENT) ACT 1933

For the purposes of the FJ(RE)A 1933 and AJA 1920 (see **17.5**), the court will have jurisdiction if the defendant either:

(a) is resident here; or

(b) has its principal place of business here; or

(c) agrees to submit to the jurisdiction; or

(d) voluntarily takes part in the proceedings.

17.4.1 Recognition

Under the FJ(RE)A 1933, registration of a foreign judgment must be set aside if:

(a) the debtor was given insufficient notice of the original proceedings;

(b) the original court lacked jurisdiction;

(c) the judgment was obtained by fraud;

(d) the judgment is not covered by the Act or was registered in breach of the Act;

(e) the applicant is not entitled to enforce the judgment;

(f) enforcement would be contrary to public policy;

(g) the debtor did not submit to the jurisdiction of the original court.

There is also a discretion to set aside the registration if there is another final and conclusive judgment between the parties on the same issue.

17.4.2 Registration

The FJ(RE)A 1933 only applies to judgments for a sum of money which are final and conclusive. If, therefore, the judgment is still liable to be set aside, it cannot be registered here.

There is a six-year time limit on registering judgments under this Act.

The application is made without notice with supporting written evidence, but the court may require a Part 8 claim form. The written evidence must, in its heading, set out the name of the Act, the court which granted the judgment and the date of the judgment. It must state:

(a) the amount outstanding under the judgment;

(b) the names, trades and addresses of the parties;

(c) that the witness believes the creditor is entitled to enforce the judgment;

(d) that the judgment is not covered by s 5 of the Protection of Trading Interests Act 1980 (see **17.6.1**);

(e) that the judgment is still enforceable;

(f) that there are no grounds for setting aside the registration;

(g) the details of any interest recoverable;

(h) any parts of the judgment which are not being registered (eg because they are not for the payment of money).

The evidence must be accompanied by the judgment and, if the judgment is not in English, also by a certified translation of the judgment. As the application of the FJ(RE)A 1933 to any State is governed by an Order in Council relating to that State, it may be necessary to consult the relevant Order in Council to see whether any other evidence is required.

The applicant may be required to give security for costs.

17.4.3 Enforcement abroad

The procedure for enforcement abroad is broadly the same as under the Civil Jurisdiction and Judgments Act 1982, but the court will also issue a further certificate stating:

(a)   the method used to serve the claim form;

(b)   objections the debtor made to the jurisdiction (if any);

(c)   what statements of case were served;

(d)   when the time for appealing expires;

(e)   whether notice of appeal has been given;

(f)   the rate of interest on the judgment.

17.5 ADMINISTRATION OF JUSTICE ACT 1920

17.5.1 Recognition

Under the AJA 1920, the judgment will not be recognised if:

(a)   recognition would be contrary to public policy;

(b)   proceedings were not properly served on the debtor;

(c)   the original court lacked jurisdiction;

(d)   the debtor was not in business or ordinarily resident in the State where the judgment was obtained and they did not submit to the jurisdiction;

(e)   the judgment was obtained by fraud; or

(f)   the defendant is appealing against the judgment.

17.5.2 Registration

The judgment must be for a sum of money. The application for leave to register is made in the usual way. It must be made within 12 months of the judgment unless the court grants an extension of time. As under the FJ(RE)A 1933, the creditor may be required to issue a Part 8 claim form. The written evidence must deal with items (a) to (d) in the list for the FJ(RE)A 1933 set out at **17.4.1**. It must also state that there are no grounds for refusing registration. Again, security for costs may be required.

17.5.3 Enforcement abroad

To enforce a judgment abroad, the evidence in support of the application for a certified copy of the judgment merely has to give details of the judgment, the territory where the debtor resides, and the names, trades and addresses of both parties.

17.6 COMMON LAW

If the judgment is one to which the above procedures do not apply (either because of the nature of the judgment or because it was made in a State which is not covered by them), its enforcement here is a matter for the common law.

17.6.1 Recognition

The judgment will not be recognised at common law if:

(a) the proceedings were contrary to natural justice (eg the defendant was not given a fair chance to be heard);

(b) it was obtained by fraud;

(c) recognition would be contrary to public policy;

(d) the foreign court lacked jurisdiction;

(e) the judgment is covered by s 5 of the Protection of Trading Interests Act 1980 (which is primarily aimed at US anti-trust legislation).

17.6.2 Enforcement here

It is always open to a foreign judgment creditor to commence fresh proceedings in England if they have a cause of action here. More usually, however, they will treat the foreign judgment as a contract containing an implied promise to pay the judgment debt. The creditor will issue proceedings alleging breach of that contract and apply for summary judgment under Part 24 of CPR 1998. (The court may award interest on the judgment.) This method is available to them only if the foreign judgment is a final judgment for the payment of a fixed sum of money. If there is an appeal in the foreign court, proceedings in this country to enforce the judgment may be stayed.

17.6.3 Enforcement there

Enforcement abroad is a matter for the law and courts of the country where the creditor is seeking to enforce an English judgment.

17.7 SUMMARY

The procedure for enforcing an English judgment in a foreign country or a foreign judgment in England depends on the place where enforcement is to take place. The starting point is to consider if the Hague Convention applies (see **17.2**). If the creditor wishes to enforce the judgment in a Commonwealth or former Commonwealth State, they will probably have to use the procedures laid down under either the FJ(RE)A 1933 or the AJA 1920 (see **17.4** and **17.5**). If there is no statute governing enforcement in the foreign State, the common law or the law of the State where the judgment is to be enforced will apply (see **17.6**).

APPENDICES

Appendix 1

Outline chart of typical case management sequence for cases in the Commercial Court

1	**Claim form** issued, served and filed
2	[**Applications** made, where necessary]
3	[**Early case management conference**, if appropriate]
4	**Acknowledgement of service** filed
5	[**Particulars of claim** served and filed, if they did not accompany the claim form and were not contained in the claim form]
6	**Defence** served and filed
7	**Reply** (if any) served and filed
8	**Case memorandum** prepared
9	**List of Common Ground and Issues** prepared **List of Disclosure Issues** prepared
10	**Case management bundle** prepared Including **Disclosure Review Document**
11	**Professional estimate of trial length** prepared
12	**Case management information sheet** lodged and served
13	[**Designated judge** identified in appropriate cases]
14	**Case management conference** a. **pre-trial timetable** [b. **ADR directions** made, if appropriate and if not already made] c. **trial date fixed** (or, exceptionally, provisional range of dates for trial specified)
15	[**ADR directions** followed, where made]
16	Pre-trial timetable followed: **Disclosure, inspection, witness statements, expert reports**
17	[**Applications** made, where necessary]
18	**Progress monitoring information sheet** lodged and served
19	**Progress monitoring date**
20	[**Reconvened case management conference**, if appropriate]
21	**Confirmed estimate of trial length** prepared
22	**Pre-trial checklist** lodged and served
23	**Fixed trial date confirmed** (or where applicable, trial date fixed within provisional range of dates for trial)
24	**Meeting of experts**

25	[**Pre-trial review**, if ordered, with consideration of trial timetable]
26	**Trial bundles** prepared and provided to the court
27	Written trial **skeleton arguments** exchanged, and provided to the court (including **trial timetable, reading list, authorities, chronology, indices and dramatis personae**)
28	**Trial** commences

Appendix 2

Case Management Information Sheet

The information supplied should be printed in bold characters

Party filing information sheet:

Name of solicitors:

Name(s) of advocates for trial:

[Note: This Sheet should normally be completed with the involvement of the advocate(s) instructed for trial. If the claimant is a litigant in person this fact should be noted at the foot of the sheet and proposals made as to which party is to have responsibility for the preparation and upkeep of the case management bundle.]

Preliminary:

(1)   (a)   Is the case suitable for retention in the Commercial Court or should it be transferred to a different Court or List?

       (b)   If the case is retained in the Commercial Court, is it suitable for the Shorter Trials Scheme or the Flexible Trials Scheme in the interest of reducing the length and cost of trial?

       (c)   Are there, or are there likely in due course to be, any related proceedings between some or all of the parties to this Claim (e.g. a Part 20 claim)? Please give brief details.

       (d)   Are there, or are there likely to be, other cases in the Commercial Court or in any different Court or List in this jurisdiction raising the same or similar issues during the currency of this case?

(2)   Please state whether the Case Management Conference (CMC) requires a High Court Judge or whether it is suitable for hearing by a Deputy High Court Judge.

(3)   If costs budgeting and costs management is applicable, do you consider that this CMC is an appropriate time to deal with those questions? Is this agreed between the parties?

(4)   Do you propose that IT is used (a) during the course of the proceedings prior to trial, (b) at trial? If so, what proposals do you make and are they agreed? If not, why not?

(5)   Please indicate whether it is considered that the case should be allocated to a designated Judge. If so please give reasons for this view and write to the Judge in Charge of the Commercial Court in accordance with section D1.5 of the Commercial Court Guide.

Issues:

(6)   Are amendments to or is information about any statement of case required? If yes, please give brief details of what is required.

(7)   Can you make any additional admissions? If yes, please give brief details of the additional admissions.

(8)   Are any of the issues in the case suitable for trial as preliminary issues, or should the trial of the case be split into separate parts?

Disclosure:

(9)   Are you satisfied that proper Initial Disclosure has been given by all parties? If not, what are the concerns and what directions are sought from the Court?

(10)   Do you, or does any other party, propose that there should be search-based Extended Disclosure (that is, Extended Disclosure using Model C, Model D or Model E) by one or

more of the parties for one of more of the Issues for Disclosure? If so, has the Disclosure Review Document been completed and agreed, and, if not, why not?

(11) By what date can you give (a) Model B Extended Disclosure, if ordered, and/or (c) search-based Extended Disclosure, if ordered?

(12) What timing and method is appropriate for inspection of documents? Is this agreed?

Evidence:

(13) (a) On the evidence of how many witnesses of fact do you intend to rely at trial (subject to the directions of the Court)? Please give their names, or explain why this is not being done.

(b) By what date can you serve signed witness statements?

(c) How many of these witnesses of fact do you intend to call to give oral evidence at trial (subject to the directions of the Court)? Please give their names, or explain why this is not being done.

(d) Will interpreters be required for any witness? What arrangements may be necessary for the translation of witness statements?

(e) Do you wish any witness to give oral evidence remotely? Please give their name, or explain why this is not being done. Please state the country and city from which the witness will be asked to give evidence by remote means.

(14) (a) On what issues may expert evidence be required? Please identify both (i) the issue or issues in the case to resolve which will reasonably require there to be expert evidence (see rule 35.1) and (ii) for each proposed expert, the issue or issues within their field of expertise it is proposed they should be instructed to address.

(b) What is the estimated cost of the proposed expert evidence?

(c) Is this a case in which the use of a single joint expert might be suitable (see rule 35.7), or in which consideration should be given to what type of directions should be made in relation to proof of foreign law (see section H.3 of the Commercial Court Guide)?

(d) On the evidence of how many expert witnesses do you intend to rely at trial (subject to the directions of the Court)? Please give their names, or explain why this is not being done. Please identify each expert's field of expertise.

(e) By what date can you serve signed expert reports? Is this a case for sequential exchange of expert reports?

(f) When will the experts be available for a meeting or meetings of experts? Is this a case for the experts to meet before reports?

(g) How many of these expert witnesses do you intend to call to give oral evidence at trial (subject to the directions of the Court)? Please give their names, or explain why this is not being done.

(h) Will interpreters be required for any expert witness? What arrangements may be necessary for the translation of reports?

(i) Do you wish any expert witness to give oral evidence by remote means? Please give his or her name, or explain why this is not being done. Please state the country and city from which the witness will be asked to give evidence by remote means.

(j) Might this be a case for any expert evidence to be taken concurrently at trial?

Trial:

(15) What are the advocates' present estimates of the minimum and maximum lengths of the trial, including reading time (see section D16.1 and J5.4(c)) of the Commercial Court Guide)?

(16) What is the earliest date by which you believe you can be ready for trial?

(17) Is this a case in which a pre-trial review is likely to be useful?

(18) Please indicate whether it is considered that the case is unsuitable for trial by a Deputy High Court Judge rather than a High Court Judge. If the case is considered to be unsuitable for trial by a Deputy High Court Judge please give reasons for this view.

Resolution without trial:

(19) Is there any way in which the Court can assist the parties to resolve their dispute or particular issues in it without the need for a trial or a full trial?

(20) (a) Might some form of Negotiated Dispute Resolution ("NDR") procedure assist to resolve or narrow the dispute or particular issues in it?

(b) Has the question at (a) been considered between the client and legal representatives (including the advocate(s) retained)?

(c) Has the question at (a) been explored with the other parties in the case?

(d) Do you request that the case is adjourned while the parties try to settle the case by NDR or other means?

(e) Would an NDR order in the form of Appendix 3 to the Commercial Court Guide be appropriate?

(f) Are any other special directions needed to allow for NDR?

(21) Has Early Neutral Evaluation been considered?

Other matters:

(22) What other applications will you wish to make at the CMC?

(23) Should provision be made in the pre-trial timetable for any application or procedural step not otherwise dealt with above? If yes, please specify the application or procedural step. An application issued later that should have been, but was not, anticipated and mentioned here may be refused on that ground.

[Signature of solicitors]

Note: This information sheet must be filed with the Commercial Court Listing Office at least 7 days before the Case Management Conference (with a copy to all other parties): see section D7.4 of the Commercial Court Guide.

Appendix 3

Standard Pre-Trial Timetable

1. [Form of disclosure, divided by issues] is to be made by [*], with inspection [*] days after notice. [Detail different forms of disclosure for different groups of issues where appropriate].

2. Signed statements of witnesses of fact, and hearsay notices where required by rule 33.2, are to be exchanged not later than [*].

3. Unless otherwise ordered, witness statements are to stand as the evidence in chief of the witness at trial.

4. Signed reports of experts
   (i) are to be confined to one expert for each party from each of the following fields of expertise: [*];
   (ii) are to be confined to the following issues: [*];
   (iii) are to be exchanged [sequentially/simultaneously];
   (iv) are to be exchanged not later than [date or dates for each report in each field of expertise].

5. Meeting of experts
   (i) The experts are to meet [before and] after reports by [*] [and by *];
   (ii) The joint memorandum of the experts is to be completed by [*];
   (iii) Any short supplemental expert reports are to be exchanged [sequentially/ simultaneously] by not later than [date or dates for each supplemental report].

6. [If the experts' reports cannot be agreed, the parties are to be at liberty to call expert witnesses at the trial, limited to those experts whose reports have been exchanged pursuant to 4. above.]

   [Or: The parties are to be at liberty to apply to call as expert witnesses at the trial those experts whose reports they have exchanged pursuant to 4. above, such application to be made not earlier than [*] and not later than [*].]

7. [The trial reading list for the Judge is to:
   (a) identify the issues that the Court will be asked to decide with the assistance of expert evidence;
   (b) in respect of each such issue, briefly state each party's case;
   (c) in respect of each such issue, identify the pages of the expert evidence that need to be read.]

8. The proposed use of IT at trial is as follows: []

9. Preparation of trial bundles in electronic or hard copy form (or part electronic, part hard copy) to be completed in accordance with Appendix 7 to the Commercial Court Guide by not later than [*].

10. The estimated length of the trial is [*]. This includes [*] pre-trial reading time.

11. Within [*] days the parties are to attend on the Commercial Court Listing Office to fix the date for trial which shall be not before [*].

12. The progress monitoring date is [*]. Each party is to provide a completed progress monitoring information sheet to the Commercial Court Listing Office at least 3 days before the progress monitoring date (with a copy to all other parties).

13. Each party is to provide a completed pre-trial checklist not later than 3 weeks before the date fixed for trial.

14. [There is to be a pre-trial review not earlier than [*] and not later than [*]].

15. Save as varied by this order or further order, the practice and procedures set out in the Admiralty & Commercial Courts Guide are to be followed.

16. Costs in the case.

17. Liberty to restore the Case Management Conference.

Appendix 4

Progress Monitoring Information Sheet

The information supplied should be printed in bold characters

[SHORT TITLE OF CASE and FOLIO NUMBER]

Fixed trial date/provisional range of dates for trial specified in the pre-trial timetable:

Party filing information sheet:

Name of solicitors:

Name(s) of advocates for trial:

[Note: this information sheet should normally be completed with the involvement of the advocate(s) instructed for trial]

(1) Have you complied with the pre-trial timetable in all respects?

(2) If you have not complied, in what respects have you not complied?

(3) Will you be ready for a trial commencing on the fixed date (or, where applicable, within the provisional range of dates) specified in the pre-trial timetable?

(4) If you will not be ready, why will you not be ready?

(5) Is any application outstanding, or is any to be made, for directions in relation to the conduct of the trial? If so, provide brief details.

(6) What are the parties' current estimates of the minimum and maximum lengths of the trial (including reading time)? If the estimated maximum length of trial exceeds the current trial listing, what solution is proposed?

[Signature of solicitors]

Note: This information sheet must be filed with the Listing Office at least 3 days before the progress monitoring date (with a copy to all other parties): see D11.2 of the Commercial Court Guide.

Appendix 5

Pre-Trial Checklist

The information supplied should be printed in bold characters

[SHORT TITLE OF CASE and FOLIO NUMBER]

a.   Trial date:

b.   Party filing checklist:

c.   Name of solicitors:

d.   Name(s) of advocates for trial:

[**Note:** this checklist should normally be completed with the involvement of the advocate(s) instructed for trial.]

1.   Have you completed preparation of trial bundles in accordance with Appendix 7 to the Commercial Court Guide?

2.   If not, when will the preparation of the trial bundles be completed?

3.   Have directions previously been made for the use of IT at trial? If so, do they remain appropriate, or do you propose any departure from or amendment of those directions? If not, what (if any) directions do you propose should now be made, or why do you make no such proposal?

4.   Which witnesses of fact do you intend to call?

5.   (a)   Which expert witness(es) do you intend to call (if directions for expert evidence have been given)?

(b)   Have the experts narrowed the areas of disputed expert opinion as far as possible?

(c)   If directions for expert evidence to be taken concurrently have not been made, will they be sought from the Judge at trial?

(d)   If this is or may be a case for expert evidence to be taken concurrently has there been a discussion between advocates as to the most suitable procedure: see H2.15 in the Commercial Court Guide?

6.   Will an interpreter be required for any witness and if so, have any necessary directions already been given?

7.   Have directions been given for any witness to give evidence by remote means? If so, have all necessary arrangements been made? If any witness of fact or expert witness you are calling will give evidence by remote means from a location outside England and Wales has any permission been obtained that is required from a court or other authority in the jurisdiction where the witness will be, or is there no requirement for such permission in that jurisdiction?

8.   What are the advocates' confirmed estimates of (i) the minimum and maximum lengths of the trial, including reading time and (ii) the reading time likely to be required for the Judge before any first sitting day? (A confirmed estimate of length signed by the advocates should be attached)?

9.   What is your estimate of costs (i) already incurred and (ii) to be incurred up to the conclusion of trial?

[Signature of solicitors]

Appendix 6

Disclosure Review Document

Section 1A: Issues for Disclosure and proposed Disclosure Models

Brief description of the Issue for Disclosure[2]			Issue agreed?		Proposed Model of Extended Disclosure (A–E)		Decision (for the court)
		Reference to statement of case	Yes	No (party not agreeing)	To be completed by claimant	To be completed by defendant	
	(Alternative proposed wording, if not agreed)[1]						

[1] If the wording of any Issue for Disclosure cannot be agreed, the alternative wording proposed should be included immediately under the claimant's formulation.

Section 1B: Model C requests for Disclosure

	Issue for Disclosure	Request for document or narrow classes of document relating to the Issue of Disclosure	Response	Decision (for the court)
1.	Issue: [ ]			
2.				
3.				
4.				
5.				
6.				
7.				
8.				
9.				
10.				
11.				
12.				

[Note: Parties should refer to the guidance on 'Completion of section 2 of the DRD' in the 'Explanatory notes for the DRD' when completing this section]

Section 2: Questionnaire

Claimant / Defendant (delete as appropriate)

	Question	Details
1.	**Hard copy documents / files** Confirm whether hard copy documents (for example, notebooks, lever arch files, note pads, drawings/plans and handwritten notes) that are not originally electronic files should be included in the collection of documents which you propose to search. Please propose an approach for the production of hard copy documents: if they will be scanned and made searchable or if they will be disclosed and made available for inspection in hard copy only.	

Claimant / Defendant (delete as appropriate)		
	Question	Details
2.	**Electronic files: data sources/locations** Please set out details on data sources to be considered at collection which you propose to search. Please include details of any sources that are unavailable but may host relevant documents or which may raise particular difficulties due to their location, format or any other reason. Examples of sources to be considered may include the following: (1) Document repositories and/or geographical locations (2) Computer systems or electronic storage devices (3) Mobile phones, tablets and other handheld devices (4) Document management systems (5) Email servers (6) Cloud based data storage (7) Webmail accounts e.g. Gmail, Hotmail, Instant messaging / collaboration systems (8) Back-up systems (9) Social media accounts (10) Third parties who may have relevant documents which are under your control (e.g. agents or advisers). The list above is not intended to be exhaustive, and it may be appropriate to consider other relevant data sources. If a data source is likely only to host documents relevant to particular Issues for Disclosure, this should be noted in this section.	
3.	Please identify and provide details of any bespoke or licensed proprietary software in which relevant documents have been created or stored which may not be available to the other party but without which it is not possible to review the relevant data (e.g. Microsoft Project, Lotus Notes, Bloomberg Chat etc.).	
4.	**Custodians and date ranges** Please set out a list of custodians whose files you propose to search and the date range(s) within which you would propose to search for documents which are relevant to Issues for Disclosure for which any party seeks Extended Disclosure. If a custodian or range of dates is only relevant to certain Issues for Disclosure, or if a certain date range is only relevant to a particular custodian, please indicate this next to their name if this might allow the scope of the search to be narrowed. If the list is extensive, please set out a proposal to prioritise key custodians.	

Claimant / Defendant (delete as appropriate)		
	Question	**Details**
5.	*(For completion after discussions between the parties)* Are the proposals at 4. agreed? If not, set out any areas of disagreement.	
6.	**Search proposals** Please list any searches and methods of searching (including any automated searches or techniques other than keyword searches) you have identified at this stage that you may use to search the data to identify documents that may need to be disclosed. If a certain method of searching, proposed search or keyword is relevant only to a particular Issue for Disclosure, please indicate this if it might allow the scope of the search to be narrowed. Note: The use of initial keywords may assist the parties to identify the likely volume of data that may need to be reviewed. However, keywords will need to be tested and refined during the disclosure process. Accordingly, any keywords proposed at this stage are for the purposes of discussion only. The fact that a party may propose a keyword at this stage should not be taken as an acceptance that the keyword should ultimately be used, particularly if, on testing the keyword against the available data, it provides false positive results. If it is not practicable to provide a list of keywords prior to the CMC, the parties should engage and seek to co-operate following the CMC to identify and agree the key words they propose using and thereafter test those key words against the data to determine whether or not they are appropriate.	
7.	*(For completion after discussions between the parties)* Are the proposals at 6. agreed? If not, set out areas of disagreement.	
8.	**Irretrievable documents** Please state if you anticipate any documents being irretrievable due to, for example, their destruction or loss, the destruction or loss of devices upon which they were stored, or other reasons.	

	Claimant / Defendant (delete as appropriate)	
	Question	**Details**
9.	**Technology / computer assisted review** Parties are to consider the use of technology to facilitate the efficient collection of data and its further use for data review. This may include the use of some of the more sophisticated forms of technology / computer assisted review software (TAR / CAR / analytics). If the parties are in a position to propose the use of any technology or computer assisted review tools in advance of the CMC, those proposals should be set out in this section. Where parties have considered the use of such tools but decided against this at this stage (particularly where the review universe is in excess of 50,000 documents), they should explain why such tools will not be used, particularly where this may mean that large volumes of data will have to be the subject of a manual review exercise. Parties should update this form and draw any material updates to the attention of all parties and the Court if they later determine it would be appropriate to use such tools.	
10.	**Estimates of costs** Where the parties have agreed searches to be undertaken, state the estimated cost of collection, processing, search, review and production of your Extended Disclosure.	
11.	Where any aspect of the approach to Disclosure is not agreed, estimate your costs of collection, processing, search, review and production of your documents based on Extended Disclosure (Models and scope of any search required) requested by the claimant(s).	
12.	Where any aspect of the approach to Disclosure is not agreed, estimate your costs of collection, processing, search, review and production of your documents based on Extended Disclosure (Models and scope of any search required) requested by the defendant(s).	

Appendix 7

Specimen skeleton argument

IN THE HIGH COURT OF JUSTICE   2023 Folio 296

BUSINESS AND PROPERTY COURTS OF ENGLAND AND WALES

KING'S BENCH DIVISION

COMMERCIAL COURT

Between   Williamson Superstores plc   Claimant

and

Haggerty Transport plc   Defendant

DEFENDANT'S SKELETON ARGUMENT FOR TRIAL

COUNSEL FOR THE PARTIES

Claimant's counsel   Joanna Smith instructed by Ballards

Defendant's counsel   Glenda Jones instructed by Tuckers

DRAMATIS PERSONAE

FOR THE CLAIMANT

(1)   James Williamson, managing director of the Claimant company.

(2)   Colin Carvell, head of production at the Claimant's dairy.

(3)   Ryan Beckham, van loader employed by the Claimant.

(4–12)   Other van loaders employed by the Claimant. [In practice each van loader would be identified by name.]

(13)   Kim Draper, branch manager of the Claimant's Houghton branch.

(14–37) Other branch managers employed by the Claimant. [In practice each branch manager would be identified by name.]

(38)   Victor Cunningham, depot manager of Price and Green, waste disposal consultants.

(39)   Graham Brace, chief accountant for the Claimant.

(40)   Joe Bloggs, a member of the general public and a customer of the Claimant.

(41–50) Other members of the public who are customers of the Claimant. [In practice each customer would be identified by name.]

FOR THE DEFENDANT

(1)   Denise Haggerty, managing director of the Defendant company.

(2)   David Hampton, van driver, employed by the Defendant.

(3–26)   Other van drivers employed by the Defendant. [In practice each van driver would be identified by name.]

(27)   Courtney Lara, maintenance supervisor, employed by the Defendant.

(28)   Ray Pallister, a consultant in food hygiene, and the Defendant's expert witness.

NATURE OF THE DISPUTE BETWEEN THE PARTIES

Under a contract dated 15 October 2008, the Defendant company agreed to transport the Claimant's produce from the Claimant's manufacturing depots to the Claimant's retail outlets. This contract was last renewed on 16 October 2021 for a period of three years.

On 13 April 2022, the Defendant company delivered 25 van loads of dairy produce from the Claimant's dairy to 25 retail outlets of the Claimant company. On arrival the produce was found to be unfit for human consumption. The Claimant alleges that the produce became unfit during transit because of some defect in the Defendant's van's refrigeration units or some other default by the Defendant or the Defendant's employees. As a result, the Claimant has repudiated its contract with the Defendant and is seeking damages for the value of the damaged produce, the costs of disposing of it, and loss of profit caused by the damage done by the incident to the Claimant's trading reputation.

The Defendant denies that it was responsible for the damage to the produce. As a result the Defendant will argue that the Claimant was not entitled to repudiate the contract and has raised a counterclaim for damages for loss of profit under the contract, including the amount payable for the delivery on 13 April 2022.

CHRONOLOGY OF EVENTS

On or about 30 March 2022, the Claimant gave instructions to the Defendant to deliver 25 consignments of dairy produce.

The delivery took place on 13 April 2022. The produce was found to be unfit for human consumption on delivery.

The Claimant purported to repudiate its contract with the Defendant on 14 April 2022.

ISSUES ARISING AT THE TRIAL
(1)   Was it the fault of the Defendant that the produce was delivered in a state in which it was unfit for human consumption?
(2)   If so, was the Claimant entitled to repudiate the contract?
(3)   If the Claimant was entitled to repudiate the contract, what damages is the Claimant entitled to?
(4)   If the Claimant was not entitled to repudiate the contract, either because the Defendant was not at fault or as a matter of law, what damages is the Defendant entitled to under its counterclaim?

DEFENDANT'S SUBMISSIONS
(1)   It was not the fault of the Defendant that the produce was delivered in a state which was unfit for human consumption. The damage was caused either directly or indirectly in the manufacturing process.

The Defendant will rely on evidence from its van drivers that the vans used to deliver the produce were in good working order on the day in question and that the refrigeration units were set to the correct temperatures for transporting dairy produce.

The Defendant will rely on evidence from its maintenance supervisor, Courtney Lara, that the vans were properly maintained and had not been tampered with.

The Defendant will rely on the expert evidence of Ray Pallister that it would not be possible for the produce to deteriorate to the extent that it was not fit for human consumption during the time in which the produce was in transit unless the produce was already defective at the time when it was loaded onto the Defendant's vans. The Defendant will also rely on the absence of expert evidence from the Claimant on this point.

(2) If the Defendant was at fault, the Defendant will argue that the Claimant was not, in law, entitled to repudiate the contract for this breach of contract.

The Defendant will rely on the following authorities in support of this contention.

[List of cases relied on.]

(3) If the Claimant was entitled to repudiate the contract, the Defendant will argue that the Claimant is not entitled to damages for loss of trading reputation.

The Defendant will rely on points arising out of cross examination of Joe Bloggs and the other sample witnesses who are alleged to be customers of the Claimant.

The Defendant will rely on the following authorities in support of this contention.

[List of cases relied on.]

ORDER SOUGHT

The Defendant will be seeking an order for judgment in its favour on both the Claimant's claim and the Defendant's counterclaim, for damages to be assessed and costs to be formally assessed if not agreed.

Appendix 8

Expert Evidence – Requirements of General Application

1. It is the duty of an expert to help the Court on the matters within the expert's expertise: rule 35.3(1). This duty is paramount and overrides any obligation to the person from whom the expert has received instructions or by whom the expert is paid: rule 35.3(2).

2. Expert evidence presented to the Court should be, and should be seen to be, the independent product of the expert uninfluenced by the pressures of litigation.

3. An expert witness should provide independent assistance to the Court by way of objective unbiased opinion in relation to matters within the expert's expertise. An expert witness should never assume the role of an advocate.

4. An expert witness should identify clearly any factual assumptions on the basis of which any opinions are expressed, explaining why the assumptions are important, and should not omit to consider material facts which could detract from the expert's opinion.

5. An expert witness should make it clear when a particular question or issue falls outside their expertise.

6. If an expert's opinion is not properly researched because the expert considers that insufficient data is available, this must be stated in the expert's report with an indication that the opinion is no more than a provisional one.

7. In a case where an expert witness who has prepared a report is unable to confirm that the report contains the truth, the whole truth and nothing but the truth without some qualification, that qualification must be stated in the report.

8. If, after exchange of reports, an expert witness changes their view on a material matter having read another expert's report or for any other reason, such change of view should be communicated in writing (through the party's legal representatives) to the other side without delay, and when appropriate to the Court.

9. All expert evidence – written or oral – should be as concise as possible.

10. An expert witness should be ready to take initiative to narrow the areas of disputed expert opinion as far as possible, including by initiating further dialogue between experts.

Please see also section H of the Commercial Court Guide.

Appendix 9

Summary of alternative procedure for claims under Part 8

The Part 8 procedure is usually used in cases where there is no substantial dispute of fact, for example in cases where the only issue is the construction of a document or a statute.

1. Claimant issues Part 8 claim form and serves the claim form and supporting written evidence[1]

NB: there are no particulars of claim.

2. Defendant acknowledges service and files written evidence in support[1]

Within 14 days of service of the claim form.

The defendant must notify the court if he does not intend to file any evidence.

NB: there is no defence and no possibility of the claimant entering judgment in default.

3. Claimant's written evidence in reply[1]

Within 14 days of receipt of defendant's written evidence (if any evidence in reply is required).

The parties may extend this time limit to a maximum of 28 days by written agreement. The agreement must be filed at court. Any longer extension requires an application to the court.

NB: no allocation questionnaires are filed.

4. The court gives directions or fixes a hearing date

The court may have given case management directions when the claim was issued, but will often consider its file for the purpose of deciding how the case should be dealt with after the expiry of the defendant's deadline for filing evidence.

If necessary the court can hold a case management conference, but in many cases no oral directions hearing is required. Instead, the court may be able to make a **final order in writing** or to **direct a hearing before a judge** (to resolve the substantive issues). The judge can require oral evidence to be given, but will more commonly rely on the parties' written evidence.

---

[1] The evidence is in the form of witness statement(s) or affidavit(s).

Appendix 10

Pre-action Protocol for Construction and Engineering Disputes 2nd edition

1 Introduction

1.1 This Pre-Action Protocol applies to all construction and engineering disputes (including professional negligence claims against architects, engineers and quantity surveyors).

2 Exceptions

2.1 A Claimant shall not be required to comply with this Protocol before commencing proceedings to the extent that the proposed proceedings (i) are for the enforcement of the decision of an adjudicator to whom a dispute has been referred pursuant to section 108 of the Housing Grants, Construction and Regeneration Act 1996 ("the 1996 Act"), (ii) include a claim for interim injunctive relief, (iii) will be the subject of a claim for summary judgment pursuant to Part 24 of the Civil Procedure Rules, or (iv) relate to the same or substantially the same issues as have been the subject of recent adjudication under the 1996 Act, or some other formal alternative dispute resolution procedure.

2.2 A Claimant shall not be required to comply with this Protocol before commencing proceedings if all the parties to the proposed proceedings expressly so agree in writing.

3 Objectives

3.1 The objectives of this Protocol are:
3.1.1 to exchange sufficient information about the proposed proceedings broadly to allow the parties to understand each other's position and make informed decisions about settlement and how to proceed;
3.1.2 to make appropriate attempts to resolve the matter without starting proceedings and, in particular, to consider the use of an appropriate form of ADR in order to do so.

4 Compliance

4.1 If proceedings are commenced, the Court will be able to treat the standards set in this Protocol as the normal reasonable and proportionate approach to pre-action conduct. It is likely to be only in exceptional circumstances, such as a flagrant or very significant disregard for the terms of this Protocol, that the Court will impose cost consequences on a party for non-compliance with this Protocol.

5 Proportionality

5.1 The overriding objective (CPR rule 1.1) applies to the pre-action period. The Protocol must not be used as a tactical device to secure advantage for one party or to generate unnecessary costs. In many cases, including those of modest value, the letter of claim and the response can be simple and the costs of both sides should be kept to a modest level. In all cases, the costs incurred at the Protocol stage should be proportionate to the complexity of the case and the amount of money which is at stake. The Protocol is not intended to impose a requirement on the parties to marshal and disclose all the supporting details and evidence that may ultimately be required if the case proceeds to litigation.

6   Overview of the Protocol

General aim

6.1   The general aim of this Protocol is to ensure that before Court proceedings commence:

6.1.1   the Claimant and the Defendant have provided sufficient information for each party to know the outline nature of the other's case;

6.1.2   each party has had an opportunity to consider the outline of the other's case, and to accept or reject all or any part of the outline case made against him at the earliest possible stage;

6.1.3   there is more pre-action contact between the parties;

6.1.4   better and earlier exchange of information occurs;

6.1.5   there is better pre-action investigation by the parties;

6.1.6   the parties have usually met formally on at least one occasion; and

6.1.7   the parties are in a position where they may be able to settle cases early, fairly and inexpensively without recourse to litigation; and

6.1.8   proceedings will be conducted efficiently if litigation does become necessary.

7   The Letter of Claim

7.1   Prior to commencing proceedings, the Claimant or his solicitor shall send to each proposed Defendant (if appropriate to his registered address) a copy of a letter of claim which shall contain the following information:

7.1.1   the Claimant's full name and address;

7.1.2   the full name and address of each proposed Defendant;

7.1.3   a brief summary of the claim or claims including (a) a list of principal contractual or statutory provisions relied on (b) a summary of the relief claimed including, where applicable, the monetary value of any claim or claims with a proportionate level of breakdown. The extent of the brief summary should be proportionate to the claim. Generally, it is not expected or required that expert reports should be provided but, in cases where they are succinct and central to the claim, they can form a helpful way of explaining the Claimant's position;

7.1.4   the names of any experts already instructed by the Claimant on whose evidence he intends to rely identifying the issues to which that evidence will be directed; and

7.1.5   the Claimant's confirmation as to whether or not it wishes the Protocol Referee Procedure to apply as provided at paragraph 11 below.

8   The Defendant's Response

The Defendant's acknowledgment

8.1   Within 14 calendar days of receipt of the letter of claim, the Defendant should acknowledge its receipt in writing and may give the name and address of his insurer (if any) and shall also confirm whether or not it wishes the Protocol Referee Procedure as provided at paragraph 11 below to apply. If there has been no acknowledgment by or on behalf of the Defendant within 14 days, the Claimant will be entitled to commence proceedings without further compliance with this Protocol.

Objections to the Court's jurisdiction or the named Defendant

8.2   If the Defendant intends to take any objection to all or any part of the Claimant's claim on the grounds that (i) the Court lacks jurisdiction, (ii) the matter should be referred to arbitration, or (iii) the Defendant named in the letter of claim is the wrong Defendant, that objection should be raised by the Defendant within 28 days after receipt of the Letter of Claim. The letter of objection shall specify the parts of the claim to which the objection relates, setting out the grounds relied on, and, where appropriate, shall identify the correct Defendant (if known). Any failure to take such objection shall not prejudice the Defendant's rights to do so in any subsequent proceedings, but the Court may take such failure into account when considering the question of costs.

8.3   Where such notice of objection is given, the Defendant is not required to send a letter of response in accordance with paragraph 8.5 in relation to the claim or those parts of it to which the objection relates (as the case may be).

8.4   If at any stage before the Claimant commences proceedings, the Defendant withdraws his objection, then paragraph 8.5 and the remaining part of this Protocol will apply to the claim or those parts of it to which the objection related as if the letter of claim had been received on the date on which notice of withdrawal of the objection had been given.

The Defendant's Response

8.5   Within 28 days from the date of receipt of the letter of claim, the Defendant shall send a letter of response to the Claimant which shall contain the following information:

8.5.1   A brief and proportionate summary of the Defendant's response to the claim or claims and, if the Defendant intends to make a Counterclaim, a brief summary of the Counterclaim containing the matters set out in paragraph 7.1.3 above;

8.5.2   the names of any experts already instructed on whose evidence it is intended to rely, identifying the issues to which that evidence will be directed;

8.5.3   the names of any third parties the Defendant intends to/is considering submitting to a Pre-action Protocol process.

8.6   If no response is received by the Claimant within the period of 28 days, the Claimant shall be entitled to commence proceedings without further compliance with this Protocol.

Claimant's Response to Counterclaim

8.7   The Claimant shall provide a Response to any Counterclaim within 21 days of the Defendant's Letter of Response. The Response shall contain a brief and proportionate summary of the Claimant's Response to the Counterclaim.

9   Pre-Action Meeting

9.1   Within 21 days after receipt by the Claimant of the Defendant's letter of response, or (if the Claimant intends to respond to the Counterclaim) after receipt by the Defendant of the Claimant's letter of response to the Counterclaim, the parties should normally meet.

9.2   It is not intended by this Protocol to prescribe in detail the manner in which the meeting should be conducted. However, the Court will normally expect that those attending will include:

9.2.1   where the party is an individual, that individual, and where the party is a corporate body, a representative of that body who has authority to settle or recommend settlement of the dispute;

9.2.2   a legal representative of each party (if one has been instructed);

9.2.3   where the involvement of insurers has been disclosed, a representative of the insurer (who may be its legal representative); and

9.2.4   where a claim is made or defended on behalf of some other party (such as, for example, a claim made by a main contractor pursuant to a contractual obligation to pass on subcontractor claims), the party on whose behalf the claim is made or defended and/or his legal representatives.

9.3   Generally, the aim of the meeting is for the parties to agree what are the main issues in the case, to identify the root cause of disagreement, and to consider (i) whether, and if so how, the case might be resolved without recourse to litigation, and (ii) if litigation is unavoidable, what steps should be taken to ensure that it is conducted in accordance with the overriding objective as defined in rule 1.1 of the Civil Procedure Rules. Alternatively, the meeting can itself take the form of an ADR process such as mediation.

9.4   If the parties are unable to agree on a means of resolving the dispute other than by litigation they should seek to agree:

9.4.1   if there is any area where expert evidence is likely to be required, how expert evidence is to be dealt with including whether a joint expert might be appointed, and if so, who that should be; and (so far as is practicable);

9.4.2   the extent of disclosure of documents with a view to saving costs and to the use of the e-disclosure protocol; and

9.4.3   the conduct of the litigation with the aim of minimising cost and delay.

9.5   Any party who attended any pre-action meeting shall be at liberty and may be required to disclose to the Court:

9.5.1   that the meeting took place, when and who attended;

9.5.2   the identity of any party who refused to attend, and the grounds for such refusal;

9.5.3   if the meeting did not take place, why not;

9.5.4   any agreements concluded between the parties; and

9.5.5   the fact of whether alternative means of resolving the dispute were considered or agreed.

9.6   Except as provided in paragraph 9.5, everything said at a pre-action meeting shall be treated as "without prejudice".

10   Other Matters

10.1   The parties may agree longer periods of time for compliance with any of the steps described above save that no extension in respect of any step shall exceed 28 days in the aggregate.

10.2   The Protocol process will be concluded at the completion of the pre-action meeting or, if no meeting takes place, 14 days after the expiry of the period in which the meeting should otherwise have taken place.

11   Protocol Referee Procedure

11.1   For the purposes of assisting the parties in participating in and complying with the Protocol, the parties may agree to engage in the current version of the Protocol Referee Procedure.

11.2   The Protocol Referee Procedure shall be published from time to time jointly by TeCSA and TECBAR on their respective websites.

12   Limitation of Action

12.1 If by reason of complying with any part of this protocol a Claimant's claim may be time-barred under any provision of the Limitation Act 1980, or any other legislation which imposes a time limit for bringing an action, the Claimant may commence proceedings without complying with this Protocol. In such circumstances, a Claimant who commences proceedings without complying with all, or any part, of this Protocol must apply to the Court on notice for directions as to the timetable and form of procedure to be adopted, at the same time as he requests the Court to issue proceedings. The Court will consider whether to order a stay of the whole or part of the proceedings pending compliance with this Protocol.

Appendix 11

Example of Scott Schedule

IN THE HIGH COURT OF JUSTICE   [Claim Number]

BUSINESS AND PROPERTY COURTS OF ENGLAND AND WALES

THE TECHNOLOGY AND CONSTRUCTION COURT (KBD)

JOHN SMITH   Claimant

– and –

BOTCHIT BUILDERS   Defendants
LIMITED

CLAIMANT'S SCOTT SCHEDULE
DELIVERED PURSUANT TO THE ORDER OF
HIS HONOUR JUDGE   DATED   2023

1 Item No	2 Claimant's description of each item of disrepair	3 Claimant's costs	4 Defendant's comments	5 Defendant's costs	6 For TCC judge
1	Inadequate bonding of the fibreboard to the steel angle generally along the perimeter of the roof	£80,000.00	Allegation denied. The fibreboard was adequately bonded to the steel angle	£25,000.00	
2	Inadequate anchoring of felt at top of perimeter upstand resulting in stripping of felt along the perimeter	£35,000.00	Allegation denied. The Defendants admit only that there would probably have been a small amount of what is known as 'birds mouthing' of the felt on the upstand which should have been dealt with by routine maintenance	£5,000.00	
3	Inadequately formed felt around rainwater sumps resulting in a raised rim around the sump delaying drainage of water and causing ponding on the flat roof	£20,000.00	Allegation denied. The Defendants' workmanship in the vicinity of the rainwater sumps was of a good standard	£7,500.00	
4	etc		etc		

Delivered by the Claimant this   day of   2023

Delivered by the Defendants this   day of   2023

Appendix 12

Specimen order for an injunction

[CLAIM NUMBER]

IN THE HIGH COURT OF JUSTICE

KING'S BENCH DIVISION

Before the honourable MR JUSTICE DASH

Between   Applicant

and

Respondent

PENAL NOTICE

If you the within named [   ] disobey this Order you may be held to be in contempt of court and liable to imprisonment or fined or your assets seized.

IMPORTANT:

NOTICE TO THE RESPONDENT

You should read the terms of the Order and Guidance Notes carefully. You are advised to consult a solicitor as soon as possible.

(1)   This Order [prohibits you from doing] [obliges you to do] the acts set out in this Order. You have a right to ask the Court to vary or discharge this Order.

(2)   If you disobey this Order you may be found guilty of Contempt of Court and may be sent to prison or fined. [In the case of a corporate respondent, it may be fined, its directors may be fined or its assets may be seized.][1]

The Order was made today [date] by Counsel for the Applicant to Mr Justice Dash [and was attended by Counsel for the Respondent]. The Judge heard the Application and read the Evidence listed in Schedule A and accepted the undertakings set out in Schedule B at the end of this Order as a result of the application.

IT IS ORDERED that:

THE INJUNCTION

(1)   Until after [date] [final judgment in this Action] the Respondent must/must not [Body of Injunction to go here]

---

[1] Include the words in square brackets in case of a corporate Respondent. This notice is not a substitute for the indorsement of a penal notice.

COSTS OF THE APPLICATION

(2)   [The Respondent shall pay the Applicant's costs of this Application.]/[The costs of this Application are reserved to be dealt with by the Judge who tries this Action.]/[The costs of this Application are to be costs in the case.]/[The costs of this Application are to be the Applicant's costs in the case.]

EFFECT OF THIS ORDER

(1)   A Respondent who is an individual who is ordered not to do something must not do it himself or in any other way. He must not do it through others acting on his behalf or on his instructions or with his encouragement.

(2)   A Respondent which is a corporation and which is ordered not to do something must not do it itself or by its directors, officers, employees or agents or in any other way.

GUIDANCE NOTES

VARIATION OR DISCHARGE OF THIS ORDER

The Respondent may apply to the Court at any time to vary or discharge this Order but if he wishes to do so he must first inform the Applicant's Legal Representatives.

INTERPRETATION OF THIS ORDER

(1)   In this Order, where there is more than one Respondent (unless otherwise stated), references to 'the Respondent' mean both or all of them;

(2)   an Order requiring 'the Respondent' to do or not to do anything applies to all Respondents.

COMMUNICATIONS WITH THE COURT

All communications to the Court about this Order should be sent to Room W11, Royal Courts of Justice, Strand, London WC2A 2LL quoting the case number. The office is open between 10 am and 4.30 pm Monday to Friday. The telephone number is 020 7936 6009.

SCHEDULE A

Evidence

The Applicant relied on the following witness statements:

[name]   [number of witness statements]   [date made]   [filed on behalf of]

(1)

(2)

SCHEDULE B

Undertaking given to the Court by the Applicant

If the Court later finds that this Order has caused loss to the Respondent, and decides that the Respondent should be compensated for that loss, the Applicant will comply with any Order the Court may make.

NAME AND ADDRESS OF APPLICANT'S LEGAL REPRESENTATIVES

The Applicant's Legal Representatives are:

[Name, address reference, fax and telephone numbers both in and out of office hours.]

Appendix 13

Specimen order for injunction before issue of a claim form

IN THE HIGH COURT OF JUSTICE
BUSINESS AND PROPERTY COURTS OF ENGLAND AND WALES
PROPERTY TRUSTS AND PROBATE LIST (ChD)

BEFORE THE HONOURABLE MR JUSTICE DAY

[CLAIM NUMBER]

DATED

IN AN ACTION INTENDED TO BE BETWEEN

Applicant

and

Respondent

PENAL NOTICE

If you the within named [   ] disobey this Order you may be held to be in contempt of court and liable to imprisonment or fined or your assets seized.

IMPORTANT:

NOTICE TO THE RESPONDENT

You should read the terms of the Order and Guidance Notes carefully. You are advised to consult a solicitor as soon as possible.

(1)   This Order [prohibits you from doing] [obliges you to do] the acts set out in this Order. You have a right to ask the Court to vary or discharge this Order.

(2)   If you disobey this Order you may be found guilty of Contempt of Court and may be sent to prison or fined. [In the case of a corporate Respondent, it may be fined, its directors may be sent to prison or fined or its assets may be seized.][1]

THE ORDER

An Application was made today [date] by Counsel for (who is to be the Claimant in an Action against) to the Judge who heard the Application supported by the Evidence listed in Schedule A and accepted the undertakings set out in Schedule B at the end of this Order as a result of the Application.

IT IS ORDERED that:

The Defendant must/must not [Body of Injunction to go here]

---

[1] Include the words in square brackets in case of a corporate Applicant. This notice is not a substitute for the indorsement of a penal notice.

EFFECT OF THIS ORDER

(1)   A Respondent who is an individual who is ordered not to do something must not do it himself or in any other way. He must not do it through others acting on his behalf or on his instructions or with his encouragement.

(2)   A Respondent which is a corporation and which is ordered not to do something must not do it itself or by its directors, officers, employees, or agents or in any other way.

GUIDANCE NOTES

VARIATION OR DISCHARGE OF THIS ORDER

The Respondent may apply to the Court at any time to vary or discharge this Order but if he wishes to do so he must first inform the Applicant's Legal Representatives.

INTERPRETATION OF THIS ORDER

(1)   In this Order, where there is more than one Respondent, references to 'the Respondent' mean both or all of them;

(2)   a requirement to serve on 'the Respondent' means on each of them. However, the order is effective against any Respondent on whom it is served;

(3)   an Order requiring 'the Respondent' to do or not to do anything applies to all Respondents.

COMMUNICATIONS WITH THE COURT

All communications to the Court about this Order should be sent to Room TM510, Royal Courts of Justice, Strand, London WC2A 2LL quoting the case number. The office is open between 10 am and 4.30 pm Monday to Friday. The telephone number is 020 7936 6827.

SCHEDULE A

Witness Statements

The Applicant relied on the following Witness Statements:

[name]   [number of witness statements]   [date made]   [filed on behalf of]

SCHEDULE B

Undertakings given to the Court by the Applicant

(1)   If the Court later finds that this Order has caused loss to the Respondent, and decides that the Respondent should be compensated for that loss, the Applicant will comply with any Order the Court may make.

(2)   As soon as practicable the Applicant will issue and serve on the Respondent a Claim Form [in the form of the draft produced to the Court] [serve on the Respondent the Claim Form] claiming appropriate relief together with this Order.

(3)   The Applicant will file a witness statement [substantially in the terms of the draft witness statement produced to the Court] (confirming the substance of what was said to the Court by the Applicant's Counsel/Solicitors).

[(4)   Where a return date has been given – as soon as practicable the Applicant will serve on the Respondent an application for the return date together with a copy of the witness statements and exhibits containing the evidence relied on by the Applicant.]

NAME AND ADDRESS OF APPLICANT'S LEGAL REPRESENTATIVES

The Applicant's Legal Representatives are:

[Name, address reference, fax and telephone numbers both in and out of office hours.]

Appendix 14

Specimen freezing injunction

FREEZING INJUNCTION	**IN THE HIGH COURT OF JUSTICE** [ ] **DIVISION**
Before The Honourable Mr Justice	[ ]
	Claim No.
	Dated
Applicant	
	Seal
Respondent	

Name, address and reference of Respondent

PENAL NOTICE

IF YOU [   ]¹ DISOBEY THIS ORDER YOU MAY BE HELD TO BE IN CONTEMPT OF
COURT AND MAY BE IMPRISONED, FINED OR HAVE YOUR ASSETS SEIZED.

ANY OTHER PERSON WHO KNOWS OF THIS ORDER AND DOES ANYTHING WHICH HELPS OR
PERMITS THE RESPONDENT TO BREACH THE TERMS OF THIS ORDER MAY ALSO BE HELD TO BE
IN CONTEMPT OF COURT AND MAY BE IMPRISONED, FINED OR HAVE THEIR ASSETS SEIZED.

1 Insert name of Respondent

THIS ORDER

1. This is a Freezing Injunction made against [   ] ('the Respondent') on [   ] by Mr Justice [   ] on the application of [   ] ('the Applicant'). The Judge read the Affidavits listed in Schedule A and accepted the undertakings set out in Schedule B at the end of this Order.

2. This order was made at a hearing without notice to the Respondent. The Respondent has a right to apply to the court to vary or discharge the order – see paragraph 13 below.

3. There will be a further hearing in respect of this order on [   ] ('the return date').

4. If there is more than one Respondent—

    (a) unless otherwise stated, references in this order to 'the Respondent' mean both or all of them; and

    (b) this order is effective against any Respondent on whom it is served or who is given notice of it.

FREEZING INJUNCTION

[For injunction limited to assets in England and Wales]

5. Until the return date or further order of the court, the Respondent must not remove from England and Wales or in any way dispose of, deal with or diminish the value of any of his assets which are in England and Wales up to the value of £   .

[For worldwide injunction]

5. Until the return date or further order of the court, the Respondent must not—

    (1) remove from England and Wales any of his assets which are in England and Wales up to the value of £   ; or

    (2) in any way dispose of, deal with or diminish the value of any of his assets whether they are in or outside England and Wales up to the same value.

[For either form of injunction]

6. Paragraph 5 applies to all the Respondent's assets whether or not they are in his own name and whether they are solely or jointly owned. For the purpose of this order the Respondent's assets include any asset which he has the power, directly or indirectly, to dispose of or deal with as if it were his own. The Respondent is to be regarded as having such power if a third party holds or controls the asset in accordance with his direct or indirect instructions.

7. This prohibition includes the following assets in particular—

    (a) the property known as [title/address] or the net sale money after payment of any mortgages if it has been sold;

    (b) the property and assets of the Respondent's business [known as [name]] [carried on at [address]] or the sale money if any of them have been sold; and

    (c) any money standing to the credit of any bank account including the amount of any cheque drawn on such account which has not been cleared.

[For injunction limited to assets in England and Wales]

8. If the total value free of charges or other securities ('unencumbered value') of the Respondent's assets in England and Wales exceeds £   , the Respondent may remove any of those assets from England and Wales or may dispose of or deal with them so long as the total unencumbered value of his assets still in England and Wales remains above £   .

[For worldwide injunction]

8. (1) If the total value free of charges or other securities ('unencumbered value') of the Respondent's assets in England and Wales exceeds £   , the Respondent may remove any of those assets from England and Wales or may dispose of or deal with

them so long as the total unencumbered value of the Respondent's assets still in England and Wales remains above £   .

(2)   If the total unencumbered value of the Respondent's assets in England and Wales does not exceed £   , the Respondent must not remove any of those assets from England and Wales and must not dispose of or deal with any of them. If the Respondent has other assets outside England and Wales, he may dispose of or deal with those assets outside England and Wales so long as the total unencumbered value of all his assets whether in or outside England and Wales remains above £   .

PROVISION OF INFORMATION

9.   (1)   Unless paragraph (2) applies, the Respondent must [immediately] [within hours of service of this order] and to the best of his ability inform the Applicant's solicitors of all his assets [in England and Wales] [worldwide] [exceeding £   in value] whether in his own name or not and whether solely or jointly owned, giving the value, location and details of all such assets.

(2)   If the provision of any of this information is likely to incriminate the Respondent, he may be entitled to refuse to provide it, but is recommended to take legal advice before refusing to provide the information. Wrongful refusal to provide the information is contempt of court and may render the Respondent liable to be imprisoned, fined or have his assets seized.

10.   Within [   ] working days after being served with this order, the Respondent must swear and serve on the Applicant's solicitors an affidavit setting out the above information.

EXCEPTIONS TO THIS ORDER

11.   (1)   This order does not prohibit the Respondent from spending £   a week towards his ordinary living expenses and also £   [or a reasonable sum] on legal advice and representation. [But before spending any money the Respondent must tell the Applicant's legal representatives where the money is to come from.]

[(2)   This order does not prohibit the Respondent from dealing with or disposing of any of his assets in the ordinary and proper course of business.]

(3)   The Respondent may agree with the Applicant's legal representatives that the above spending limits should be increased or that this order should be varied in any other respect, but any agreement must be in writing.

(4)   The order will cease to have effect if the Respondent—

(a)   provides security by paying the sum of £   into court, to be held to the order of the court; or

(b)   makes provision for security in that sum by another method agreed with the Applicant's legal representatives.

COSTS

12.   The costs of this application are reserved to the judge hearing the application on the return date.

VARIATION OR DISCHARGE OF THIS ORDER

13.   Anyone served with or notified of this order may apply to the court at any time to vary or discharge this order (or so much of it as affects that person), but they must first inform the Applicant's solicitors. If any evidence is to be relied upon in support of the application, the substance of it must be communicated in writing to the Applicant's solicitors in advance.

INTERPRETATION OF THIS ORDER

14. A Respondent who is an individual who is ordered not to do something must not do it himself or in any other way. He must not do it through others acting on his behalf or on his instructions or with his encouragement.

15. A Respondent which is not an individual which is ordered not to do something must not do it itself or by its directors, officers, partners, employees or agents or in any other way.

PARTIES OTHER THAN THE APPLICANT AND RESPONDENT

16. Effect of this order

It is a contempt of court for any person notified of this order knowingly to assist in or permit a breach of this order. Any person doing so may be imprisoned, fined or have their assets seized.

17. Set off by banks

This injunction does not prevent any bank from exercising any right of set off it may have in respect of any facility which it gave to the respondent before it was notified of this order.

18. Withdrawals by the Respondent

No bank need enquire as to the application or proposed application of any money withdrawn by the Respondent if the withdrawal appears to be permitted by this order.

[For worldwide injunction]

19. Persons outside England and Wales

(1) Except as provided in paragraph (2) below, the terms of this order do not affect or concern anyone outside the jurisdiction of this court.

(2) The terms of this order will affect the following persons in a country or state outside the jurisdiction of this court —

  (a) the Respondent or his officer or agent appointed by power of attorney;

  (b) any person who—

   (i) is subject to the jurisdiction of this court;

   (ii) has been given written notice of this order at his residence or place of business within the jurisdiction of this court; and

   (iii) is able to prevent acts or omissions outside the jurisdiction of this court which constitute or assist in a breach of the terms of this order; and

  (c) any other person, only to the extent that this order is declared enforceable by or is enforced by a court in that country or state.

[For worldwide injunction]

20. Assets located outside England and Wales

Nothing in this order shall, in respect of assets located outside England and Wales, prevent any third party from complying with—

(1) what it reasonably believes to be its obligations, contractual or otherwise, under the laws and obligations of the country or state in which those assets are situated or under the proper law of any contract between itself and the Respondent; and

(2) any orders of the courts of that country or state, provided that reasonable notice of any application for such an order is given to the Applicant's solicitors.

COMMUNICATIONS WITH THE COURT

All communications to the court about this order should be sent to—

[Insert the address and telephone number of the appropriate Court Office]

If the order is made at the Royal Courts of Justice, communications should be addressed as follows—

Where the order is made in the Chancery Division

Chancery Associates, Ground Floor, The Rolls Building, 7 Rolls Buildings, Fetter Lane, London EC4A 1NL, quoting the case number. The telephone number is 020 7947 6733.

Where the order is made in the King's Bench Division

Room E07, Royal Courts of Justice, Strand, London WC2A 2LL quoting the case number. The telephone number is 020 7947 6010.

Where the order is made in the Commercial Court

7 Rolls Building, Fetter Lane, London, EC4A 1NL, quoting the case number. The telephone number is 020 7947 6826.

The offices are open between 10 am and 4.30 pm Monday to Friday.

SCHEDULE A

AFFIDAVITS

The Applicant relied on the following affidavits—

[name]   [number of affidavit]   [date sworn]   [filed on behalf of]

SCHEDULE B

UNDERTAKINGS GIVEN TO THE COURT BY THE APPLICANT

(1)   If the court later finds that this order has caused loss to the Respondent, anddecides that the Respondent should be compensated for that loss, the Applicant will comply with any order the court may make.

[(2)   The Applicant will—

    (a)   on or before [date] cause a written guarantee in the sum of £ to be issued from a bank with a place of business within England or Wales, in respect of any order the court may make pursuant to paragraph (1) above; and

    (b)   immediately upon issue of the guarantee, cause a copy of it to be served on the Respondent.]

(3)   As soon as practicable the Applicant will issue and serve a claim form [in the form of the draft produced to the court] [claiming the appropriate relief].

(4)   The Applicant will [swear and file an affidavit] [cause an affidavit to be sworn and filed] [substantially in the terms of the draft affidavit produced to the court] [confirming the substance of what was said to the court by the Applicant's counsel/solicitors].

(5)   The Applicant will serve upon the Respondent [together with this order] [as soon as practicable]—

    (i)   copies of the affidavits and exhibits containing the evidence relied upon by the Applicant, and any other documents provided to the court on the making of the application;

    (ii)   the claim form; and

    (iii)   an application notice for continuation of the order.

[(6)   Anyone notified of this order will be given a copy of it by the Applicant's legal representatives.]

(7)   The Applicant will pay the reasonable costs of anyone other than the Respondent which have been incurred as a result of this order including the costs of finding out whether that person holds any of the Respondent's assets and if the court later finds that this order has caused such person loss, and decides that such person should be

compensated for that loss, the Applicant will comply with any order the court may make.

(8) If this order ceases to have effect (for example, if the Respondent provides security or the Applicant does not provide a bank guarantee as provided for above) the Applicant will immediately take all reasonable steps to inform in writing anyone to whom he has given notice of this order, or who he has reasonable grounds for supposing may act upon this order, that it has ceased to have effect.

[(9) The Applicant will not without the permission of the court use any information obtained as a result of this order for the purpose of any civil or criminal proceedings, either in England and Wales or in any other jurisdiction, other than this claim.]

[(10) The Applicant will not without the permission of the court seek to enforce this order in any country outside England and Wales [or seek an order of a similar nature including orders conferring a charge or other security against the Respondent or the Respondent's assets].]

NAME AND ADDRESS OF APPLICANT'S LEGAL REPRESENTATIVES

The Applicant's legal representatives are –
[Name, address, reference, fax and telephone numbers both in and out of office hours and e-mail]

Appendix 15

Specimen search order

SEARCH ORDER	**IN THE HIGH COURT OF JUSTICE**
	[ ] DIVISION
Before The Honourable Mr Justice	**[ ]**

Claim No.

Dated

Applicant

Seal

Respondent

Name, address and reference of Respondent

PENAL NOTICE

IF YOU [   ]^1 DISOBEY THIS ORDER YOU MAY BE HELD TO BE IN CONTEMPT OF COURT AND MAY BE IMPRISONED, FINED OR HAVE YOUR ASSETS SEIZED.

ANY OTHER PERSON WHO KNOWS OF THIS ORDER AND DOES ANYTHING WHICH HELPS OR PERMITS THE RESPONDENT TO BREACH THE TERMS OF THIS ORDER MAY ALSO BE HELD TO BE IN CONTEMPT OF COURT AND MAY BE IMPRISONED, FINED OR HAVE THEIR ASSETS SEIZED.

1 Insert name of Respondent

THIS ORDER

1. This is a Search Order made against [   ] ('the Respondent') on [   ] by Mr Justice [   ] on the application of [   ] ('the Applicant'). The Judge read the Affidavits listed in Schedule F and accepted the undertakings set out in Schedules C, D and E at the end of this order.

2. This order was made at a hearing without notice to the Respondent. The Respondent has a right to apply to the court to vary or discharge the order – see paragraph 27 below.

3. There will be a further hearing in respect of this order on [   ] ('the return date').

4. If there is more than one Respondent—

    (a) unless otherwise stated, references in this order to 'the Respondent' mean both or all of them; and

    (b) this order is effective against any Respondent on whom it is served or who is given notice of it.

5. This order must be complied with by—

    (a) the Respondent;

    (b) any director, officer, partner or responsible employee of the Respondent; and

    (c) if the Respondent is an individual, any other person having responsible control of the premises to be searched.

THE SEARCH

6. The Respondent must permit the following persons[8]—

    (a) [   ] ('the Supervising Solicitor');

    (b) [   ], a solicitor in the firm of [   ], the Applicant's solicitors; and

    (c) up to [   ] other persons[9] being [their identity or capacity] accompanying them,

    (together 'the search party'), to enter the premises mentioned in Schedule A to this order and any other premises of the Respondent disclosed under paragraph 18 below and any vehicles under the Respondent's control on or around the premises ('the premises') so that they can search for, inspect, photograph or photocopy, and deliver into the safekeeping of the Applicant's solicitors all the documents and articles which are listed in Schedule B to this order ('the listed items').

7. Having permitted the search party to enter the premises, the Respondent must allow the search party to remain on the premises until the search is complete. In the event that it becomes necessary for any of those persons to leave the premises before the search is complete, the Respondent must allow them to re-enter the premises immediately upon their seeking re-entry on the same or the following day in order to complete the search.

RESTRICTIONS ON SEARCH

8. This order may not be carried out at the same time as a police search warrant.

9. Before the Respondent allows anybody onto the premises to carry out this order, he is entitled to have the Supervising Solicitor explain to him what it means in everyday language.

10. The Respondent is entitled to seek legal advice and to ask the court to vary or discharge this order. Whilst doing so, he may ask the Supervising Solicitor to delay starting the search for up to 2 hours or such other longer period as the Supervising Solicitor may permit. However, the Respondent must—

    (a) comply with the terms of paragraph 27 below;

    (b) not disturb or remove any listed items; and

    (c) permit the Supervising Solicitor to enter, but not start to search.

11. (1) Before permitting entry to the premises by any person other than the Supervising Solicitor, the Respondent may, for a short time (not to exceed two hours, unless the Supervising Solicitor agrees to a longer period)—

   (a) gather together any documents he believes may be incriminating or privileged; and

   (b) hand them to the Supervising Solicitor for him to assess whether they are incriminating or privileged as claimed.

   (2) If the Supervising Solicitor decides that the Respondent is entitled to withhold production of any of the documents on the ground that they are privileged or incriminating, he will exclude them from the search, record them in a list for inclusion in his report and return them to the Respondent.

   (3) If the Supervising Solicitor believes that the Respondent may be entitled to withhold production of the whole or any part of a document on the ground that it or part of it may be privileged or incriminating or if the Respondent claims to be entitled to withhold production on those grounds, the Supervising Solicitor will exclude it from the search and retain it in his possession pending further order of the court.

12. If the Respondent wishes to take legal advice and gather documents as permitted, he must first inform the Supervising Solicitor and keep him informed of the steps being taken.

13. No item may be removed from the premises until a list of the items to be removed has been prepared, and a copy of the list has been supplied to the Respondent, and he has been given a reasonable opportunity to check the list.

14. The premises must not be searched, and items must not be removed from them, except in the presence of the Respondent.

15. If the Supervising Solicitor is satisfied that full compliance with paragraphs 13 or 14 is not practicable, he may permit the search to proceed and items to be removed without fully complying with them.

DELIVERY UP OF ARTICLES/DOCUMENTS

16. The Respondent must immediately hand over to the Applicant's solicitors any of the listed items, which are in his possession or under his control, save for any computer or hard disk integral to any computer. Any items the subject of a dispute as to whether they are listed items must immediately be handed over to the Supervising Solicitor for safe keeping pending resolution of the dispute or further order of the court.

17. The Respondent must immediately give the search party effective access to the computers on the premises, with all necessary passwords, to enable the computers to be searched. If they contain any listed items the Respondent must cause the listed items to be displayed so that they can be read and copied.[10] The Respondent must provide the Applicant's Solicitors with copies of all listed items contained in the computers. All reasonable steps shall be taken by the Applicant and the Applicant's solicitors to ensure that no damage is done to any computer or data. The Applicant and his representatives may not themselves search the Respondent's computers unless they have sufficient expertise to do so without damaging the Respondent's system.

PROVISION OF INFORMATION

18. The Respondent must immediately inform the Applicant's Solicitors (in the presence of the Supervising Solicitor) so far as he is aware—

   (a) where all the listed items are;

   (b) the name and address of everyone who has supplied him, or offered to supply him, with listed items;

(c) the name and address of everyone to whom he has supplied, or offered to supply, listed items; and

(d) full details of the dates and quantities of every such supply and offer.

19. Within [   ] working days after being served with this order the Respondent must swear and serve an affidavit setting out the above information.[11]

PROHIBITED ACTS

20. Except for the purpose of obtaining legal advice, the Respondent must not directly or indirectly inform anyone of these proceedings or of the contents of this order, or warn anyone that proceedings have been or may be brought against him by the Applicant until 4.30 pm on the return date or further order of the court.

21. Until 4.30 pm on the return date the Respondent must not destroy, tamper with, cancel or part with possession, power, custody or control of the listed items otherwise than in accordance with the terms of this order.

22. [Insert any negative injunctions.]

23. [Insert any further order.]

COSTS

24. The costs of this application are reserved to the judge hearing the application on the return date.

RESTRICTIONS ON SERVICE

25. This order may only be served between [ ] am/pm and [ ] am/pm [and on a weekday].[12]

26. This order must be served by the Supervising Solicitor, and paragraph 6 of the order must be carried out in his presence and under his supervision.

VARIATION AND DISCHARGE OF THIS ORDER

27. Anyone served with or notified of this order may apply to the court at any time to vary or discharge this order (or so much of it as affects that person), but they must first inform the Applicant's solicitors. If any evidence is to be relied upon in support of the application, the substance of it must be communicated in writing to the Applicant's solicitors in advance.

INTERPRETATION OF THIS ORDER

28. Any requirement that something shall be done to or in the presence of the Respondent means—

(a) if there is more than one Respondent, to or in the presence of any one of them; and

(b) if a Respondent is not an individual, to or in the presence of a director, officer, partner or responsible employee.

29. A Respondent who is an individual who is ordered not to do something must not do it himself or in any other way. He must not do it through others acting on his behalf or on his instructions or with his encouragement.

30. A Respondent which is not an individual which is ordered not to do something must not do it itself or by its directors, officers, partners, employees or agents or in any other way.

COMMUNICATIONS WITH THE COURT

All communications to the court about this order should be sent to—

[Insert the address and telephone number of the appropriate Court Office]

If the order is made at the Royal Courts of Justice, communications should be addressed as follows—

Where the order is made in the Chancery Division

Chancery Associates, Ground Floor, The Rolls Building, 7 Rolls Buildings, Fetter Lane, London EC4A 1NL, quoting the case number. The telephone number is 020 7947 6733.

Where the order is made in the King's Bench Division

Room E07, Royal Courts of Justice, Strand, London WC2A 2LL quoting the case number. The telephone number is 020 7947 6010.

Where the order is made in the Commercial Court

7 Rolls Building, Fetter Lane, London, EC4A 1NL, quoting the case number. The telephone number is 020 7947 6826.

The offices are open between 10 am and 4.30 pm Monday to Friday.

SCHEDULE A

THE PREMISES

SCHEDULE B

THE LISTED ITEMS

SCHEDULE C

UNDERTAKINGS GIVEN TO THE COURT BY THE APPLICANT

(1)   If the court later finds that this order or carrying it out has caused loss to the Respondent, and decides that the Respondent should be compensated for that loss, the Applicant will comply with any order the court may make. Further if the carrying out of this order has been in breach of the terms of this order or otherwise in a manner inconsistent with the Applicant's solicitors' duties as officers of the court, the Applicant will comply with any order for damages the court may make.

[(2)   As soon as practicable the Applicant will issue a claim form [in the form of the draft produced to the court] [claiming the appropriate relief].]

(3)   The Applicant will [swear and file an affidavit] [cause an affidavit to be sworn and filed] [substantially in the terms of the draft affidavit produced to the court] [confirming the substance of what was said to the court by the Applicant's counsel/solicitors].

(4)   The Applicant will not, without the permission of the court, use any information or documents obtained as a result of carrying out this order nor inform anyone else of these proceedings except for the purposes of these proceedings (including adding further Respondents) or commencing civil proceedings in relation to the same or related subject matter to these proceedings until after the return date.

[(5)   The Applicant will maintain pending further order the sum of £ [   ] in an account controlled by the Applicant's solicitors.]

[(6)   The Applicant will insure the items removed from the premises.]

SCHEDULE D

UNDERTAKINGS GIVEN BY THE APPLICANT'S SOLICITORS

(1)   The Applicant's solicitors will provide to the Supervising Solicitor for service on the Respondent—

(i)   a service copy of this order;

(ii)   the claim form (with defendant's response pack) or, if not issued, the draft produced to the court;

(iii)   an application for hearing on the return date;

(iv)   copies of the affidavits [or draft affidavits] and exhibits capable of being copied containing the evidence relied upon by the applicant;

(v)   a note of any allegation of fact made orally to the court where such allegation is not contained in the affidavits or draft affidavits read by the judge; and

(vi) a copy of the skeleton argument produced to the court by the Applicant's [counsel/ solicitors].

(2) The Applicants' solicitors will answer at once to the best of their ability any question whether a particular item is a listed item.

(3) Subject as provided below the Applicant's solicitors will retain in their own safe keeping all items obtained as a result of this order until the court directs otherwise.

(4) The Applicant's solicitors will return the originals of all documents obtained as a result of this order (except original documents which belong to the Applicant) as soon as possible and in any event within [two] working days of their removal.

SCHEDULE E

UNDERTAKINGS GIVEN BY THE SUPERVISING SOLICITOR

(1) The Supervising Solicitor will use his best endeavours to serve this order upon the Respondent and at the same time to serve upon the Respondent the other documents required to be served and referred to in paragraph (1) of Schedule D.

(2) The Supervising Solicitor will offer to explain to the person served with the order its meaning and effect fairly and in everyday language, and to inform him of his right to take legal advice (including an explanation that the Respondent may be entitled to avail himself of the privilege against self-incrimination and legal professional privilege) and to apply to vary or discharge this order as mentioned in paragraph 27 above.

(3) The Supervising Solicitor will retain in the safe keeping of his firm all items retained by him as a result of this order until the court directs otherwise.

(4) Unless and until the court otherwise orders, or unless otherwise necessary to comply with any duty to the court pursuant to this order, the Supervising Solicitor shall not disclose to any person any information relating to those items, and shall keep the existence of such items confidential.

(5) Within [48] hours of completion of the search the Supervising Solicitor will make and provide to the Applicant's solicitors, the Respondent or his solicitors and to the judge who made this order (for the purposes of the court file) a written report on the carrying out of the order.

SCHEDULE F

AFFIDAVITS

The Applicant relied on the following affidavits—

[name]   [number of affidavit]   [date sworn]   [filed on behalf of]

NAME AND ADDRESS OF APPLICANT'S SOLICITORS

The Applicant's solicitors are—

[Name, address, reference, fax and telephone numbers both in and out of office hours.]

FOOTNOTES

...

8   Where the premises are likely to be occupied by an unaccompanied woman and the Supervising Solicitor is a man, at least one of the persons accompanying him should be a woman.

9   None of these persons should be people who could gain personally or commercially from anything they might read or see on the premises, unless their presence is essential.

10   If it is envisaged that the Respondent's computers are to be imaged (i.e. the hard drives are to be copied wholesale, thereby reproducing listed items and other items indiscriminately), special provision needs to be made and independent computer

specialists need to be appointed, who should be required to give undertakings to the court.

11   The period should ordinarily be longer than the period in paragraph (2) of Schedule D, if any of the information is likely to be included in listed items taken away of which the Respondent does not have copies.

12   Normally, the order should be served in the morning (not before 9.30 am) and on a weekday to enable the Respondent more readily to obtain legal advice.

Appendix 16

Disclosure Certificate

Notes: This Disclosure Certificate is for use in all claims where Practice Direction 57AD (Disclosure in the Business and Property Courts) applies.

In the	
Claim No.	
Claimant (including ref)	
Defendant (including ref)	
Date	
Party returning form	

Initial Disclosure

Either:

On [date] [party], [with its Statement of Case] [or state if the parties agreed to defer the time for provision of Initial Disclosure] , provided [to party/parties] by way of Initial Disclosure [a List, and/or] copies of the following:

- the key documents on which it has relied (expressly or otherwise) in support of the claims or defences advanced in its statement of case (and including the documents referred to in that statement of case); and

- the key documents that are necessary to enable the other parties to understand the claim or defence they have to meet.

    (These comprise Initial Disclosure as defined at paragraphs 5.1 and 5.2 of Practice Direction 57AD.)

[The Initial Disclosure List is found at [at Appendix A]] or [The parties agreed to dispense with the requirement to produce an Initial Disclosure List of Documents, as permitted by paragraph 5.8 of Practice Direction 57AD.]

<u>*Or*</u>

[No Initial Disclosure was required because [the parties agreed to dispense with it] [the Court ordered that it was not required] [it would involve [name of party] providing (after removing duplicates, and including documents referred to at paragraph 5.4(3)(a)) more than (about) whichever is the larger of 1000 pages or 200 documents (or such higher but reasonable figure as the parties may agree)].

Where the parties agreed to dispense with Initial Disclosure, please set out here your reasons for this agreement.

```
┌─────────────────────────────────────────────────────────────┐
│                                                             │
│                                                             │
│                                                             │
└─────────────────────────────────────────────────────────────┘
```

Extended Disclosure

Please list the orders made in the proceedings that have imposed Extended Disclosure obligations (together, "the Disclosure Order/s"):

```
┌─────────────────────────────────────────────────────────────┐
│                                                             │
│                                                             │
│                                                             │
└─────────────────────────────────────────────────────────────┘
```

Please state if the Extended Disclosure List of Documents has been dispensed with, by agreement or order.

```
┌─────────────────────────────────────────────────────────────┐
│                                                             │
│                                                             │
│                                                             │
└─────────────────────────────────────────────────────────────┘
```

Unless already particularised in the Disclosure Review Document or in any Extended Disclosure List of Documents, if any of Models C, D or E (search-based Extended Disclosure) were ordered in respect of any Issues for Disclosure, set out here the limits of the search conducted, by reference to custodians, date ranges, locations, document types, keyword searches and any relevant limits specified.

```
┌─────────────────────────────────────────────────────────────┐
│                                                             │
│                                                             │
│                                                             │
└─────────────────────────────────────────────────────────────┘
```

To the extent any of these limits were not contained in the Disclosure Order/s or recorded in an agreement in writing between the parties either in the Disclosure Review Document or elsewhere, please identify them and explain why they were necessary and why they were not agreed with the other part[y/ies]

```
┌─────────────────────────────────────────────────────────────┐
│                                                             │
│                                                             │
│                                                             │
└─────────────────────────────────────────────────────────────┘
```

I, [name] certify [for and on behalf of the above-named Party] that I am aware of and, to the best of my knowledge and belief, have complied with [my / Party's] duties under Practice Direction 57AD, including having:

A) taken and caused to be taken reasonable steps to preserve documents in [the Party's] control that may be relevant to any issue in the proceedings;

B) disclosed documents I am aware (or, in the case of a company or organisation, of which the company or organisation is aware, within the meaning of paragraph 2.9 of Practice Direction 57AD) are or have been in [my] or [the Party's / company's] control and adverse to [my/the Party's] case on any issue in the proceedings, unless they are privileged;

C) [*in the case of an order for Extended Disclosure of Model C, D or E only*] undertaken and caused to be undertaken any search for documents in a responsible and conscientious manner to fulfil the stated purpose of the search and in accordance with [my/the Party's] obligations as set out in Practice Direction 57AD and [the Disclosure Order/s];

D) acted honestly in relation to the process of giving disclosure;

E) used reasonable efforts to avoid providing documents to another party that have no relevance to the Issues for Disclosure in the proceedings.

F) produced electronic copies of documents in their native format, in a manner which preserves metadata and produced disclosable hard copy documents by providing scanned versions or photocopied hard copies.

I certify [on behalf of the Party] that I am aware of and, to the best of my knowledge and belief, have complied with the Disclosure Order.

I understand that I [and Party] must inform the court and the other parties if any further document required to be disclosed (whether under Practice Direction 57AD or the Disclosure Order/s) comes into [the Party's] control at any time before the conclusion of the case.

I wish to withhold production of the following [document, part of a document, or class of documents] which would otherwise fall within [my/the Party's] obligations:

Description of document, part of a document or class of documents	**Grounds upon which production is being withheld**
	e.g. Privilege, already in other party's possession (inter-partes correspondence etc)
	Documents no longer within party's control

I am aware that proceedings for contempt of court can be brought against me if I sign a false Disclosure Certificate without an honest belief in its truth.

Signed [   ]   **Date** [   ]

(Party) (Party's representative or
legal representative)

*If the party making disclosure is a company or other organisation, the person signing
this Disclosure Certificate should be someone from within the organisation with
appropriate authority and knowledge of the disclosure exercise or the party's legal
representative. This person will have received confirmation from all those people with
accountability or responsibility within the company or organisation either for the events
or circumstances the subject of the case or for the conduct of the litigation that they have
provided for disclosure all adverse documents of which they are aware, and will have
taken reasonable steps to check the position with any such person who has since left the
company or organisation. Identify here who the person making the disclosure
statement is and why he or she is the appropriate person to make it:*

Name:
Role and explanation of why you are the appropriate person to sign this Certificate:

Appendix A

List/s of Documents

Please either attach copies of any Initial Disclosure and/or Extended Disclosure Lists of Documents,
or incorporate the text of the lists here.

Appendix 17

Notice of appeal

Appellant's notice

(All appeals except small claims track appeals and appeals to the Family Division of the High Court)

For Court use only	
Appeal Court Ref. No.	
Date filed	

Notes for guidance are available which will help you complete this form. Please read them carefully before you complete each section.

SEAL

Section 1 Details of the claim or case you are appealing against

Claim or Case no. [ ]

Fee Account no. (if applicable) [ ]

Help with Fees - Ref no. (if applicable) H W F – [ ][ ][ ] – [ ][ ][ ]

Name(s) of the ☐ Claimant(s) ☐ Applicant(s) ☐ Petitioner(s)

[ ]

Name(s) of the ☐ Defendant(s) ☐ Respondent(s)

[ ]

Details of the party appealing ('The Appellant')

Name

[ ]

Address (including postcode)

[ ]

Tel No.	
Fax	
E-mail	

Details of the Respondent to the appeal

Name

[ ]

Address (including postcode)

[ ]

Tel No.	
Fax	
E-mail	

Details of additional parties (if any) are attached   ☐ Yes   ☐ No

Section 2   Details of the appeal

From which court is the appeal being brought?

☐ The County Court at

☐ The Family Court at

☐ High Court

    ☐ Queen's Bench Division

    ☐ Chancery Division

    ☐ Family Division

☐ Other (please specify)

What is the name of the Judge whose decision you want to appeal?

What is the status of the Judge whose decision you want to appeal?

☐ District Judge or Deputy   ☐ Circuit Judge or Recorder   ☐ Tribunal Judge

☐ Master or Deputy   ☐ High Court Judge or Deputy   ☐ Justice(s) of the Peace

What is the date of the decision you wish to appeal against?

Is the decision you wish to appeal a previous appeal decision?   ☐ Yes   ☐ No

Section 3   Legal representation

Are you legally represented?   ☐ Yes   ☐ No

If Yes, is your legal representative (please tick as appropriate)

☐ a solicitor

☐ direct access counsel instructed to conduct litigation on your behalf

☐ direct access counsel instructed to represent you at hearings only

Name of your legal representative

The address (including postcode) of your legal representative

	Tel No.	
	Fax	
	E-mail	
	DX	
	Ref.	

Are you, the Appellant, in receipt of a
Civil Legal Aid Certificate?   ☐ Yes   ☐ No

Is the respondent legally represented?   ☐ Yes   ☐ No

If 'Yes', please give details of the
respondent's legal representative below

Name and address (including postcode) of the respondent's legal representative

	Tel No.	
	Fax	
	E-mail	
	DX	
	Ref.	

Section 4   Permission to appeal

Do you need permission to appeal?   ☐ Yes   ☐ No

Has permission to appeal been granted?

☐ **Yes** (Complete Box A)   ☐ **No** (Complete Box B)

Box A   **Box B**

Date of order granting permission

[   ]

Name of Judge granting permission

[   ]

I [   ]

the Appellant('s legal representative) seek permission to appeal.

If permission to appeal has been granted **in part** by the lower court, do you seek permission to appeal in respect of the grounds refused by the lower court?   ☐ Yes   ☐ No

Section 5   Other information required for the appeal

Please set out the order (or part of the order) you wish to appeal against

[   ]

Have you lodged this notice with the court in time?   ☐ Yes   ☐ No
(There are different types of appeal -
see Guidance Notes N161A)   If **'No'** you must also complete
                                                             Part B of Section 10 and Section 11

Section 6   Grounds of appeal

Please state, in numbered paragraphs, **on a separate sheet** attached to this notice and entitled 'Grounds of Appeal' (also in the top right hand corner add your claim or case number and full name), why you are saying that the Judge who made the order you are appealing was wrong.

☐ I confirm that the grounds of appeal are attached to this notice.

Section 7   Arguments in support of grounds for appeal

☐ I confirm that the arguments (known as a 'Skeleton Argument') in support of the 'Grounds of Appeal' are set out **on a separate sheet** and attached to this notice.

OR   (in the case of appeals other than to the Court of Appeal)

☐ I confirm that the arguments (known as a 'Skeleton Argument') in support of the 'Grounds of Appeal' will follow within 14 days of filing this Appellant's Notice. A skeleton argument should only be filed if appropriate, in accordance with CPR Practice Direction 52B, paragraph 8.3.

Section 8   Aarhus Convention Claim

For applications made under the Town and Country Planning Act 1990 or Planning (Listed Buildings and Conservation Areas) Act 1990

I contend that this claim is an Aarhus Convention Claim   ☐ Yes   ☐ No

If Yes, and you are appealing to the Court of Appeal, any application for an order to limit the recoverable costs of an appeal, pursuant to CPR 52.19, should be made in section 10.

If Yes, indicate in the following box if you do not wish the costs limits under CPR 45 to apply. If you have indicated that the claim is an Aarthus claim set out the grounds below

Section 9   What are you asking the Appeal Court to do?

I am asking the appeal court to:-
(please tick the appropriate box)

☐ set aside the order which I am appealing

☐ vary the order which I am appealing and substitute the following order. Set out in the
following space the order you are asking for:-

☐ order a new trial

Section 10   Other applications

Complete this section **only** if you are making any additional applications.

Part A

☐ I apply for a stay of execution. (You must set out in Section 11 your reasons for seeking a stay
of execution and evidence in support of your application.)

Part B

☐ I apply for an extension of time for filing my appeal notice. (You must set out in Section 11 the
reasons for the delay and what steps you have taken since the decision you are appealing.)

Part C

☐ I apply for an order that:

(You must set out in Section 11 your reasons and your evidence in support of your
application.)

Section 11 Evidence in support

In support of my application(s) in Section 10, I wish to rely upon the following reasons and evidence:

Section 12   Vulnerability

Vulnerability

Do you believe you, or a witness who will give evidence on your behalf, are vulnerable in any way which the court needs to consider?

☐ Yes. Please explain in what way you or the witness are vulnerable and what steps, support or adjustments you wish the court and the judge to consider.

```
┌──────────────────────────────────────────────┐
│                                              │
│                                              │
│                                              │
│                                              │
│                                              │
│                                              │
└──────────────────────────────────────────────┘
```

☐ No

Statement of Truth

This must be completed in support of the evidence in Section 11

I understand that proceedings for contempt of court may be brought against a person who makes, or causes to be made, a false statement in a document verified by a statement of truth without an honest belief in its truth.

☐ **I believe** that the facts stated in section 11 are true.

☐ **The applicant believes** that the facts stated in section 11 are true. **I am authorised** by the applicant to sign this statement.

Signature

☐ Applicant

☐ Litigation friend (where applicant is a child or a Protected Party)

☐ Applicant's legal representative (as defined by CPR 2.3(1))

Date

Day   Month   Year

Full name

Name of applicant's legal representative's firm

If signing on behalf of firm or company give position or office held

Section 13   Supporting documents

To support your appeal you should file with this notice all relevant documents listed below. To show which documents you are filing, please tick the appropriate boxes.

If you do not have a document that you intend to use to support your appeal complete the box over the page.

In the County Court or High Court:

☐ three copies of the appellant's notice for the appeal court and three copies of the grounds of appeal;

☐ one additional copy of the appellant's notice and grounds of appeal for each of the respondents;

☐ one copy of the sealed (stamped by the court) order being appealed;

☐ a copy of any order giving or refusing permission to appeal; together with a copy of the judge's reasons for allowing or refusing permission to appeal; and

☐ a copy of the Civil Legal Aid Agency Certificate (if legally represented).

In the Court of Appeal:

☐ three copies of the appellant's notice and three copies of the grounds of appeal on a separate sheet attached to each appellant's notice;

☐ one additional copy of the appellant's notice and one copy of the grounds of appeal for each of the respondents;

☐ one copy of the sealed (stamped by the court) order or tribunal determination being appealed;

☐ a copy of any order giving or refusing permission to appeal together with a copy of the judge's reasons for allowing or refusing permission to appeal;

☐ one copy of any witness statement or affidavit in support of any application included in the appellant's notice;

☐ where the decision of the lower court was itself made on appeal, a copy of the first order, the reasons given by the judge who made it and the appellant's notice of appeal against that order;

☐ in a claim for judicial review or a statutory appeal a copy of the original decision which was the subject of the application to the lower court;

☐ one copy of the skeleton arguments in support of the appeal or application for permission to appeal;

☐ a copy of the approved transcript of judgment; and

☐ a copy of the Civil Legal Aid Certificate (if applicable)

☐ where a claim relates to an Aarhus Convention claim, a schedule of the claimant's financial resources

Reasons why you have not supplied a document and date when you expect it to be available:-

Title of document and reason not supplied	Date when it will be supplied

Section 14 The notice of appeal must be signed here

Signed [   ]   Appellant('s legal representative)

Appendix 18

Example of a statutory demand against a company

Rule 7.3
SD 1

Statutory Demand
under section 123(1)(a) of the Insolvency Act 1986 [*]
under section 222(1)(a) of the Insolvency Act 1986 [*]
*[Delete whichever is not applicable]

Warning
• This is an **important** document. This demand must be dealt with **within 21 days** after its service upon the company or a winding-up order could be made in respect of the company.   • Please read the demand and notes carefully.

Notes for Creditor

- The person making this demand must complete the whole of sections 1, 2 (including Part B if applicable) and 3 and the authentication (including the date) at the end.

- The details given in Section 1 must comply with rule 1.6 of the Insolvency (England and Wales) Rules 2016 (IR 2016).

- The Details of Debt (Section 2) must include all the relevant matters listed in the margin notes at Section 2. These should be set out in the order given unless the person completing the demand considers that a different order would be more convenient for the recipient.

- The creditor must give details of an individual with whom the Company can communicate about the Demand in Section 3.

- The authentication must comply with rule 1.5 of the IR 2016. If signatory of the demand is a solicitor or other agent of the creditor the name of his/her firm should be given.

Section 1 - DEMAND

To

Name: Gates Launderettes Limited   (The Company)
[If registered, insert its registered name; if unregistered, its name]

Registered No. 234567
[If incorporated in England and Wales under the Companies Act 2006 or a previous Companies Act, its registered number]

Address: 73 Cider Street, Slough SL1 1PP

[If registered, insert its registered office; if unregistered, the postal address of any principal place of business]

[Or, if the Debtor Company was incorporated outside the UK insert the following details]*

Country or territory in which incorporated:

Registered No. (if any):

No. (if any) **under which registered under Part 34 of Companies Act 2006:**
*[delete if not applicable]

This demand is made under section 123(1)(a) of the Insolvency Act 1986 and is served on you by the creditor [insert details of Creditor below]

Name: Brewsters Limited
[If a registered company, insert its registered name; if unregistered, its name; if an individual, his or her full name]

Registered No. 765432
[If a company incorporated in England and Wales under the Companies Act 2006 or a previous Companies Act, insert its registered number]

Address: Unit 12 Brownside Industrial Estate, Reading RG2 6DS

[If a registered company, insert its registered office; if unregistered, the postal address of any principal place of business; if an individual, his or her personal or professional address (as appropriate)]

[Or, if the Creditor is a company incorporated outside the UK insert the following details]*

Country or territory in which incorporated:

Registered No. (if any):

No. (if any) **under which registered under Part 34 of Companies Act 2006:**
*[delete if not applicable]

The creditor claims that the Company owes the sum of £65,350.80, full details of which are set out in section 2 of this Demand.

Section 2

A. Details of Debt

These details must include the following information:

(a) the amount of the debt as at the date of this demand;

(b) the consideration for the debt (or if is there is no consideration the way in which it arose); the date on which the debt arose should also be included;

(c) if the demand is founded on a judgment or order of a court, details of the judgment or order;

(d) if the creditor is entitled to the debt by way of assignment, a statement to that effect and that the details of the relevant assignment(s) are given in Part B below (which must then also be filled in);

(e) if the sums demanded include (i) any charge by way of interest not previously notified to the company as included in its liability and/or (ii) any other charge accruing due from time to time, each such charge must be separately identified (if claimed) with the amount or rate of the charge and the grounds upon which payment is claimed: the amount claimed for such charges must be limited to that which has accrued due at the date of the demand.

On 1 March 2023 the creditor agreed to sell to the debtor company machinery to the value of £63,450. The machinery was delivered to the debtor company on 14 March 2023 and payment in full was due on 21 March 2023. The debtor company has failed to make any payment to the creditor. The creditor also claims interest pursuant to the Late Payment of Commercial Debts (Interest) Act 1998 at the rate of 8.1% per annum (8% over the relevant reference rate) for the period 22 March 2023 to 3 August 2023 being 135 days and amounting to £1,900.80. The total debt due at the date of this demand is therefore £65,350.80.

Part B [For completion if the creditor is entitled to the debt by way of assignment]

	Name	Date(s) of Assignment
Original creditor		
Assignees		

SD1 - Statutory Demand under section 123(1)(a) or 222(1)(a) of the Insolvency Act 1986 (04.17)

Section 3

The Company must pay the above debt within 21 days of service of this demand on the Company after which the creditor may present a winding-up petition unless the Company offers security for the debt and the creditor agrees to accept security or the Company compounds the debt with the creditor's agreement.

The individual or individuals to whom any communication regarding this demand may be addressed is/are:

Name COLLAWS

Address 14 Ship
Street, Weyford
WE18 HQ

Electronic address

Telephone Number
01904 876550

Reference
BM/ABC/BREWSTER

How to comply with a statutory demand

If the Company wishes to avoid a winding-up petition being presented it must pay the debt shown on page 1, details of which are set out on page 2 of this notice, within the period of **21 days after** its service upon the Company. Alternatively, the Company can attempt to come to a settlement with the creditor. To do this an officer or representative of the Company should:

- inform the individual (or one of the individuals) named in Part A above immediately that it is willing and able to offer security for the debt to the creditor's satisfaction; or

- inform the individual (or one of the individuals) named in Part A immediately that it is willing and able to compound for the debt to the creditor's satisfaction.

If the Company disputes the demand in whole or in part it should contact the individual (or one of the individuals) named in Part A immediately.

REMEMBER!	**The Company has only 21 days after the date of service on it of this document before the creditor may present a winding-up petition.**
NOTE:	**The Company has the right to make an application to the court(*) for an injunction restraining the creditor from presenting a winding-up petition or from advertising it.**
Insert the name of the court (hearing centre) to which, according to present information, the company must make the application	(*) The court to which an application should be made is: Reading

Note: The demand must be dated, and authenticated either by the creditor, or a person authorised to make the demand on the creditor's behalf. A demand which is authenticated by a person other than the creditor must state that the person is authorised to make this demand on the creditor's behalf and state the person's relationship to the creditor.	**Authentication** Signature of individual: *Collaws* Name: COLLAWS (Block Letters) Date: 3 August 2023 Address: 14 Ship Street, Weyford WE1 8HQ Telephone number: 01904 876550 Ref: BM/ABC/BREWSTER [I, the above-signed, not being the creditor herein, state as follows: I am authorised to make this demand on the creditor's behalf. My position in/relationship to the creditor is Solicitor. [*if the creditor is a body corporate of which the signatory is the sole member*] I am the sole member of the creditor]]

SD1 - Statutory Demand under section 123(1)(a) or 222(1)(a) of the Insolvency Act 1986 (04.17)

Appendix 19

The Business and Property Courts – Advisory Note

This note is likely to be updated on a regular basis

Introduction

1. The Business and Property Courts ("B&PCs") were launched in July 2017 and became operational on 2nd October 2017. They have been created as a single umbrella for specialist civil jurisdictions across England and Wales. In London, these specialist civil jurisdictions operate together in the Rolls Building on Fetter Lane, forming the largest specialist centre for financial, business and property litigation in the world.

2. Business and Property Courts have also been established in the five main centres outside London where specialist business similar to that in the Rolls Building is undertaken, namely, Birmingham, Bristol, Cardiff, Leeds and Manchester. They will also be established in Newcastle and Liverpool shortly. The main centre for the Business and Property Courts in Wales is in Cardiff, but judges of the courts will sit in other venues in Wales when appropriate and practicable. Specialist County Court cases that fall within the ambit of the B&PCs will internally be marked "Business and Property Courts Work" (encompassing what was previously "Chancery Business" for specialist work of a Chancery nature and TCC work in the County Court (CPR PD 60 para 3.2; 3.4 and CPR 60.4(c))) (please see paragraph 4.3 of the draft practice direction which is awaiting publication but is attached in its current draft form). The Mercantile Court has been renamed the Circuit Commercial Court, and Mercantile Judges are now Circuit Commercial Judges.

3. The Business and Property Courts are divided into separate specialist courts or lists, some of which are further subdivided into sub-lists. These courts and lists are dealt with in more detail below.

4. Although the various specialist civil work has been brought together under one umbrella, the courts themselves will continue to operate in the same way as at present, applying the same practices and procedures under the Civil Procedure Rules and Insolvency Rules as before and retaining their own procedural Guides. The way in which cases are dealt with in each type of court will not change. Claims which have been proceeding in the Chancery Division before 2nd October remain under the control of the same Master (or Judge) as before until further order. The Practice Direction setting up the Business and Property Courts contains new provisions, particularly as regards issue and transfer of proceedings (see paragraphs 13 to 19).

5. The new arrangements will allow, over time, for greater flexibility in cross-deployment of judges with suitable expertise and experience to sit on appropriate business and property cases. It will also be simpler to issue claims in any of the B&PCs and to transfer claims between the Rolls Building and the other specialist centres.

Issuing Proceedings in the Business and Property Courts

6. Presently electronic filing and issue is only available in London. For the time being, claim forms should continue to be issued in the same way as before in the other Business and Property Courts centres.

7. The new types of case numbers (available on CE-File) will not, however, be provided in the other centres until electronic filing begins in those centres in 2018.

8.   Court users will at present, when issuing proceedings electronically on CE-File, see the heading "Business and Property Courts of England and Wales" on the system. They will then be asked to say which court or list, and if applicable, which sub-list, they wish their case to be assigned to. This will depend on the principal subject matter of the dispute. For example, if the dispute involves land, even if the land is for commercial use, it should be assigned to the Property, Trusts and Probate List. Similarly, a dispute about pensions should be assigned to the Business List, sub-list Pensions, even if professional negligence is also involved. Where several issues arise, involving different courts, lists or sub-lists, the user must consider whether there are issues requiring the expertise of a specialist judge and if so must select the court, list or sub-list in which the relevant specialist judges sit.

9.   Cases issued in centres outside London, after 2nd October 2017 and before electronic filing becomes available outside London, should identify the list or court in which the claimant wishes the case to proceed, as above. Users issuing in the centres outside London will have to indicate on the claim form or to listing staff in those centres the court, list or sub-list to which their claim should be allocated.

10.   Users must choose one of the following:

(1)   Admiralty Court (QBD)

(2)   Business List (ChD) (with further choice of Financial Services and Regulatory or Pensions sub-lists available)

(3)   Commercial Court (QBD) (with the option to issue in the London Circuit Commercial Court instead in London, or a single option of issuing in the Circuit Commercial Court in other centres)

(4)   Competition List (ChD)

(5)   Financial List (ChD/QBD)

(6)   Insolvency and Companies List (ChD) (with further option of Insolvency or Companies sub-lists)

(7)   Intellectual Property List (ChD) (with further choice of Patents Court or IPEC)

(8)   Property,Trusts and Probate List (ChD)

(9)   Revenue List (ChD)

(10) Technology and Construction Court (QBD)

11.   Once CE-File has been extended to the other centres, the user will also be asked to identify on CE-File the hearing centre in which they wish to issue the proceedings. In the meantime, users issuing in the centres outside London will have to issue in the centre on the circuit with which the claim has significant links. Links, as specified in the Practice Direction, are established where:

a.   one or more of the parties has an address or registered office in the circuit (particularly if the party is non-represented);

b.   at least one of the witnesses expected to give oral evidence is located within the circuit;

c.   the dispute occurred in a location within the circuit;

d.   the dispute concerns land, goods or other assets located in the circuit; or

e.   the parties' legal representatives are based in the circuit.

12.   Claims with significant links to a particular circuit must be issued in the District Registry located in the circuit. Although a claimant must base a decision on any information available about links to a particular circuit, there is no obligation to make extra inquiries to determine whether there may be other links outside the claimant's current knowledge.

13.   Care should be taken to ensure that any proceedings are brought in the correct court and hearing centre. If users are uncertain as to the availability of a specialist judge in an

area they should contact the relevant Listing Office. It is important to note however that if a claim is issued in the wrong court, list or sub-list, or in the wrong hearing centre, this will not invalidate the issue of the claim. If there is such an error the court may remedy it by making an order under CPR rule 3.10(b).

The Constituent Courts and Lists

14.   In order to help users identify the correct court, list or sub-list in which to issue, a brief description of each one of the Business and Property Courts follows. The various examples of cases dealt with in each category are not exhaustive:

(1) Admiralty Court (QBD)

The Admiralty Court deals with shipping and maritime disputes. This list deals with cases such as:

- collisions between ships
- disputes over the transport of cargo
- salvage of a ship, cargo or crew
- disputes over goods supplied to a ship
- disputes over mortgages and other security over ships
- claims by passengers for injuries suffered
- claims by ship crew for unpaid wages
- claims by ship-owners to limit liability for loss or damage

The Admiralty Court deals with claims brought against the owner of a ship ('in personam' claims) and claims brought against the ship itself ('in rem' claims). The court can seize ('arrest') ships and cargos to prevent them being moved and can also sell them within England and Wales.

(2) Business List (ChD)

The scope of the Chancery Business List is broad. It includes a wide range business disputes, often with an international dimension. Frequently these concern a business structure (company, LLP, LP, partnership etc), claims against directors for breach of fiduciary duty, or disputes about contractual arrangements between investors such as share purchase agreements. They also include claims in tort, such as conspiracy or fraud, claims for professional negligence (e.g. against solicitors, accountants, surveyors, valuers), claims for breach of contract, specific performance, rectification and injunctive relief as well as other equitable remedies.

The Business List also includes pensions claims, and a sub-list exists to reflect that. The sub-list covers all claims where pensions are the subject matter of the dispute. Many pension schemes, particularly occupational pension schemes, are established under a trust. Not all pensions cases however are brought under the court's trusts jurisdiction. For example, trustees and/or employers may bring claims for professional negligence against former advisers, or action taken under statutory powers, for example by the Pensions Regulator, or statutory appeals, for example from the Pensions Ombudsman.

The Business List also includes a Financial Services and Regulatory sub-list, to cover financial claims where the Financial Conduct Authority is a party, claims under the Financial Services and Markets Act 2000, and claims involving regulators (other than the Pensions Regulator).

(3) Commercial Court (QBD)

(a) Commercial Court

The Commercial Court deals with complex cases arising out of business disputes, both national and international, encompassing all aspects of commercial disputes, in the fields of banking and finance, shipping, insurance and reinsurance and commodities. The Court also acts as a supervisory court for arbitration, dealing with the granting of freezing and other relief in aid of arbitration, challenges to arbitration awards and enforcement of awards.

This list deals with cases such as:

- disputes over contracts and business documents
- insurance and reinsurance
- sale of commodities
- import, export and transport ('carriage') of goods
- issues relating to international and commercial arbitration
- banking and financial services
- agency and management agreements
- sale and purchase of businesses and commercial share sale agreements
- oil, gas and energy disputes
- professional negligence in commercial circumstances

(b) Circuit Commercial Court (QBD) (formerly the Mercantile Court)

Formerly known as the Mercantile Court, it deals with business disputes of all kinds apart from those which, because of their size, value or complexity, will be heard by the Commercial Court. As well as large cases, it also decides smaller business disputes. There are no restrictions on the size of claims which can be brought to the Circuit Commercial Court. The Court also acts as a supervisory court for arbitration, dealing most often with the challenges to arbitration awards and enforcement of awards. Cases will ordinarily be heard if they are of a genuine business nature and appropriate for the court. This list deals with cases such as:

- disputes over contracts and business documents
- insurance and reinsurance
- sale of goods
- import, export and transport ('carriage') of goods
- professional negligence in commercial circumstances (eg solicitors and accountants)
- issues relating to arbitration awards
- restraint of trade
- banking and financial services
- agency and management agreements
- share sale agreements
- confidential information
- injunctions

(4) Competition List (ChD)

This list deals with claims brought under Article 101 and Article 102 of the Treaty on the Functioning of the European Union ("TFEU"), and also claims brought under the corresponding provisions of UK domestic law contained in Chapters I and II of Part 1 of the Competition Act 1998.

Article 101 (EU law claims) and Chapter I of Part 1 of the Competition Act 1998 (UK domestic law claims) prohibit agreements, concerted practices, or decisions by associations of undertakings whose object or effect is to prevent, restrict or distort competition.

Article 102 (EU law claims) and Chapter II of Part 1 of the Competition Act 1998 (UK domestic law claims) are aimed at preventing abusive behaviour by undertakings who hold a dominant position in a relevant geographic and product market (eg by imposing unfair prices or unfair trading arrangements).

A claim may be for an injunction to restrain an alleged breach or threatened breach of the competition rules, and/or for damages resulting from such a breach. Proceedings frequently involve consideration of economic or technical issues on which expert evidence is called. The procedure is governed by the Practice Direction on Competition Law (See further Ch.29 (7) of the Chancery Guide).

(Note: claims such as those identified above may also be brought in the Competition Appeal Tribunal, whose jurisdiction was expanded by the Consumer Rights Act 2015 to bring it largely into line with that of the High Court. However, by virtue of the 2015 Act the Competition Appeal Tribunal has the exclusive jurisdiction over certain proceedings for collective redress for infringement of the competition rules.)

Although a claim under paragraph 1 of the Practice Direction on Competition Law may be issued in any of the district registries with which it has significant links (see paragraph 7 above), its case management and/or trial will be dependant on the availability of a suitable judge.

(5) Financial List (ChD/Commercial Court - QBD)

The Financial List is a specialist cross-jurisdictional list set up to address the particular business needs of parties litigating on financial matters. Disputes that are eligible for inclusion are those that principally relate to financial disputes of over £50m or equivalent, and which require particular market expertise or raise issues of general market importance. The list can deal with cases:

- generally worth more than £50 million
- which need expert judicial knowledge of financial markets
- which raise important issues for the sector

(6) Insolvency and Companies List (ChD)

This list deals with both personal and corporate insolvency on the one hand, and companies work on the other hand.

Specifically, the work includes:

Insolvency

- applications concerning company voluntary arrangements;
- administration applications and applications concerning administrations;
- petitions to wind up companies and partnerships;
- applications concerning the winding up of companies and partnerships (whether in members or creditors voluntary liquidation or following winding up by the court);
- applications concerning individual voluntary arrangements;
- bankruptcy petitions and applications concerning bankruptcy;
- applications relating to transaction avoidance in both personal and corporate insolvency;
- applications under the Cross-Border Insolvency Regulations

- petitions and applications under the Insolvency Act 2016 or the Administration of Insolvent Estates of Deceased Persons Order 1986.

Directors' disqualification

- claims for the disqualification of unfit directors;
- applications for permission to act as a director after disqualification.

Company law

- unfair prejudice petitions/shareholder disputes;
- applications for the confirmation of a reduction of capital;
- applications concerning schemes of arrangement
- other claims and applications under the Companies Act 2006, FISMA 2000, or the Companies (Cross-Border Mergers) Regulations 2007

This list of examples is not exhaustive.

(7) Intellectual Property List (ChD)

The following matters must be dealt with in either the Patents Court or the IPEC (multi-track):

(1)   claims under the Patents Act 1977

(2)   claims under the Registered Designs Act 1949

(3)   claims under the Defence Contracts Act 1958

(4)   claims relating to Community registered designs, semiconductor topography rights or plant varieties

(collectively "registered rights claims")

Claims under the Trade Marks Act 1994 and the other intellectual property claims set out at paragraph 16.1 of Practice Direction 63 (collectively "general intellectual property claims") must be dealt with in either the Intellectual Property List generally or the IPEC.

There is no lower limit on the value of claims that may be commenced in the Intellectual Property List. Where, however, the damages or sums payable on an account of profits are likely to be £500,000 or less, consideration should be given to issuing the claim in the IPEC.

Intellectual property claims outside London

Intellectual property claims may be issued in B&PCs District Registries. However the case management and/or trial of a claim in the Patents Court or the IPEC in the B&PCs District Registry in question will be dependent on an appropriate judge being made available in the district registry in question.

(8) Property, Trusts and Probate List (ChD)

This list covers a large amount of Chancery work which is separate from the Business List. The examples given below are not intended to be a definitive list. The Property list deals mainly with land, and the Trusts list with matters that fall within Part 64 of the CPR, i.e. the administration of estates and the execution of trusts, and with charities. The Probate list covers all matters which fall within Part 57 of the CPR.

Property

Landlord & Tenant residential
Landlord &Tenant commercial
Trespass/squatters
Mortgages

Land Registry
Land – title, easements, restrictive covenants etc
Orders for sale to enforce charging orders
Trusts of Land and Appointment of Trustees Act 1996 (TOLATA)

Trusts

Variation of trusts
Removal of trustees
Claims against trustees for breach of trust
Issues of construction/rectification
Trustees/Personal Representatives seeking directions including Beddoe applications
Disputes about trust property
Applications for prospective costs order
Charities
Applications for administration order

Probate

Contentious Probate claims
Rectification of wills
Substitution or removal of Personal Representatives
Inheritance Act
Presumption of Death Act

(9) Revenue List (ChD)

Claims involving major points of principle relating to taxation where HMRC is a party. (This List does not include claims for the recovery of taxes or duties or where a taxpayer disputes liability to pay tax. Such claims fall within the Business list).

(10) Technology & Construction Court (QBD)

This list can be divided into three areas of work as follows:

(a)   **Adjudication disputes.**

These are claims to enforce or challenges to adjudicators' decisions arising out of the Housing Grants' Construction and Regeneration Act 1996 (as amended).

(b)   **Public procurement.**

This concerns all kinds of public procurement (not limited to construction or engineering projects) and involves, amongst other things, applications to lift the automatic suspension, and challenges to tender evaluations and decisions to award contracts.

(c)   **The General TCC list.**
    This includes:
    - Building and engineering disputes.
    - Claims by and against architects, engineers, surveyors, accountants and other specialised advisors relating to the services they provide.
    - Claims involving issues that are technically complex.
    - Claims relating to the design, supply and installation of computers, software and related network systems.
    - Claims relating to the supply and provision of materials, goods, plant and other services.
    - Claims by and against local authorities relating to their statutory duties concerning the development of land or the construction of buildings.
    - Dilapidation claims as between landlord and tenant.

- Environmental claims, including pollution and reclamation.
- Nuisance claims relating to land use.
- Claims arising out of fires, explosions and other catastrophic events.
- Insurance disputes relating to construction, engineering and technology.
- Contractual disputes involving oil and gas installations, onshore and offshore, and ship building.
- Any arbitration claim under the Arbitration Act 1996, including challenges to decisions of arbitrators in construction and engineering disputes and/or application for permission to appeal and appeals in such cases.

Titles of Claims

15. All claims issued in the Business and Property Courts must be titled as in the following examples:

IN THE HIGH COURT OF JUSTICE

BUSINESS AND PROPERTY COURTS OF ENGLAND AND WALES PROPERTY TRUSTS AND PROBATE LIST (ChD)

or

IN THE HIGH COURT OF JUSTICE

BUSINESS AND PROPERTY COURTS IN MANCHESTER BUSINESS LIST (ChD)

or

IN THE HIGH COURT OF JUSTICE

BUSINESS AND PROPERTY COURTS IN WALES TECHNOLOGY AND CONSTRUCTION COURT (QBD)

16. For claims which belong in one of the sub-lists, it is not necessary to include the overarching list/court in the title (although parties can do so if they would prefer to do so). The sub-list title suffices, as follows:

IN THE HIGH COURT OF JUSTICE

BUSINESS AND PROPERTY COURTS OF ENGLAND AND WALES LONDON CIRCUIT COMMERCIAL COURT (QBD)

or

IN THE HIGH COURT OF JUSTICE

BUSINESS AND PROPERTY COURTS IN BIRMINGHAM PATENTS COURT (ChD)

or

IN THE HIGH COURT OF JUSTICE

BUSINESS AND PROPERTY COURTS OF ENGLAND AND WALES COMPANIES COURT (ChD)

17. When lodging an appeal to the Technology and Construction Court or the Patents Court, the case should be marked accordingly. For all other appeals to the Business and Property Courts, the title should be as follows:

IN THE HIGH COURT OF JUSTICE

BUSINESS AND PROPERTY COURTS OF ENGLAND AND WALES APPEALS (ChD)

or

IN THE HIGH COURT OF JUSTICE

BUSINESS AND PROPERTY COURTS IN BRISTOL APPEALS (ChD)

18. When issuing proceedings, the general rule, which has not changed, is that below the title of the court in which the claim is issued, the title of the claim should contain only the names of the parties to the proceedings. There are however various exceptions. Examples include:

(i)   Proceedings relating to arbitrations

(ii)   Proceedings relating to the administration of an estate should be entitled "In the estate of AB deceased"

(iii)   Contentious probate proceedings should be entitled "In the estate of AB deceased (probate)"

(iv)   Proceedings under the Inheritance (Provision for Family and Dependants) Act 1975 should be entitled "In the Matter of the Inheritance (Provision for Family and Dependants) Act 1975"

(v)   Proceedings relating to pension schemes should be entitled "In the Matter of the [ ] Pension Scheme"

(vi)   Proceedings in the Companies Court should be entitled "in the matter of [the relevant company or other person] and of [the relevant legislation]

(vii)   A claim form to which Section I of Part 63 applies (patents and registered designs) must be marked "Patents Court" below the title of the court in which it is issued (PD 63 paragraph 3.1(a))

(viii) a claim form to which Section II of Part 63 applies (e.g. copyright, registered trade marks, Community trade marks and other intellectual property rights) must, except for claims started in the Intellectual Property Enterprise Court (IPEC), be marked Intellectual Property below the title of the court in which it is issued (PD 63 paragraph 17). Claims relating to trade marks and Community trade marks must state the registration number of the trade mark

(ix)   proceedings under the Presumption of Death Act 2013 should be entitled "In the matter of an application for a declaration of the presumed death of [*name*].

19.   The new headings indicated above should be used throughout the Business & Property Courts for new cases issued after 2nd October 2017. The headings of orders made subsequently to 2nd October 2017 may (but are not required to) refer to the Business and Property Courts and the list or court in which the case would be were it to have been issued on or after 2nd October 2017, or they may continue to refer to the jurisdiction in which they were originally issued. A date will shortly be identified after which the headings of orders will be required to be in the new Business and Property Courts form.

20.   The daily cause list published in the Business and Property Courts will list all the courts and lists in alphabetical order, indicating for each court/list which judge is sitting (in order of seniority), at what time, and in which court room. Those Business and Property Courts centres that operate fewer courts and lists than the Business and Property Courts of England & Wales may list all Business and Property Courts cases in a single daily list, or divide the cases by court/list, as preferred.

21.   Existing claims, issued before 2nd October 2017, will retain their claim numbers. These will not change at any stage.

22.   All claims issued in London on or after 2nd October 2017 are given a claim number with a prefix that reflects the Court, List or sub-list in which they are issued, in accordance with the table below, which can be found on CE-File.

List	Sub-List	Pre-Fix
Admiralty Court	Admiralty Court	AD
Appeals (ChD)*	Appeals (ChD)	CH
Business List	Business	BL
	Financial Services and Regulatory	FS
	Pensions	PE

List	Sub-List	Pre-Fix
Commercial Court	Commercial Court	CL
	London Circuit Commercial Court	LM
	Circuit Commercial Court (other than London)*	CC
Competition List	Competition List	CP
Financial List	Financial List	FL
Insolvency & Companies List	Insolvency List	BR
	Companies Court	CR
Intellectual Property List	Intellectual Property	IL
	Intellectual Property and Enterprise Court (IPEC)	IP
	Patents Court	HP
Property Trusts and Probate List	Property Trusts and Probate	PT
Revenue List	Revenue List	RL
Technology and Construction Court	Technology and Construction Court	HT

*NB: "Appeals (ChD)" is not a list in itself (and indeed does not exist in any centre other than London), but rather an option that can be selected on CE-File to lodge an appeal from Chancery-type cases decided in the County Court. TCC County Court cases will continue at present to be appealed through QBD appeals, although this may change when the centres outside London option an electronic filing system.

*NB: outside London the "Commercial Court" list option will be replaced by the Circuit Commercial Court and no sub list will exist. The Circuit Commercial Court replaces the Mercantile Court, and in London it will be called the London Circuit Commercial Court. On the CE-File system the London Circuit Commercial Court appears as a sub-list of the Commercial Court (although strictly speaking it is not). The prefix for the Circuit Commercial Court other than the London Circuit Commercial Court will in due course be CC.

23. At present, case numbers in the centres outside London are not changing, and will only change once CE-File is introduced in those centres.

Claim Form marking

24. All claim forms and all subsequent court documents relating to business or property work issued in the High Court must be marked "Business and Property Courts"; and all such claims issued in the County Court must marked "Business and Property Courts Work" by court staff, for proper triage.

25. In addition:

- Claims in the Shorter Trials Scheme must be marked in the top right hand corner "Shorter Trials Scheme".

- Where the claim is a probate claim, the claim form and all subsequent court documents must be marked at the top "In the estate of [name] deceased (Probate)".

- A claim form to which Section I of Part 63 applies (patents and registered designs) must be marked "Patents Court" below the title of the court in which it is issued.

Transfer of Proceedings

26. Cases that have specific links with a locality must be capable of being tried in that locality by a specialist judge. Therefore, although the transfer criteria in CPR rule 30.2 (transfer between the County Court and the High Court) and 30.5 (transfer between High Court Divisions and to or from a specialist list) continue to apply, new transfer rules set out in the Practice Direction will also apply alongside the existing criteria for a transfer order in CPR rule 30.3.

27. When considering whether to make an order for transfer between the Royal Courts of Justice and the District Registries when the proceedings are in the Business and Property Courts, the court must, in addition to the criteria in CPR rule 30.3, also have regard to:

    (a) significant links between the claim and the circuit in question, considering the factors listed in paragraph 11 above;

    (b) whether court resources, deployment constraints, or fairness require that the hearings (including the trial) be held in some other court than the court it was issued into;

    (c) the wishes of the parties, which bear special weight in the decision but may not be determinative;

    (d) the international nature of the case, with the understanding that international cases may be more suitable for trial in centres with international transport links;

    (e) the availability of a judge specialising in the type of claim in question to sit in the court to which the claim is being transferred.

28. An application for a transfer from the Rolls Building to or from a B&PCs District Registry or from a B&PCs District Registry to another such District Registry or to the Rolls Building must be made to the court from which transfer is sought and must additionally be discussed with and consented to by the receiving court. It will be sensible practice for the parties to discuss transfer with the appropriate judge at the receiving court before they apply for an order for transfer. If the parties are uncertain about the availability of a specialist judge, they should discuss this with the Listing Manager at the receiving court.

29. In addition to the provisions set out in CPR 30.3, the Business and Property Courts considering whether to make an order for transfer from the Business and Property Courts to a county court hearing centre must have regard to:

    (a) to the nature of the claim, in accordance with guidance as to what business falls within the specialist work of the B&PCs, provided at paragraphs 4.2 to 4.5 of the Practice Direction; and,

    (b) to the availability of a judge specialising in the corresponding type of claim to sit in an appropriate court in the circuit.

30. The following guidelines, which relate to transfers to a District Registry outside London, the County Court, or another Division of the High Court, are still relevant and should also be followed.

- Only cases which may properly be regarded as being suitable for management and trial in London will be retained there. All other claims will be transferred out. Active consideration will be given at all stages of the management of a claim to the appropriate venue for the claim to be managed and tried. If a case is suitable for transfer, it is generally preferable for it to be transferred before detailed case management has taken place, leaving the receiving court to case manage the claim in accordance with its usual approach.

- Consideration will be given, where relevant, to:

- PD 29 paragraphs 2.1 to 2.6 which provide guidance for case management within the High Court in London;
- Part 49 and PD 49A and PD 49B – Specialist Proceedings;
- Part 57 – Probate and Inheritance;
- Part 63 – Intellectual Property.

- Under PD 29 paragraph 2.2 a claim with a value of less than £100,000 will generally be transferred to the County Court unless it is required by an enactment to be tried in the High Court, it falls within a specialist list, or it falls within one of the categories specified in the list at PD 29 paragraph 2.6.

- The figure of £100,000 in PD 29 paragraph 2.2 accords with the current minimum value of money claims which may be issued in the High Court. It does not follow that money claims of over £100,000 (or over £200,000 (the value figure beyond which court fees do not increase)) will be retained. The value of a claim is not a consideration which has greater weight than the other criteria set out in CPR rule 30.3(2) but it is likely to be a factor with considerable influence in making a decision about transfer to the County Court or a specialist list. Similarly, for probate and equity claims, the figures of £30,000 and £350,000 respectively are not determinative.

- If the value of the claim is ascertainable, the court will consider the possibility of transferring Part 7 claims with a value of less than £500,000. Factors which may point to retention of such claims in the High Court include complex facts and/or complex or non-routine legal issues or complex relief; parties based outside the jurisdiction; public interest or importance; large numbers of parties; any related claim; and the saving of costs and efficiency in the use of judicial resources.

- The availability of a judge with the specialist skills to deal with the claim is always an important consideration when considering whether or not to transfer it. There are for example two circuit judges at Central London County Court who are specialised in Chancery work, and the waiting times at Central London are likely to be shorter than in the High Court for a trial before a judge. The delay in having a case heard should also be a consideration when deciding whether to transfer a case to the County Court or not and regard will be had to listing information provided by the Central London CC Business and Property Court team. The order for transfer of a claim to Central London County Court, may include a direction that the case is considered to be suitable for trial only by a specialist circuit judge. Such a direction is not binding on the County Court but should be taken into account.

- PD 29 paragraphs 2.6(1), (3) and (7) indicates that professional negligence claims, fraud and undue influence claims and contentious probate claims are suitable for trial in the High Court, but it does not follow that claims within these categories should necessarily remain in the High Court. Less complex and/or lower value claims of these types are suitable for trial in Central London County Court, as Business and Property Court Work. Serious cases of fraud, however, should generally remain in the High Court. Certain professional negligence claims may be better suited to the Queen's Bench Division.

- Part 7 and Part 8 claims may sometimes be dealt with more efficiently by a Master rather than transferring the claim, especially since the amendments to PD 2B which came into effect on 6 April 2015.

- Many claims under the Inheritance Act will be suitable for trial in the County Court and should generally be transferred to Central London County Court, Business and Property Court List unless the Master is willing to try the claim and it is efficient to do so. Inheritance Act claims by a spouse will usually be suitable for transfer to the Family Division. Where there is a related Probate claim, or other Part 7 claim, the overall scope of the issues before the Court should be considered and generally all related claims should either be retained in the High Court or transferred out. The

County Court limit for probate claims is £30,000, but claims well above that figure should be transferred to the County Court nonetheless.

- Most claims relating to joint ownership under the Trusts of Land and Appointment of Trustees Act 1996 will be suitable for transfer to the County Court.

31. An application to transfer a case into the shorter trials scheme may be made to a Judge or, in the relevant list, to a Master.

Sir Geoffrey Vos
Chancellor of the High Court
13th October 2017

Appendix 20

Practice Direction 57AA – Business and Property Courts

Contents of this Practice Direction

Title	Number
Scope	Para. 1
Starting proceedings	Para. 2
Transfers	Para. 3
Specialist work in the district registries and the County Court	Para. 4
Appeals	Para. 5

Scope

1.1 The Chancery Division of the High Court, the Commercial Court, the Technology and Construction Court, the Circuit Commercial Court, and the Admiralty Court located in the Royal Courts of Justice, Rolls Building together with the Chancery Division of the High Court, the Technology and Construction Court and the Circuit Commercial Courts in the District Registries of the High Court in Birmingham, Bristol, Leeds, Liverpool, Manchester, Newcastle and Cardiff together constitute the Business and Property Courts.

1.2 The Business and Property Courts located at the Royal Courts of Justice, Rolls Building, are collectively described as the Business and Property Courts of England and Wales. Those Business and Property Courts in the District Registries of the High Court in Birmingham, Bristol, Leeds, Liverpool, Manchester, Newcastle, and Cardiff, are, respectively, described as the Business and Property Courts in Birmingham, the Business and Property Courts in Bristol, the Business and Property Courts in Leeds, the Business and Property Courts in Liverpool, the Business and Property Courts in Manchester, the Business and Property Courts in Newcastle and the Business and Property Courts in Wales. In this Practice Direction the Business and Property Courts in Birmingham, Bristol, Leeds, Liverpool, Manchester, Newcastle and Cardiff are referred to together as the B&PCs District Registries.

1.3 The work of the Business and Property Courts is divided and listed into the following courts or lists: the Admiralty Court, the Business List, the Commercial Court, the Circuit Commercial Courts, the Competition List, the Financial List, the Insolvency and Companies List, the Intellectual Property List, the Property, Trusts and Probate List, the Revenue List, and the Technology and Construction Court.

1.4 The courts or lists of the Business and Property Courts include sub-lists, as follows:

    (1) The Pensions sub-list and Financial Services and Regulatory sub-list are sub-lists of the Business List;

    (2) The Patents Court and the Intellectual Property Enterprise Court are sub-lists of the Intellectual Property List.

1.5 (1) The Business and Property Courts operate within and are subject to all statutory provisions and rules together with all procedural rules and practice directions applicable to the proceedings concerned.

    (2) In particular, the following provisions of the CPR apply—

    Part 49 (Companies Court)

Part 57 (Probate, Inheritance and Presumption of Death)

Part 58 (Commercial Court)

Part 59 (Circuit Commercial Courts)

Part 60 (Technology and Construction Court Claims)

Part 61 (Admiralty Claims)

Part 62 (Arbitration Claims)

Part 63 (Intellectual Property Claims)

Part 63A (Financial List)

Part 64 (Estates, Trusts and Charities)

Practice Direction – Insolvency Proceedings

Practice Direction: Directors Disqualification Proceedings

Practice Direction PD51O (Electronic Working)

EU Competition Law Practice Direction

1.6 This Practice Direction applies to cases in the Business and Property Courts or cases which are to be issued in those courts. In the event of inconsistency between this Practice Direction and any other Practice Direction the provisions of this Practice Direction shall prevail.

1.7 Parties will also need to give careful consideration to the Chancery Guide, the Admiralty and Commercial Courts Guide, the Technology and Construction Court Guide, the Financial List Guide, the Circuit Commercial Court Guide, the Patents Court Guide, and the Intellectual Property Enterprise Court Guide (where applicable).

Starting proceedings

2.1 Starting proceedings in the Business and Property Courts is subject to CPR Parts 7 and 8.

2.2 (1) A claimant wishing to issue a claim in the Business and Property Courts chooses which court, list or sub-list from within the Business and Property Courts in which to issue its claim, based (subject to sub-paragraph (2)) on the principal subject matter of the dispute.

(The courts, lists and sub-lists are set out in paragraphs 1.3 and 1.4.)

(2) In cases where different aspects of the dispute indicate that the case be issued in different lists, sub-lists or courts, the claimant must consider whether there are aspects requiring the expertise of a specialist judge and choose the list, sub-list or court in which the relevant specialist judges sit.

2.3 (1) Before a claimant issues a claim in the Business and Property Courts, the claimant must determine the appropriate location in which to issue the claim.

(2) With the exception of claims started under Parts 58, 60, 61 and 62, claims which are intended to be issued in the Business and Property Courts and which have significant links to a particular circuit outside London or anywhere else in the South Eastern Circuit must be issued in the B&PCs District Registry located in the circuit in question. If a claim has significant links with more than one circuit, the claim should be issued in the location with which the claim has the most significant links.

(3) A link to a particular circuit is established where—

(a) one or more of the parties has its address or registered office in the circuit in question (with extra weight given to the address of any non-represented parties);

(b) at least one of the witnesses expected to give oral evidence at trial or other hearing is located in the circuit;

(c)   the dispute occurred in a location within the circuit;

(d)   the dispute concerns land, goods or other assets located in the circuit; or

(e)   the parties' legal representatives are based in the circuit.

(4)   A claim which raises significant questions of fact or law in common with another claim already proceeding before a B&PCs District Registry may be regarded as having significant links with the circuit in question.

2.4   (1)   In a claim issued in London in the following courts, a hearing may, where appropriate, take place in a court in a circuit—

(a)   the Commercial Court;

(b)   the Admiralty Court;

(c)   the Financial List;

(c)   the Technology and Construction Court.

(2)   A judge of the Commercial Court may, where appropriate and subject always to available judicial resources, be made available to hear a claim issued in a Circuit Commercial Court.

2.5   While any appropriate claim may be issued in any of the B&PCs District Registries, the following are circumstances in which case management or trial may instead occur in the Business and Property Courts of England and Wales—

(1)   Where a claim is issued in the Revenue List in one of the B&PCs District Registries, HM Revenue and Customs may nevertheless seek to have the proceedings case managed and/or tried in the Business and Property Courts of England and Wales, in accordance with CPR 30.3(2)(h) and Annex 1 of Practice Direction 66.

(2)   A claim meeting the definition established in paragraph 1.1 of the EU Competition Law Practice Direction may be issued in an appropriate BPCs District Registry, but its case management and/or trial in the district registry in question will be dependent on an appropriate judge being made available in the district registry in question.

(3)   A claim in the Intellectual Property List, which includes the Patents Court and the Intellectual Property Enterprise Court ("IPEC") (and includes the IPEC small claims track to which rule 63.27 applies), may be issued in an appropriate BPCs District Registry. However the case management and/or trial of a claim in the Patents Court or the IPEC in the BPCs District Registry in question will be dependent on an appropriate judge being made available in the district registry in question.

Transfers

3.1   (1)   Subject to CPR 30.2, 30.5 and 59.3, the Business and Property Courts may, having regard to the criteria in 3.1(3), order proceedings in the Business and Property Courts of England and Wales or of a BPCs District Registry, or any part of such proceedings (such as a counterclaim or an application made in the proceedings), to be transferred—

(a)   from the Business and Property Courts of England and Wales to the Business and Property Courts in a BPCs District Registry; or

(b)   from the Business and Property Courts in a BPCs District Registry to the Business and Property Courts of England and Wales or to the Business and Property Courts in another BPCs District Registry.

(2)   An application for an order under paragraph 1(b) must be made to the Business and Property Court from which the transfer is sought, and notified to the intended receiving Business and Property Court at the same time by the applicant,

and must be consented to by the receiving Business and Property Court before any order for transfer is made.

(3) When considering whether to make an order under rule 30.2(4) (transfer between the Royal Courts of Justice and the district registries) when the proceedings are in the Business and Property Courts, the court must also have regard to—

(a) significant links between the claim and the circuit in question, considering the factors listed in paragraph 2.3(3) and (4) above;

(b) whether court resources, deployment constraints, or fairness require that the hearings (including the trial) be held in another court than the court into which it was issued;

(c) the wishes of the parties, which bear special weight in the decision but may not be determinative;

(d) the international nature of the case, with the understanding that international cases may be more suitable for trial in centres with international transport links;

(e) the availability of a judge specialising in the type of claim in question to sit in the court to which the claim is being transferred.

3.2 In addition to the provisions set out in CPR 30.3, the Business and Property Courts must have regard, when considering whether to make an order for transfer from the Business and Property Courts to a county court hearing centre:

(a) to the nature of the claim, in accordance with the guidance provided at paragraphs 4.1 to 4.4; and,

(b) to the availability of a judge specialising in the corresponding type of claim to sit in an appropriate court in the circuit;

3.3 When considering the availability of a judge under paragraph 3.1(e), the listing office of the court to which the claim is being transferred will be consulted before the order is made by the court.

Specialist work in the County Court

4.1 Subject to any enactment or rule relating to the jurisdiction of the County Court, the County Court at Central London, Birmingham, Bristol, Cardiff, Manchester, Newcastle, Leeds, Liverpool, and Preston are appropriate venues for any cases which are suitable to be heard in the County Court which fall within the definition in paragraph 4.2 as the specialist work of the type undertaken in the Business and Property Courts.

4.2 The specialist work of the type undertaken in the Business and Property Courts includes all the work that falls under the jurisdiction of the courts and lists that make up the Business and Property Courts, except for—

(a) Claims for possession of domestic property and rent and mesne profits, or in respect of domestic mortgages;

(b) Claims for possession of commercial premises or disputes arising out of business tenancies that are routine in nature;

(c) Claims falling under the Trusts of Land and Appointment of Trustees Act 1996, unless combined with other specialist claims;

(d) Hearings of applications to set aside statutory demands, unopposed creditors' winding-up petitions or unopposed bankruptcy petitions;

(e) Building claims, other than adjudication claims, of a value under £75,000;

(f) Invoice and other straightforward business claims of a value under £75,000;

(g) Boundary and easement disputes involving no conveyancing issues;

(h) Claims to enforce a charging order;

(i)   Applications under the Access to Neighbouring Land Act 1992;

(j)   Proceedings under the Inheritance (Provision for Family and Dependants) Act 1975.

4.3   Claims issued in the County Court which are issued in the County Court at the hearing centres defined in paragraph 4.1 and relate to the specialist work of the type undertaken in the Business and Property Courts will be marked "Business and Property work" by the court upon allocation if they have not already been marked in that way by the claimant, and will be managed and heard only by judges specialising in this work.

4.4   Judges specialising in the County Court Business and Property work must spend a minimum of 20 percent of their time handling Business and Property work, either in the Business and Property Courts or in the County Court.

Appeals in BPCs District Registries

5.1   Specific appeal slots will be created in listing in the BPCs District Registries to accommodate blocks of applications for permission to appeal and appeals which are to be heard by a Group A judge (as defined in PD52A) in accordance with PD52A.

5.2   So far as possible these slots will be concomitant with the slots identified for cases listed in BPCs District Registries requiring a Group A judge as defined in PD52A to hear them and transferred cases referred to in paragraph 3.

Updated: Tuesday, 7 February 2023

Index